THE COMPLETE BOOK OF HOME DECORATING

Publishers   ·   **GROSSET & DUNLAP**   ·   **New York**

CONTENTS

A majority of the material in this volume has been reprinted from previously copy-
righted issues of Woman's Day Guide to Good Decorating and Woman's Day
Decorating Guide, which are owned and published by Fawcett Publications, Inc.

Traditional
design taps sources which have enjoyed well-deserved popularity for generations

Consider the French and Italian influence

This "Continental" collection by American of Martinsville amiably borrows design inspiration from French and Italian furnishings for its wood and antiqued dining room pieces. Especially noteworthy are the cane back chairs with the crested solid brass fleur-de-lys inset and the cut-out trellised base of the table.

When you hear a room described as being decorated in the traditional manner, it means it follows the patterns set in European court circles, modified somewhat in America. We have the Louis of France, the monarchs and cabinetmakers of England, and even American craftsmen like Duncan Phyfe lending their names to both formal elegance and provincial charm. Stores abound both in reproductions and scaled-down versions of beloved styles so that you can handle a traditional decorating scheme with authenticity.

Do it with English authenticity

The graceful lines and fine detailing of the furniture reproductions shown here fit perfectly into the architectural formality of the room plan. The beauty of age-old design is captured in the Oriental rug, which keys the colors used in the room and determines the placement of furniture for varied activities.

Traditional

Underscore antique furnishings with plank flooring

The totally traditional room benefits from the warm glow and the eye-catching pegged flooring such as the Tempo walnut plank flooring by Wood-Mosaic, shown here. Ornately carved fireplace and shapely andirons are compatible with the walnut Chippendale secretary and other antique furnishings. The Oriental rug, with its subtle faded coloring, highlights the mellow wood tones throughout.

Traditional

Festoon a canopy

The soft draping and festooning, which fashions this canopy is reminiscent of treatments used in mansions of yester-year. Combined with a simple quilted and shirred bedspread, it can add a feeling of elegance to the bedroom of today.

Traditional

Create elegance with carefully chosen furnishings

An average-sized living room can assume the elegance of a high-budget home with furnishings carefully chosen in local stores, as this room cheerfully proves. All fabrics, carpets, draperies and furniture are by Burlington House and are available at local stores.

Extend space

Space-extending and country-flavored, this "Tyndale Hunt" mural by Wall Trends International adds a note of distinction to an otherwise drab foyer area.

Save space

Space-shy hallways respond brightly to hanging shelf, mirror, sconces and reproductions, all from Arabesque. The cultured slate-topped table measures 32 x 10 x 10½″ deep.

Beam the ceiling, lattice the shutters

Home handyman projects can give expression to your own individuality and good taste and whisk a room out of the ordinary category. Here, the addition of wooden beams, color-matched to the room's paneling and strongly contrasting the blue ceiling, give cozy country flavor to a bedroom. Spanking white lattice-work has been placed over blue fabric-covered shutters to frame the window treatments and make them an important decorative point. Same blue fabric is fashioned into a dust ruffle and round table cover, pleasing partners to the colorful blue and green wildflower print used on the bed and for the wallhanging. Celery-colored carpeting unifies entire scheme. All fabrics, curtains, furniture and carpeting are by Burlington House.

Plan a reading corner

If your living room is large enough, why not devote a corner area for reading? Nothing could be more comfortable than having one such as this, with a reading table (by Stiffel) of distressed fruitwood with burled turnings and sizeable enough to hold a large reference book. Apt companions are the modified wing chair and the tall black-shaded Stiffel lamp.

Go Classic French

Hibriten's "Traditions III" collection offers classic designs, geared to the space realities of today. The wall unit serves as a storage/display center, and can be supplemented with additional units used as a group or separately. Table serves multi-uses, as dining area or as game table or writing desk.

Traditional

Focus on fireplace

Nothing is more heartwarming or homier than a roaring fire in the fireplace. If you are one of the lucky ones to have one in your home, play it to the hilt. Try a textured area rug (such as this one by Cabin Crafts) in front of it; then add a comfortable chair and hassock and keep pipes and slippers within easy reach for complete relaxation.

Create a marvelous feeling of formality

Broyhill's "Trouville" grouping gives the essence of formal French Court designs, while avoiding the extravagant lavishness. The shapely curved pieces, plus the richness of the fabrics, capitalize on the underlying characteristics of the style. The deep constrasting walls, enriched with moldings, dramatize the furnishings and are highly effective in this room of tradition. The full-length draperies combined with sheer curtaining, the crystal lamp bases, and the ornately-framed grouping over the sofa, are well-thought-out touches that underscore the feeling of formality.

Stay in style . . . right down to the shade trims

In this handsome bedroom decked out with furniture from Thomasville's "Charlton Hall" collection, even the window shades are in the correct period. Stauffer's washable Tontine cloth shades have hems which echo the graceful curves of the highboy and are trimmed with the same fringe used on the bed canopy.

Salute Spirit of '76

An inspiring wall decoration for a boy's room makes American history come to life in a molded version of the famous 19th century painting by Archibald Willard. The simulated antique pine woodtone finish is brightened with vivid color accents. By Arabesque, a division of Burwood Products.

Recapture the casual charm and honest simplicity of our country's origins with

Early American

From the time of the arrival of the Pilgrims, continuing with other early settlers such as the Pennsylvania Dutch and, later on, the Shakers, Early American design has been characterized by sturdiness, simplicity and serviceability. Because of its nostalgic reference to our beginnings, it continues its popularity today. Woods, like maple and pine, native to America, furniture including rockers, corner cupboards and four posters; hooked rugs, patchwork quilts . . . these are the essence of the Early American look.

Create a gallery wall

Hanging treasured pictures and artifacts on one wall rather than scattering them about a room makes a strong decorative impact. This interesting collection, massed over the sofa in a family living room, is the focal point in a modern version of an Early American "keeping" room. Wall-to-wall textured carpet of Du Pont nylon by Wunda Weve unifies the room and provides necessary quiet underfoot.

Feature a patchwork bedspread

A delightfully "patchy" fringed bedspread by Bates has all sorts of patterns and colors mixed in a hither-and-yon yet well thought-out design to make this spirited example of a beautiful craft a merry maverick. Complemented by the traditionally-minded spool headboard, the bedspread, aptly named "Serendipity," is machine washable and dryable and requires no ironing.

Panel a room

Wide painted pine panels provide traditional background for genuine Colonial and fine reproductions. Antique brass, copper and pewter, chintz, braided rugs and an impressive collection of Chinese Export china are authentic antiques.

Paper a room

Colonial charm prevails in this bedroom under the eaves. It has all the classic elements: shutters, quilt, needlepoint rug, tilt-top table, rush seat chair, and floral wallcovering, "Spring Thing" by Columbus Coated Fabrics.

Tile a room

"Zuider Zee," a cheery pattern from GAF's Softred tile, has inner layer of Quiet-Cor vinyl foam to absorb sound. It is used to frame hooded fireplace and doorway as well as cover the floor of a country dining room, sitting room combination.

Hang a rogues gallery

An effective, amusing way to show off portraits and candid shots of family, friends, old school chums, pets and "crushes," is to mount them on panels of a folding screen, using two-way adhesive tape, strips of molding, or little hooks. You can make screen from pine boards hinged together. Paint them or cover them with fabric. Perfect for a bar area in an Early American family room.

Use modern shag with provincial

Texture of a deep shag rug complements country provincial furniture from Broyhill's "Georgetown" collection. Other Early American details: diamond-paned leaded windows and reproduction oil lamps.

Use oval rug in square space

Furniture from Broyhill's "Chevy Chase" collection groups neatly around oval rug in this charming living room. Note random wall paneling and board-and-batten door which serve as background.

Be Shaker-inspired

Perfect choice for vacation house or first apartment is this wrought iron and natural pine wood group by Carolina Forge. Table top is laminated. Chairs have stencilled backs and bold, checked, vinyl upholstery. Simulated pegged, random-width flooring and machine-made braided rug, look as authentic as the genuine barn side wall, old shutters, primitive painting on wood, and antique weather vanes.

Salvage dormer space

To find needed space, utilize your attic. Here, calico-covered walls are framed with matching woodwork. Antiqued white Colonial designed furniture by Kling has spanking fresh, easy-to-make, checked gingham spreads with ruffled pillow shams, a cafe curtain hung low to catch the view. A trio of unmatched, hand-hooked area rugs, an electrified old oil lamp and gayly-matted prints are beguiling accessories.

Build storage-bed unit

For extra guest space or a family hideaway, a talented home carpenter can build a neat sofa plus storage unit from a 2x4-frame covered with plywood. Latex foam mattress and bolster are covered with same colorful print used for the wall covering. Drawers beneath store bedding. A rotovinyl floor covering, Armstrong's "Imperial Accotone," has a textured surface, sound deadening core.

Early American

Swing with
Modern
if you're turned on by space-age materials and an absence of clutter

Choose sectionals

One of the best ways to assure plenty of seating space in a room on the smallish side is by using sectionals. Today's versions, like Broyhill's tufted sofas from their "Freeform" collection, are neat, trim, and, best of all, really function.

Use snappy designs

Today's baths blaze up in new colors, patterns and products. What's new here is the acrylic shower wall, plexiglas bench, and "Vibrations" shower curtain, rug and towels by Pierre Cardin for Fieldcrest. Note large glass jug used to hold tree branch.

24

Modern is where it's at this very minute. It can't really be defined as it's still evolving, still happening. It has tossed away slavish reliance on the past and evokes a picture of the home that is fresh, young, and contemporary. It means the utilization of developments from the laboratories . . . plastics whose names you can't pronounce, silhouettes in sofas and chairs never seen before, everything-proof fabrics. It's multi-use furniture, things you assemble yourself, the zip of pattern, the zap of lots of color.

Use carpet and steel everywhere

Carpet and steel make ideal companions in the modern room. Here, the floor and even part of the walls are covered in Armstrong's medallion pattern "Prodigy," a new carpeting with an embossed surface and a three-dimensional sculptured look. Walls and ceiling are delineated by strips of steel cemented in place. Their shine echoes their furniture use.

Modern

Go natural

The natural, hand-crafted look is swiftly gaining acceptance. One of its handsomest interpretations is seen in Founders' "Stowaways" collection in which the pieces are of maple veneers finished in an almost-clear, grain-exposing tone. Storage unit can be arranged in many ways.

Grow with style

This boy's room, furnished with Ward's "Madison Park" collection, has the kind of units which can grow from this young setting into a bachelor apartment. All pieces boast good-looking, close-to-the-floor silhouettes.

Style in a romantic manner

Modern and romantic can go hand-in-hand. This bedroom, designed by Virginia Frankel, shows how it is done. In the modern idiom is the stainless steel bed frame. For touches of sentiment, there is a furry spread, lots of lacy ferns and an attractive window treatment in which identical fabric is used for Roman shades and draperies. Toss pillows on the bed, folk-like in theme, are another touch of the contemporary which looks to past inspiration.

Tuft it

Tufting is as much a part of the modern furniture scene as angular lines. Deep-seated tufts on wool, covering flexible foam, high-light these seating units in the "Brenda" style by Domani, a division of Burris Industries. Chrome casters are used on sofa, loveseat and chair.

Unify it

Now you can buy fabrics which match floorcoverings. Here, we show Armstrong's "Flower Garden" shag carpet on the floor and matching fabric on wall panels. As you can see it simplifies decorating, creates feeling of co-ordination.

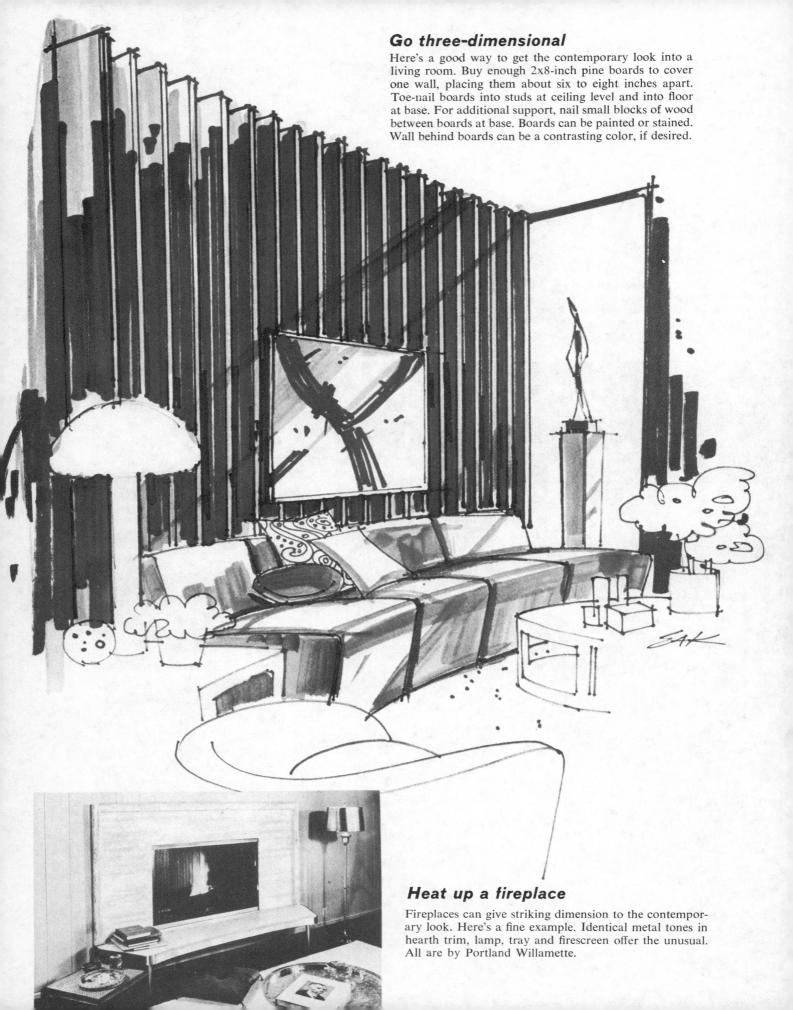

Go three-dimensional

Here's a good way to get the contemporary look into a living room. Buy enough 2x8-inch pine boards to cover one wall, placing them about six to eight inches apart. Toe-nail boards into studs at ceiling level and into floor at base. For additional support, nail small blocks of wood between boards at base. Boards can be painted or stained. Wall behind boards can be a contrasting color, if desired.

Heat up a fireplace

Fireplaces can give striking dimension to the contemporary look. Here's a fine example. Identical metal tones in hearth trim, lamp, tray and firescreen offer the unusual. All are by Portland Willamette.

Modern

Dazzle with the shapes of today

For a home featuring the off-beat, try these super-contemporary, molded-plywood, frame chairs from Flair. In dining room, you might use a glass-and-chrome set with a bamboo motif which updates a traditional theme. The meteor-shaped lamp, Corfam-covered chrome etagere and abstract painting are also tuned in with today. So is the built-in storage and fireplace unit against one wall.

Use take-aparts

If your space is small and you're decorating shoe-horn style, use multi-functional furniture such as this fraction dining table by Wondum Designs (it comes apart to form snack tables), this "Geometrix" sofa by Simmons (bolsters come off to form single bed), and the modular storage units by Lane (they stack in many ways). Graphics and accessories are by Raymor. On floor is "Misty" shag by Modern Carpets, made of Enka nylon staple fiber.

Accent it

Modern furniture calls for modern accent pieces. Here we see a collection of smart sophisticated ones from Haeger: wall planter, candleholders, fruit bowl and lamp. All come in seven mod colors and in various sizes. Note the unity they bring to just a cabinet top.

Go modular

The great value of modular units is they arrange in many ways, bring diversity to decorating, fit as well in one home as in another. Here, an interesting collection from Domani. Even the little coffee table with its glass top has been upholstered in virgin wool. Note fireplace wall. It's made from Dacor Stones, which are lightweight plastic, covered with adhesive mortar and pressed into place. See them at building supply stores.

Open up a small room with a blaze of color

Modern houses and apartments often have rooms on the minuscule side. To make this den look larger, bright turquoise was liberally used with a punctuation of green. The furniture, chosen with care, emphasizes a sofa bed positioned under the window. Colorful maps are a great decorative touch as are the colorfully-bound books.

Modern

Unify with a lively pattern

For a modern teenager's room, use African style sheets and spread for bed (here, it's "Botanical Zoo" by J. P. Stevens), then cut up another sheet to cover walls and Roman shade. Unifies room and gives it a great look.

Build a bookcase for architectural interest

The modern room which lacks architectural interest needs the personal touch. Here, a combination bookcase and planter (built of plywood and wooden dowels) extends to help create "doorway" into dining area. Unit was painted same color as wall so it blends in nicely. A green foyer and furniture contrast nicely with the blue walls.

Modern

Do it with red, white and blue wallcoverings

Dining-Living room begins with red, white and blue striped and floral wall-coverings from Columbus Coated Fabrics. Walls and ceiling get the floral pattern, while folding screens flanking sliding glass doors take the striped pattern. Graber vertical cloth blinds in washable, textured, linen cotton rotate for light control and open to move door.

Take your cue from red, white and blue beads

Family room walls are painted red, all furniture is white, all cushions and accessories are blue, and at the windows strands of red, white and blue Bead-angles hang in interesting array as the color co-ordinator.

Let a red, white and blue area rug set the pace

Small study has lower portion of walls painted blue, upper portion painted red, and woodwork painted white. Floor is white vinyl tile with a smashing little area rug, "Chevron Shag," new from Cabin Crafts, holding stage center.

Go "today" with tawny browns

Dark parquet floors and brown walls are a perfect complement to Selig's modern furniture with its strong dominant browns. Orange accents are picked up in pillows, pictures, baskets, etc. That unusual chair, "The Orsala", has sausage-shaped cushions on a curving chromesteel frame. Performing as a chaise is the "Chairester" with its matching ottoman. Carpet is by Lees. Room designed by Elroy Edson, AID.

Oriental

Use the subtle approach

Subtlety is one of the most interesting aspects of an Oriental room. Textures and tactile elements play a leading role. Here, the fabric weave effect of General Tire's "Brio" vinyl wallcovering pleasingly combines with stone and brick to create a garden corner. Interesting notes: the modern sculpture and the simple hanging light.

Make a grand entrance

A simple but effectively furnished entryway lets the bold fabric on walls come on strong. Hand-dyed "Sargon" batik fabric sets a memorable scene, accented by strategically placed Oriental sculptures and a corner full of tangerine mums. Wooden beams edged with tinted mirror squares give the walls a three dimensional effect. The luminous paneled skylight brightens the subtle blue and green color scheme which is repeated in the shag rug. Everything from Sears.

Create a little tea room

Thayer Coggin's low chairs and simple table give a touch of the Orient to this room with its built-in platform and trellis wall. A mirror, set behind the trellis, gives a feeling of space with sand and plants in between. Grass cloth wall is balanced by oak plank flooring.

Scrutinize the
Far East for
Oriental
grace and line,
form and decoration

Chinese and Japanese furnishings and art have long had a definite influence on the Western world. Chinese Chippendale has been part of the decorating lexicon ever since the 18th century. A bit later, clipper ships, sailing from the Orient to America, brought with them a bounty of porcelain, textiles, and art objects. And now, with East and West growing nearer, the crisp lines of Chinese and Japanese furniture, the subtle colors of painted tea boxes, shoji screens, bamboo, and teak are seen everywhere.

Go Eastern in the modern manner
Look how Oriental touches make today's Modern furniture look like it's right out of the Far East. Touches are plywood folding screens covered with Eastern-style wallpaper, Mandarin picture over fireplace, statuary and art objects. Covering floor is "Snip 'n Stick", Ozite's new self-stick broadloom carpeting.

Go Eastern in the traditional vein
Look how Oriental touches make Traditional furniture seem to be part of a foreign land. Touches are ebony screen mounted to wall above sofa, coffee table with graceful bamboo legs, heavily-tasseled, pagoda-styled draperies, Oriental rug and artifacts. Room by Colby's of Northbrook, Illinois.

Oriental

Build corner seating unit

In corner of dining area, build a 2x4 frame, cover with plywood, then with same Oriental-style wallcovering used on walls. Make cushions from latex foam rubber, cover with upholstery fabric (here, it's "Fanfare" a blend of Kodel and cotton, by John Wolf Textiles.) Note little shelf in corner for vase and Oriental-like dining chairs.

Build folding screens

Make two folding screens, each two pieces of plywood or pine hinged together and covered with same covering used on wall (here, its "Lo Long" by Lloyd). Place screens in front of wall, as was done here, to get dimension and to emphasize mirror between them. On floor is Cabin Craft's carpet of Kodel polyester fiber.

Build Chinese parsons table

For something really smashing, build a plywood or pine table which encloses three sides of your sofa, looks like a parsons table with Oriental trim, and becomes a marvelous "shelf" for lamps, books, ashtrays, etc. Another build-it project here is the Oriental screen which can be made from plywood or pine boards covered with a Far Eastern wall-covering or fabric and then hinged together.

Oriental

Building a home? Consider one with Japanese spaciousness

Ernest Silva is one of New York's best-known interior photographers. He and his wife, Arlene, live in this handsome home on Long Island in New York. Home blends architectural interest with Oriental-flavored interior design concepts, creating a "Total Look".

Cathedral ceilings, clerestory windows, built-ins, and the genuine hardwood used throughout the house, add to the spacious effect of the rooms.

The living room (left) has interest focused toward the brick, stone and plaster fireplace, complemented by the elm paneling and the dark oak floors. Oriental rug, Far Eastern art and accessories augment Japanese design scheme.

Built-in cabinet (top, right) holds television set and stereo components and provides extra storage space for the dining room. Inspired by a Japanese wall shrine, area features same elm paneling used on walls. A chigai-dana shelf displays a collection of ceramics and books.

The Silva's kitchen (bottom, right) is done in the Japanese manner, too, featuring simple lines and a plenitude of storage and work space. Elm paneling is matched to kitchen cabinets, while center island is modeled after a Japanese children's kite, and has a butcher block counter top.

Use it in an outdoorsy way

In tune with the times, decorating has gone back to nature, too. Small area captures a fresh and natural look with a multitude of plants, light and airy wicker furniture, bamboo blinds and white tile flooring. In perfect harmony with this "natural" mood are Fieldcrest's "Nature Walk" sheets, used on the daybed. This pretty floral of swaying green ferns is repeated for the table covering, made from a twin-size sheet.

Use it as an accent

Kitchen-dining area assumes a fresh, new appearance with a touch of wicker. Sweetheart chairs with delicate curlicues and decorative wicker panels are pleasing accents against the cool background of floor tiling and kitchen cabinets. Panels can be easily hooked or nailed to the walls, providing a three-dimensional feeling. They can be left in their natural color or painted in the color of your choice. A row of potted plants and scalloped fabric shade at the window add a touch of color.

Keep it white and light

The perfect accessory for summer living is wicker. Here, the living room of a summer home is enhanced by the crisp, cool look of white wicker furniture by Tropi-Cal, a fresh contrast against the large floral print used for sofa, seat cushions and draperies. For unexpected guests, sleep-sofa by Southern Cross is easily converted into a queen-size bed.

Put it to work in the bathroom

With a little imagination, unattractive bathroom can be converted into a pretty and colorful area. Bold, floral wall covering is a handsome contrast for the light look of wicker arched cabinets and swivel chair, all available "natural" or in painted finishes. Switchable seat lid by American-Standard can be changed in seconds for decorating flexibility and comes in a variety of designs and colors.

Wicker

Use pieces of it in the bedroom

The light-toned wicker and bamboo headboard, chair and night table by Ficks Reed are perfect complement to the modern furniture of this small bedroom, which has been made to look larger by keeping the walls and carpeting in light colors. Bed is a Simmons king-size "Beautyrest Supreme."

Use it as dining room furniture

To add a touch of drama to a small dining room, the Wallcovering Industry Bureau suggests first covering walls with a bold wallcovering. Then build a lambrequin from plywood and cover it with the same wallcovering. Then put wicker to work; normally informal rattan chairs assume a more formal air when used as shown here and when fitted with moire seat covers made from same material used for draperies. Round area rug repeats the round lines of the table and creates a pretty contrast against white vinyl flooring.

Wicker

Use it for spring-time feeling

Wicker automatically suggests the outdoors, so here it was used to create a bedroom that remains springtime fresh all year around. Bed was bought unpainted, then painted blue. Delhi chair and butterfly drum table were also bought unpainted, then painted pink. Carpet is green. Gay floral print containing all these colors, covers bed, makes canopy top. "Stoplite" shades by Breneman.

Keep it casual

Small room reflects cool and casual air, combining soft shag rug with rattan furniture. Lace-like design in furniture is enhanced by exotic floral design in wallcovering ("Samoa" by Columbus Coated Fabrics). Striped wallcovering and rattan bird cage are in perfect harmony with light-hearted mood of room.

Don't be a square

Even bamboo furniture comes in circular, modular units today. This one by Ficks Reed is comprised of three sections, making it ideal for smaller living-space. Glass-top table repeats circular theme of seating module. Brightly-covered cushions enhance natural look of bamboo furniture.

Create the exotic

Colorful striped fabric and wicker furniture is the perfect combination for a young girl's room. Make bedspread and pillow cover from striped fabric. Band top of wall all the way around with one long stripe. Cut tents three or four stripes wide, staple or glue to wall, as shown. Cut tops of tents from three pie-shaped pieces, glue together on wall. Once up, they will assume a dimensional look and appear to be real tents instead of the flat pieces they are.

Wicker

Create a garden-like room

Lattice panels on walls and cool vinyl on floor (by Congoleum), give this room a fresh, "outdoorsy" look. Casual wicker furniture adds to the informal atmosphere. An abundance of flower plants brightens one corner, a further reflection of the outdoor feeling.

Create a room to grow in

Six today and sixteen tomorrow, or so it seems, so why not decorate your little girl's room with some thought for the future. Patchwork quilt carpet design sets the color scheme for this delightful room. Made of 100% Allied Chemical nylon fiber, it is practical as it is pretty and can be used for many years. Delicately striped wallpaper is a charming background for the white wicker furniture and ruffly curtains. With the exception of the bed, basic pieces of furniture can remain for years—a change of accessories will provide a whole, new look.

Eclectic

Put "the mix" on your walls, too

Eclectic refers to walls, too. The Wallcovering Industry Bureau suggests mixing them up, too. Paint one wall and paper the other three . . . or vice versa, as shown here, where bold swirls on one wall complement modern plexiglas parsons tables, paintings and sofa, and at the same time work well with traditional chairs and little table. All furniture here is from Chesapeake-Siegel-Land.

Mix styles

This model bedroom from Colby's of Northbrook, Illinois, is a carefree medley of styles. It contains an Oriental rug, a Wicker chair, Early American wall cabinet, Modern chair and parsons table, Traditional bed and chair, all blended together into an interesting room.

Mix textures

A tawny shag carpet, "Midnight Sun" by Lees, made of Allied Chemical's nylon fiber, is a stunning backdrop for the textural variety of this living room: the plaid-covered sofa, the furry throw, the cane Sedan chair, and all the wooden furniture. Even the walls are eclectic: wooden beams on painted surfaces. Sofa and coffee table are from Drexel's "Wellington Park" collection.

Reflect the mix

Shimmery foil wallcovering by Columbus Coated Fabrics reflects a stunning mixture of Modern furniture (plastic parsons table, glass-and-steel etageres, sofa and loveseat) with Traditional pieces (chairs, tables, pictures). Lovely Traditional bibelots are displayed in the Modern etageres. A clever decorating scheme which joins the old with the new.

Do it geometrically

Geometrics from the floor up highlight this interesting room. There's small diamond shapes on the carpet, larger ones on the sofa, there's plaid on the chairs, and there's a ceiling of squares formed by wooden beams. As for the furniture, Modern and Traditional live happily together. Room designed by Colby's of Northbrook, Illinois.

Eclectic

Make a Modern mirrored screen to show off Traditional treasures

Cut plywood or pine panels to desired height and 18-inches wide. Hinge together. Buy 18-square-inch mirrors in kit form. Use adhesive to attach mirrors to panels. An inexpensive way to make a really expensive-looking, mirrored, folding screen.

Dramatize a wall

One of the most important ingredients of well-decorated rooms is the accessories. They are the "finishing touches" which make or break. Here, the assymetrical placement of Mayan relics by Arabesque over a two-door chest, creates a meaningful point of interest and aids a strong Mediterranean look. Notice how the clock and the figures are done in deep-relief, capturing the hand-chiseled texture of weathered stone.

Decorate Hispana-style

The easy-going warmth of a Hispana-styled kitchen will foster congenial entertaining. Colby's of Northbrook, Illinois, suggests that gleaming copper pots be hung on black iron meat hooks over table in gleaming "chandelier" fashion. Other important accessorizing includes the handsomely-filled niches and the family treasures placed on the Spanish-patterned vinyl floor.

Try Spanish-inspired furniture in a corner grouping

Designed for conviviality and easy entertaining, this "Spanada" seating group by Broyhill sports brilliantly-colored crushed velvet upholstery which bounces against the white plastered walls. Simplicity of arched, wrought-iron treated windows blends with aplomb with the beamed ceiling and corners. Portraits, framed in antique gold and black, and the shimmering glass lamp bases, enrich the Mediterranean decorating scheme.

Add a Spanish-inspired built-in and shutters

Boxed units fashioned of 2x4 frames, covered with plywood and then decorated with Moroccan tiles to match the flooring, can easily convert your room into a Spanish-inspired one. Tall windows are treated to full-length wooden panels, affording scenic view or complete shut-off in evening or in inclement weather.

Add a Spanish-styled wine rack

Make the neighbors goggle by adding this handsome wine rack by Woodard to your Mediterranean living or dining room. Unit has three shelves for serving space and plenty of room for stocking wine bottles of all kinds. Unit makes good room divider, too.

Add a Spanish-type mirror

A fireplace automatically becomes the focal point of a room, and with this new wrought iron mirror from Thomas Industries, your Mediterranean fireplace can really become a "swinging" center of interest. Delicate scrollwork pattern gates open or close, depending upon your mood.

LIVING ROOMS

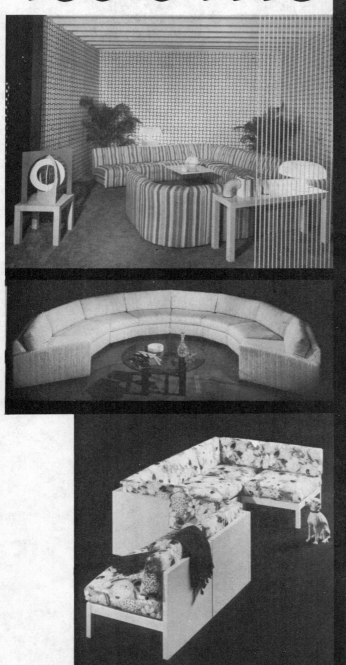

Consider new seating arrangements

Sofas are no longer what they used to be. Nowadays they bend, circle, twist, reverse . . . as these new designs show: (1st photo) Curved loveseats and sofa by Thayer Coggin almost complete circle. (2nd) Five seating units by Thayer Coggin almost complete a square, provide seating for quite a crowd. (3rd) Oval sectional by Thayer Coggin can be arranged in many ways. (4th) Half-circle by Selig is really four-piece sectional. (5th) Continuous seating in serpentine style is from Thayer Coggin. (6th) American of Martinville's sectional has various pieces for many arrangements.

Put a greenhouse in your window

Unusual feature of this Colonial living room is greenhouse in window. It's really just a series of shelves nailed in place, then used to hold plants, books, etc. Another interesting feature of room is folding screen made from three panels of plywood covered with same hound's-tooth check upholstery fabric used on sofa. All furniture is from "Country Hearth" collection by Kling Colonial. Sofa converts to bed.

LIVING ROOMS

SUMMER IS A TAPE THING.

**If you're wildly adventurous,
do it up adventurously wild!**

If you really want to be "with it," create a living room with interesting furniture and highly imaginative accessories . . . such as this room designed by John Weber, A.I.D., for a young married couple who entertain a lot and really want to swing! Furniture is all from Broyhill's new "Chapter One" collection, features Pucci print on sofa and ottoman. Three walls were covered with silvery, reflecting paper, fourth wall with interesting geometric print. Wall trims are plastic gears, mod painting, etc. Child's rocking horse is an added "fun" thing.

LIVING ROOMS

Include a guest room

Simplest way to solve that guest room problem in a small house is to use a sofa which opens up into a bed. One shown here is new "Magic Bed" by Flexsteel. It has foam seating and foam mattress.

Note interesting wall treatment in this living room. Lattice grillwork from local lumberyard was bought in panels, nailed to floor and ceiling a few inches away from the wall, then painted a gay color. Arches were cut from plywood, nailed in place as shown and painted a contrasting color.

Beam the ceiling

Simplest way to put attractive wooden beams on your walls and ceiling in a hurry is to use the new lightweight polyurethane ones now on the market. They come with their own adhesive and are easily put in place. Ones shown here are from Town and Country Reproductions "Room Kits." Each kit is one carton, includes everything needed to beam a room in a parallel design; beams can be ordered in lengths up to 16 feet.

Note interesting use of striped carpet on the floor, the stripes running opposite to the beams on the ceiling. Curved lines in painting add further geometric interest.

Use venetian blinds and shelves to cover up windows with unsightly view

To cover up windows which looked out on a brick wall next door, this homeowner installed Levolor Venetian Blinds over windows, then mounted wooden beams with adjustable shelves and turned the whole thing into an interesting storage unit. Two of the blinds were fixed, two others open and close.

LIVING ROOMS

Build your own coffee table ensemble

It's all made from plywood. A square makes the table top, four smaller squares are glued and nailed underneath to form legs and provide storage for four small cubes . . . also made from squares of plywood, glued and nailed together. Cover table and cubes with fabric, Con-Tact, wall paper, or paint on designs of your own.

Dramatize with matching wallcovering and fabric

Matching wallcoverings and fabrics are commonplace today, and offer infinite possibilities for dramatizing any room. Here, wall was covered with an interesting design, then strips of matching fabric were positioned around windows as shown to give room its special effect. Venetian blinds by Levolor Lorentzen, in color used in print, carry out the color scheme of the room.

Use sofa as a room divider

What simpler way to divide a narrow living room in half than to use a sofa as positioned here? Beautiful wrap-around rosewood of this model by Selig, forms a delightful backdrop for small-scaled plexiglass dining room table and chairs, also by Selig. Area rug is by Lees.

For elegance and comfort, add a sculptured chaise

The sculptured look is evident in this far-out chaise lounge covered in a soft, furry fabric on a foam-upholstered wood structure. Chaise is from Selig's "Monroe" collection.

LIVINQ ROOMS

Let an exciting area rug provide a color scheme

This luxurious living room by Peg Walker keys its color scheme—and its dramatic look—to a bold-patterned abstract rya rug from Egetaepper. The design, "Finnmark," is in multiple tones of blue, with green and accents of gold. The brightest of the blues is picked up in the wall color, while the antique gold is echoed in vinyl flooring. Lots of shiny steel-and-glass adds gleam—and space to show off decorative pieces and plants, accented by the light that streams through shuttered windows. Upholstered pieces are by Selig, steel furniture by Brueton. Flooring by Flintkote.

Use glass beads for see-through room divider

Strings of glass beads hung from a wooden rafter divide living room from sunken dining room. Glass beads make excellent dividers because they separate yet let the light through. Note that rooms are unified with raftered ceiling, painted wall, and use of similar art work and furniture in both rooms. All furniture is from Thayer Coggin's "New Concept II" collection by Milo Baughman.

Add a swivel rocker for comfort

Here's a good addition for any living room . . . a chair of modern design, which is really a rocking chair . . . which swivels around when needed. It's made by Burris Industries, comes in several colors, will fit in nicely with most furnishings.

Use see-through draperies for interesting color effect

Undulating color is captured in see-through drapery treatment which features a layer of electric blue ninon-type sheers and an overdrape in white leno weave fabric from PPG Industries' new "Fashionglass" collection. The subtly soft color treatment molds the mood of the room and provides a feeling of spaciousness to the room. "Fashionglass" collection emphasizes variety of weaves, textures and colors currently available which focus attention on the new fashion appeal of fiber glass. Fabrics by Hess, Goldsmith & Co. in PPG fiber glass yarns. Furniture by Dunbar/Dux.

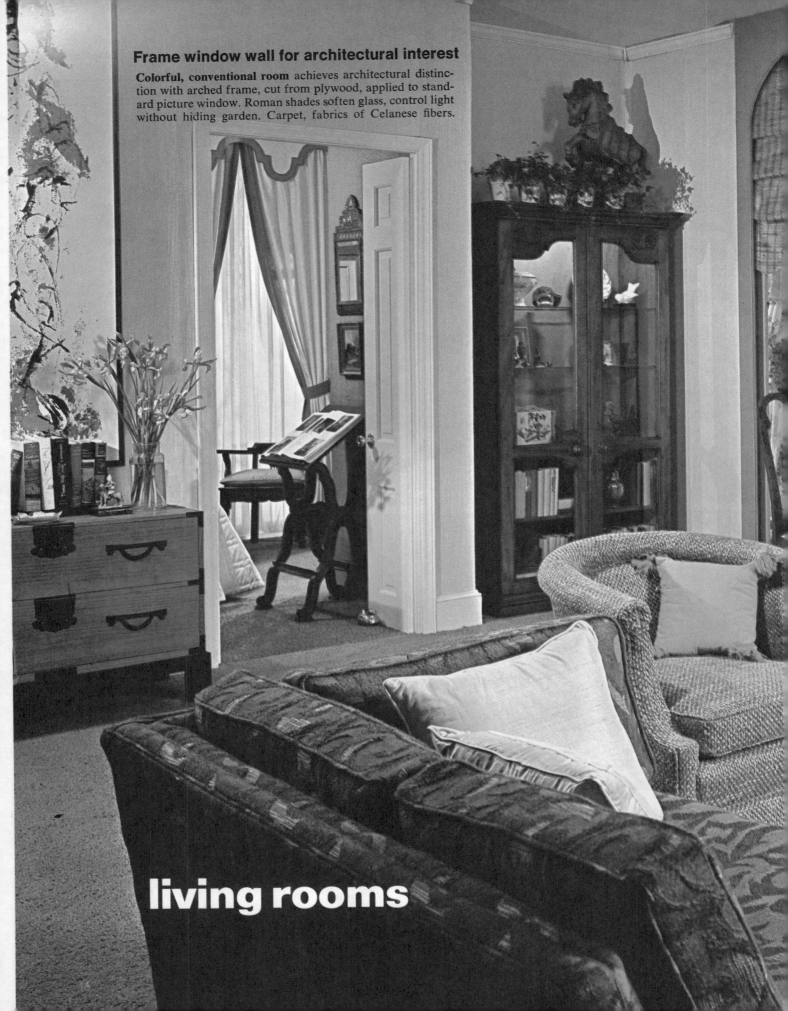

Frame window wall for architectural interest

Colorful, conventional room achieves architectural distinction with arched frame, cut from plywood, applied to standard picture window. Roman shades soften glass, control light without hiding garden. Carpet, fabrics of Celanese fibers.

living rooms

Coordinate tall windows with rest of room

Designer John Van Koert adds structural stature to tall windows with a seemingly simple treatment that unifies the whole living room. Illinois' textured "Calcutta" shades, trimmed with carpet fringe for stronger definition, are framed by fabric-covered plywood panels which climb the walls in subtle, grey-on-beige design. This soft neutrality melts into the beige carpet and continues downward to the sunken conversation area. There, built-in sofas upholstered in warm grey encircle the great stone fireplace wall—from which the medley of grey and beige tones naturally eminate.

Make it delightfully modern

Making good use of slanting ceiling, this homemaker built narrow storage unit into wall, then placed sofa directly underneath for easy access to the various items in the unit. A beautiful tweed shag rug ("The Clincher" by Armstrong) is a perfect foil for the simple-line modern furniture used in the room.

Include a bedroom, study and dining room

This one-room apartment by Paul Krauss, A.I.D., functions in four ways. First, it's a living room, ideal for conversation. A light scaled faux bamboo chair and a comfortable armchair make grouping with sofa. Note same covering, a wide-wale corduroy in nearly same gold as wall, is used for both large upholstered pieces. This makes them appear smaller. Feeling of spaciousness is furthered by use of small glass top table.

Second, this is a bedroom. "The Warwick" Hide-A-Bed sofa by Simmons unfolds to make a queen-size bed. Storage for clothes is neatly built in on opposite wall.

Third, this is a study. Parsons table serves as desk. Nearby shelves hold books, typewriter. Fourth, this is a room for dining. Desk is placed in center of room, used as table.

And there are the marvelous fabrics with their true-to-life illustrations of real flowers and birds. From Greeff's new "Nature's Heritage" collection, "Snowy Egrets" appear on draperies and seat cushion. A pair of Audubon prints on the wall are actually fabric panels named "Caribbean Hummingbirds." The center painting is the "Deep Woods."

Colonial chandelier and matching sconce is by Progress Lighting. Glass table is by Raymor. "Contrast" goblets are by Fostoria Glass.

lIVING
ROOMS

Make a vacation house living room spacious and spectacular

Here's a really casual living room complete with gray slate floor, handsome fieldstone fireplace, rattan and wicker furniture and a swing-sofa that's bound to be the hit of any gathering. Note simple storage and bookshelf units built into walls and game table in corner. Small photo shows view from other side of room with dining room down the hall.

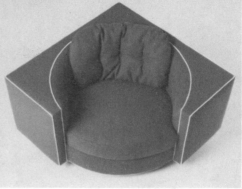

Arrange and rearrange for conversational needs

What could be more fun than this new "Circle-in-the-Square" chair by Selig? One of them fits beautifully in a corner, also functions well in the middle of a room. Two of them form a unit, so do three, so do four! Chair has loose-back cushion.

Hide unsightly architecture

Ugly looking beams and pipes ruined appearance of this room in old-style house, were covered by latticed panel built in as shown. Lattice was covered with thin paper in back. Lighting fixture was attached behind the panel and provides subdued lighting when turned on by switch on wall. Furniture shown here is by State of Newburgh, rug by Regal.

Mix your patterns

Today almost anything goes . . . certainly you can have great fun mixing several patterns in one room, as was done in photo below, right. Blue velvet sofa is surrounded by floral and striped decked chairs and checkered table covering. All furniture is by State of Newburgh.

Add a charming little chair

The addition of one, smart, little chair can alter the appearance of a whole room. Here it's the "Lohmeyer" chair designed for Burris Industries by German designer Hartmut Lohmeyer. Chair is flexible urethane with stretch velvet covering, comes in several colors.

77

PLOT OUT a
living room
WHICH really
LIVES UP TO ITS name

Follow your life-style . . . make your living room strikingly simple . . .

What could be simpler than the warmth of a fine wood floor, wood-paneled walls, a ponderosa pine patio door and wall-to-wall picture window with hopper windows underneath? Complementing these is a simple collection of furniture, highlight of which is the hair-pin backed chair found at an antique shop. Final touch: the lovely view.

. . . or fabulously fancy, as in these two contrasting interpretations

What could be fancier than several tall mirrored screens placed against one wall to reflect the glamor and gleam of a Thayer Coggin's lavishly upholstered sofa, chrome and glass cocktail table, and armless lounge chairs with mirror chrome bases? Underlying the scene is a white rug with smaller white shag area rugs adding an interesting texture.

Dramatize entranceway with colorful folding screens

To make screens, cut pieces of plywood to appropriate height and width, then cover with wallpaper (here, it's "Villa D'Este" by Imperial). Position screens on both sides of doorway to make a dramatic entranceway. Screens work most effectively when doorway to living room is quite large; the screens bring the opening down to size. One-of-a-kind coffee table looks just grand seated on simple area rug. Room designed by the Wallcovering Industry Bureau.

Dramatize exit with a floor-to-ceiling bookcase

Make bookcase from inexpensive pine or plywood. Build to fit entire wall area around door, as shown. Paint bookcase desired color; black or brown are good colors to use because they show off contrasting colors of book jackets.

living rooms

Create an architectural look with platforms and dividers

Tiled platform and mirrored divider: They set off a library-dining room from the living room. Divider is made by gluing small three-dimensional mirrors to a large sheet of plywood nailed to ceiling and floor. Teak-stained beams and thick library shelving complement sparkly tiles, the glint of a metal screen and the texture of white-painted bricks. Room designed by Bloomingdale's.

Carpeted conversation pit: Built into home, it has armless seating and cushions that provide a surprising seating capacity for so small a space. Furniture by Thayer Coggin.

Balustrades and bannisters: They make decorative, practical, see-through dividers to define areas. Available at lumberyards, they can be antiqued or painted. A lucky find at a demolition site may unearth a genuine vintage example for a modest price. Furniture here by Kroehler.

Raised platform: It divides room into two conversational areas—one formal, one informal. Dropped portion will find great favor with floor sitters; low-slung chairs hug the furry area rug used on wall-to-wall carpeting. Furniture by Basic Witz.

Use upholstery fabric to cover homemade screens

The rugged wool-look upholstery in a large-scale plaid which covers the perimeter seating in this modern living room is repeated on homemade plywood screens at the window. Sheer white curtains and white "Opulence" shag carpeting by Viking counterbalance the strong pattern. All furniture and accessories are from Selig.

A handsome sofa deserves center-of-room position

Instead of being scrunched against a wall, this imposing tuxedo sofa commands prominence in placement as well as distinction in design. Its tightly-tufted seat of urethane foam sweeps into a lush roll of arms and back. Flanking one end of the upholstered piece is an oak flip-top table. Its spiral-turned base contrasts with the simplicity of the yew-veneered cocktail table. Furniture by Ethan Allen.

Plan a setting to provide enough seating

Too many living rooms offer too little seating space. But that's not the case here. In addition to the antique velvet sofa, which, incidentally, opens into a bed when needed, there is a matching love seat. A pair of low chairs can be pulled up for intimacy in conversation while the swivel rocker and ottoman offer comfort for reading. Note how each of the upholstered pieces is linked with a convenient table. Furnishings are from Bassett's new "Entrant" collection, a Debut '72 highlight.

living
rooms

living rooms

Use storage system as focal point

Stretching ceiling-to-floor, an 88-inch imported wall storage system is multi-purpose gem, has space for everything from built-in bar to desk complete with safe. Books, stereo, TV storage may be arranged to suit needs. Cupboards are ideal for dead storage. Lighted shelves house collections handsomely. Wall system and furniture a Debut '72 feature by Flair.

Use area rugs as colorful accents

Imaginative racing stripe design rya rug ("Primula" by Egetaepper) is a bold accent for black and white shag carpet and a strong support for floor-level airplane-type seats by Selig. Concentric circle chain rug ("Kamelia") is color related to seating unit.

Be seated on one of these make-it-yourself creations

Window Seat: Turn an old fashioned bay window into a charming perch by building in a window seat and topping it with a bevy of bright pillows. Complete the colorful window treatment with Tontine "Peruvian Stripe" shades and valance. For contrast, walls were covered in white with Stauffer's "Pueblo," a fabric-backed vinyl with a stucco-like texture. The cathedral-back chair? It came right from a thrift shop!

Niche sofa: Here, a wooden sofa was built right into a window bay area, then upholstered in the same fabric used to cover a dropped ceiling (which conceals lighting), bookcases, window sill and radiator (which becomes a broad, backrest table in which a narrow insert of red grill permits the heat to escape). Same damask material was laminated onto window shade, hung reverse-roll, and was used to make draperies, bolsters and pillows.

Storage Sofa: Need an extra sofa? Need storage space, too? Get them both by putting together the seating unit shown here. It's just a series of storage trunks (like those found at Sears), two of them serving as the sofa, two of them becoming end tables, and one making out like a coffee table. Cushions and bolsters (also available at Sears) fit atop trunks for comfortable seating.

Utilize the architecture

This living room using furniture from American of Martinsville's "Affinity" collection, takes the utmost advantage of the room's architecture. The unusual fireplace serves as a pivot for the conversational grouping; the traffic flows easily to out-of-doors, via the ceiling-to-floor window-doors; and the bookcases fit snugly against the far wall.

Set up a conversational corner

Encourage the almost-lost art of conversation by planning interesting groupings of comfortable chairs. Set upon a scalloped area rug by Lees, these well-scaled brunch chairs surround a "propeller" base glass cocktail table, all by Selig.

Living Rooms

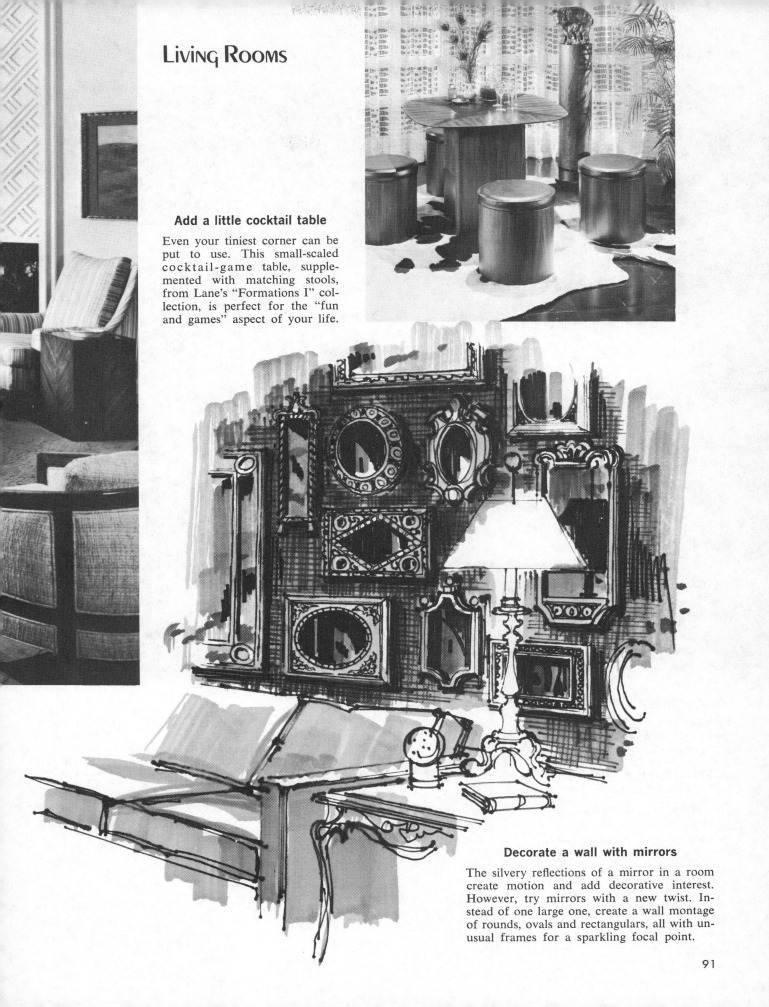

Add a little cocktail table

Even your tiniest corner can be put to use. This small-scaled cocktail-game table, supplemented with matching stools, from Lane's "Formations I" collection, is perfect for the "fun and games" aspect of your life.

Decorate a wall with mirrors

The silvery reflections of a mirror in a room create motion and add decorative interest. However, try mirrors with a new twist. Instead of one large one, create a wall montage of rounds, ovals and rectangulars, all with unusual frames for a sparkling focal point.

Combine modern and traditional

This room by Colby's of suburban Chicago is a gracious example of indulging one's individual taste to successfully combine modern and traditional in design. The new modern is seen in the foam loveseat, plexiglass etagere, parsons tables, etc., all combined with more traditional pieces. Daring feature of this raised living room is indoor terrace with real brick flooring, outdoor furniture, plants and railing.

Blend textures for interesting effect

Like color, texture is a major ingredient for creating an unusal room. Here, texture has been adroitly blended in carpeting, loveseat upholstery, blinds, shelves and tables to create an exciting room. Carpeting is "Empress," a Woolmark textured surface from Aldon Industries.

Add a new chair

Bring new life to an old room simply by adding an interesting piece of furniture, such as this "Parameter Chair" by Virtue of California. It features attractive, mini-rub upholstery fabric of Enkalure nylon, and is indicative of the new spirit of functional freedom in furniture for today's living.

Go modern

This living room (left) is a good example of today's mode of decorating. Furniture is from Thayer Coggin's "New Dimension" collection and features a sofa covered in 100% Trevira polyester print from Joseph Woods. Jazzy pattern sets mood for room. Colors are repeated in modern paintings on wall.

Build this easy-to-make coffee table from leather-textured paneling

Here's a coffee table that is both husky and handsome with its posh look of rich leather. And the plastic-finished top is soilproof, too.

It is easy to build and can be completed in several evenings' work. The base is of ½-inch plywood and a new leather-textured Marlite paneling. For the top ¾-inch plywood is covered with a panel of the same plastic-finished leather textured Marlite and trimmed with ¾ x 1½-inches hardwood mitered at the corners. To make it:

(1.) Start with the square legs. Cut 8 panels 10½-inches wide by 13⅞-inches high from ½" plywood. Glue the overlapping edges and assemble using 6d finishing nails to form butt joints as shown in leg assembly.

(2.) Glue and nail a ¾" x 6" x 10" plywood top block into the top of each leg. Drill and countersink holes in opposite corners of the top blocks for 1¼"—No. 10 wood screws.

(3.) Carefully cut the leather textured panels for the legs and miter the long edges to fit. Use sharp jack plane for the final fitting. Spread glue liberally on the back of the Marlite and clamp to the leg using wood blocks to help spread the pressure.

(4.) Set the legs aside and cut the ¾" x 20½" x 64½" plywood panel for the top to size. Next cut the leather-textured Marlite top to 21⅛" x 65⅛" size.

(5.) The ¾" x 1½" hardwood trim is next. Birch was used on this table to contrast with the dark leather. If light leather is your choice (it comes in brown, green, tan and white), use mahogany or walnut for trim. Cut a ⅛" x ⅜" groove in the trim to take the top. Level the top edges as shown. Then saw the trim pieces to length mitering the corners using a miter box and back saw for accuracy.

(6.) Drill and countersink for 1¾" No. 10 wood screws, one every 6" to 6½". Countersink approximately ½" below the surface. Use a plug cutter to make ¼" plugs from the scrap piece of trim.

(7.) Use a slow-setting adhesive to secure the Marlite top to the plywood base. Knead it to assure a strong bond. To assemble the trim to the top, slip it onto the edge. This automatically aligns the trim and will make it easy to drill lead holes for the screws. Glue and screw fasten the trim in place.

(8.) Screw fasten the legs in place and your table is complete except for plugging the screw holes and finishing the trim. The table shown was antiqued in brown to compliment the leather-textured hardboard. Staining the screw plugs a different color will add a decorator touch.

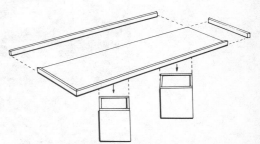

Include everything

Here's a living room (above) that's all things to everyone in the house. It has conversational groupings, a big lounging pillow, a game table, a writing desk, reading facilities, even a little garden in the corner! And it all fits together charmingly. Designed by Colby's of suburban Chicago.

LIVING ROOMS

Let modern art set the pace for a room that says Today

In photo below, Dux furniture of polyurethane cushions and chrome bases rests on a shag rug, forms perfect setting for large, rectangular painting. In second photo, one wall of room was covered with black patent, which serves as perfect backdrop for wildly shaped piece of modern art. Furniture in room was custom-made by Lakeside Furniture Co. Room designed for Dunbar Apartments in Chicago.

Build a sofa, then cover it with same carpeting used on the floor

Sound incredible? Build your own sofa? Well, it can be done, as our diagram here indicates. All you do is determine size you'd like to make sofa, then build a sturdy, square frame from 2x4's, and cover frame with plywood. Study our diagram for the basic construction idea, then turn your home handyman loose on it. Note that unit has a wide table area on back of sofa.

When sofa is built, cover it with same carpeting used on floor . . . in this case, "Candescent" by Venture Carpets, using Enkalite polyester. Carpeting should be glued, stapled and tacked in place. Use as few pieces as possible. The fuzzy quality of the fibers should hide all joints.

Cushions can be store-bought or made at home from latex foam rubber and fabric coverings. Since making a sofa is a big job, plan carefully to determine dimensions, amount of materials needed, sizes of cushions, etc.

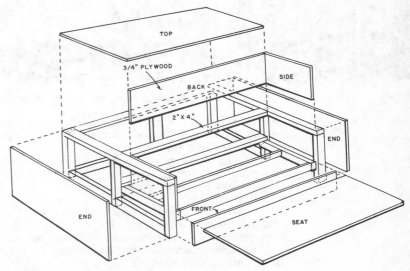

97

decorating
Living Rooms

Make use of new materials and new designs

Never were there so many new products, new designs and new materials to work with. One of the most interesting is Frontera sculptured polymer, a new chemical fabric process capable of reproducing any textured surface.

The first commercially-produced Frontera product—a suede-like, velvet-soft surface—is being used on many new upholstered pieces by such manufacturers as Charlton, Craft Associates, Directional, Dux, Flair, Flexsteel, Forecast, Founders, Lane, Selig, John Stuart, Southland, Thayer Coggin, and Tomlinson.

Shown here is the man-made suede used on sofa and chairs by Directional. Both sofa and chairs have chrome frames. Pirella webbing supports cushions on sofa and lounge chair, while arms of the two large pieces extend downward to become leg supports.

Although Frontera suede has the feel of actual doeskin, it is waterproof and can be cleaned with soap and water, unlike the real thing.

Mix patterns for "Today"

Today almost anything goes . . . particularly when mixing patterns. Here, for example, a geometric, a small grille and a simple floral pattern are used together happily in a small living room. Patterns are all from Drexel's new "Shelby" upholstery collection. Added decorating fillip is geometric print used as border on draperies.

Be different with a valance

There's no rule that says a valance has to go over a window . . . it really can go anywhere . . . so build one from heavy cardboard, plywood, masonite, etc., cover it with fabric, wall paper, etc., and mount it to the wall so it is positioned over an interesting cabinet of some kind. Use matching fabric on the cabinet to form a unit.

Co-ordinate upholstery fabric and wall coverings for a beautifully unified look

Here are three excellent examples of co-ordinating upholstery fabric with wall coverings.

In photo above, a ginger and white floral print adds vitality to facing traditional love seats and carries the same excitement to the walls. Ginger linen arm chair and white linen skirted table make separate complements. Steel and glass coffee tables and antique brass fire tools provide eclectic contrast.

In photo, top, opposite page, a floral print is used on chair, pillows and table covering. Same pattern then was used to cover one wall of the room.

In photo, below, opposite page, plaid wall covering is echoed in pillows and ottoman.

All three of these charming rooms were designed by Allen Scruggs, using furniture by State of Newburgh. Rugs are by Regal, lamps by Wilmar.

Divide a long room into two rooms with a simple frame wood divider

Here's an excellent, easy-to-do project that will turn any long room into two rooms. Just build a simple frame structure, hang woven bamboo blinds in it.

Use 1x2-inch pine for frame. To estimate wood needed, measure the height of your ceiling and the width you wish the divider to be. Cut pieces to size, and nail together with 4-penny nails, as in diagram. Paint desired color. Hang rods for bamboo blinds. Other kinds of blinds, or strings of glass beads, could be used if you're doing a room of a different style than this one.

This room reflects a Far Eastern motif, utilizes furniture by American of Martinsville. Group is called "East Wind" and is a contemporized Oriental collection, available in three finishes: dark Burmese, warm Malasyian and vibrant Mandarin red.

The red leather party chairs have the same slick look of the lacquered cubes. The large storage pieces in the dining area are balanced by the lighted curio cabinets in the living room, placed to show off an undersea collection.

Two campaign chests, with their low, unbulky proportions, are ideal bases for the bamboo room divider.

The sofa, with pontoon-like arms, floats on a sea blue carpet. All-in-all, a perfect haven for a sophisticated salt.

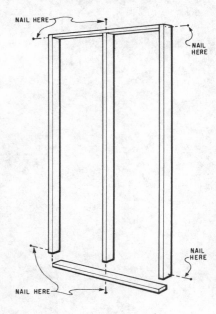

Living Rooms

Cover walls with barn-siding wood panels
to set the stage for a Country French look

Any room can undergo a complete change of appearance by covering the walls with wood paneling of some kind. Today there are hundreds of designs, patterns and textures to choose from. The panels are usually mounted to the walls on furring strips which are simply nailed to the wall. Check with your local hardware or lumberyard for construction details.

Room shown here has been paneled in gray, barn-siding design. Then room was carpeted in gold and outfitted with furniture to suggest a Country French look.

Dominating the gentle scene is an antique yellow breakfront, lighted from within to assure family treasures the attention they deserve. A pale blue strié loveseat, complemented by a minute table, vase and bouquet on a small petit point rug, is opposite a comfortable large, beige, velvet sofa. Plaid-cushioned chairs, blue floral upholstered armchair and a master's chair with tiny wood wings contribute to the more rustic flavor.

A pedestal party table and gold-cushioned chairs under a tole chandelier entice game-players as well as family snacks. Accessories include marble-topped yellow bunching tables, rush bench, tall, slender lamps for the sideboard, large copper lavabo, and gleaming metal flowers which "bloom" around the room.

Room designed by Colby's Home Furnishings of suburban Chicago.

Hang an alphabetical tapestry panel as part of a conversational unit

Called "Writing on the Wall," this tapestry panel by The Jack Denst Designs, Inc., is a geometric study of a stylized alphabet. It can be used horizontally or vertically. Panel is printed on linen, mounts to wall permanently or can be hung like a picture.

Emphasize windows with built-in bookcases

To give added structural weight to this big picture window, bookcases were built on both sides and extended around each corner. This simple built-in completely changes the look of this room, gives it an added feeling of intimacy. Note interesting arrangement of furniture to create a conversational mood.

Run carpeting up the wall,
let it serve as background for sculpture and paintings

Carpet the floor. Then run the same carpeting up the wall to the ceiling, tacking and gluing it in place. Then cover a long piece of wood with carpeting and nail in place as lower shelf. Then nail pine boards in place, creating the various niches for displaying art objects and painting. Carpeting makes an excellent background.

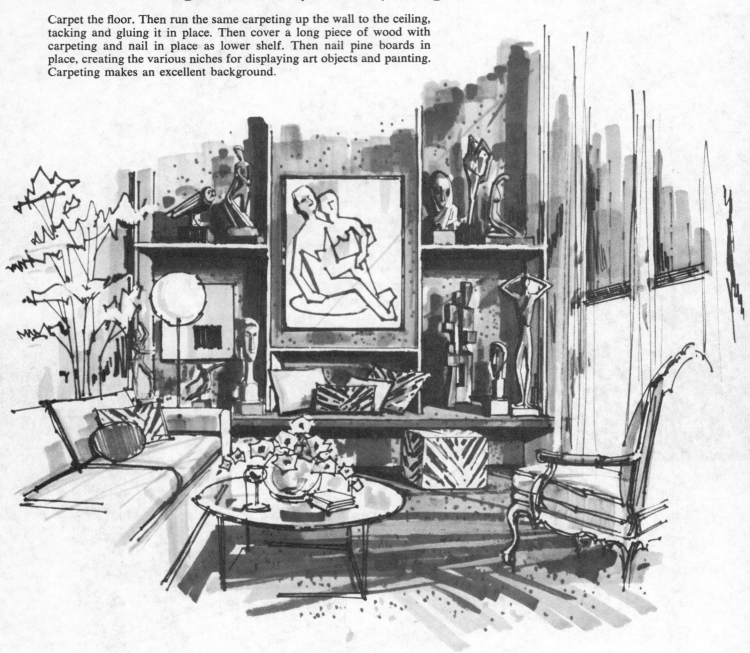

Living Rooms

Find a special corner
for a blue chair

This chair by Nemschoff is a circle of upholstered comfort supported by a graceful curve of shiny chrome. Chair comes in both fabric and vinyl, was designed by Larry Peabody, A.I.D.

This little charmer is a ladies chair in every respect. It has an overstuffed cushion and a recessed base on casters, with sloping, cut-away arms. By Flair.

Arm chair by Selig is from their "Magnum Collection," is made of foam with an inner construction of wood and springs. It comes in blend of nylon and wool, has Scotchgard finish. This chair, like all the others here, not only comes in blue, but in other colors, too.

Club chair by Flair is the ultimate in comfort for any man. It has all fortrel pillows and flaircrown cushion, is smartly tailored with contrasting suede belts and sleigh base.

Made of 19-ply birch, this chair by Jensen is assembled by visible screws, from four pieces—sides, seat and back. The cushions come in two pieces. One section attaches to inside of arm with Velcro tape, wraps around arm, across seat and over other arm in same fashion. Back cushion also attaches to frame with tape. Frame is white lacquer.

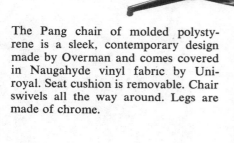

The Pang chair of molded polystyrene is a sleek, contemporary design made by Overman and comes covered in Naugahyde vinyl fabric by Uniroyal. Seat cushion is removable. Chair swivels all the way around. Legs are made of chrome.

Named for its segmented construction as well as its softness, the Petal chair from Selig's "Imperial Collection" has rounded edges and the smooth simplicity of foam-padded slabs.

Living Rooms

Add a spot of sunshine here and there

Love seats are more popular today than ever, mainly because of their simplicity and charm. This one by Directional from its "Sedgefield Collection" has good clean lines and will blend easily with other furniture styles.

The delicate tracery of white bamboo, sharply etched against crisp yellow is the feature of this charming parsons table. It's part of a collection (cabinets, chests, mirrors, etc.) designed by Australian designer, Lemeau, for Raymor.

Here's an accent piece that would grace any room . . . a small bombé commode (29 inches wide) in Mimosa yellow with scroll design. From Drexel's "Et Cetera" group, it can be used as an end table or as an occasional chest.

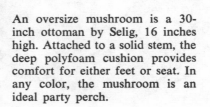

An oversize mushroom is a 30-inch ottoman by Selig, 16 inches high. Attached to a solid stem, the deep polyfoam cushion provides comfort for either feet or seat. In any color, the mushroom is an ideal party perch.

Use imitation beams and carved doors to set the stage for a Spanish living room

One of the most interesting new products on the market today is lightweight, urethane foam beams, which can easily be stuck in place with adhesive. Several companies now manufacture these beams in a variety of styles; check your local lumber yard or hardware store for patterns.

Here, they have been placed on walls and ceilings to create a mood for a Spanish-style room.

Additional mood was created by nailing two carved wooden doors to the walls, hanging an old-style tropical fan from the ceiling, and filling the room with an antiqued armoire, sleek foalskin chairs with leather-sling armrests, burnt orange lacquered parson's table, wicker chair, big, boxy tufted black couch, tasseled, striped and furry cushions, iron and sheepskin stools, a terra cotta tile floor, and a great Moroccan rug with huge pigtail tassels. All of these encourage applause for the sheer bravado that is the Spanish primitive prerogative to stir together favored decorative ideas—the mixing of textures, colors and patterns.

Designed by Colby's of suburban Chicago, this two-level Spanish room illustrates the growing relationship between the living room and an adjacent room, in this case the Spanish dining room-kitchen, crowned with a huge iron loop with its meat hooks employed to dangle a dazzling array of copper pans. Its entrance is marked by gay striped orange, brown and eggshell draperies, trimmed with string tassels.

Utilized here as a dining and serving area, the "kitchen" takes delicious advantage of a distressed oak wine cabinet for storage, a tea trolley and a sideboard, studded with Moorish tiles to echo, but not match floor tiles, and topped with a 19th century stove.

Four ladderback chairs accessorize a round maple table for dining and game-play.

Swirled plaster walls are pierced to provide niches for display of earthenware and sculpture; animal themes add to the country flavor.

Create an exciting Oriental living room

Living Rooms

Far from inscrutable, designer Robert Turner's intentions for this Oriental living room are marvelously obvious; the room is designed to provide a serene, cool-blue atmosphere for any family activity from pure contemplation (staring into the fire), to conversation, to puzzle construction, a fine project for the massive black-lacquered cane coffee table.

Pale gray walls, softly patterned blue and white strié couch, and a magnificent white Oriental rug with velvety blue border and floral design are subtle as wind-bells; an imposing 18th century bronze figure, chrome yellow cushioned chairs, and a very contemporary, horn-curved, brass-accented chair really strike a gong with sensational effect. Rattan chairs and settee, cushioned in natural cotton, and a glass-topped rattan end table, establish cordial relations between Oriental design and American comfort.

Carved engaged columns focus the eye on the fireplace with its lofty decorations, a Chinese Chippendale mirror flanked by bronze jars bursting with peacock and ostrich feathers. Further coaxing fireside attention are twin cushioned stools, upholstered completely in a blue Dalmatian print, terminating at the foot with tasseled "paws."

Also present is a modern regard for storage; block-design stacking units offer the family space for art, reading, music and study material. Room was designed for Colby's Home Furnishings of suburban Chicago.

Make a foyer with a partition

No hallway or foyer? Make one by installing a floor-to-ceiling partition, thereby creating "doors" at either side. Build partition frame from 2x4's, cover with plywood, cover both sides of frame with fabric, wall paper, etc. Add wood strips or moulding around edges. Place mirror wall set on one side ("Saxony" by Syroco here), put painting on other side.

Dramatize your living room with a dramatic sofa

An interesting sofa can easily be the starting point of your living room, especially if it's as exciting as this one by Directional. Sofa has molded rosewood wrapped around the curvilinear frame. Plump, squashy, vinyl cushioning fills in the shape and laps over the arms.

Living Rooms

Use new cordless clocks for decorative accents

Today clocks are faithfully reproduced in every design period, and now come battery controlled, thereby eliminating cords which always have to be hidden in some way. Clocks shown here are from a new collection by Syroco, have batteries good for a minimum of 12 months. Styles shown here are: Mediterranean, Early American and Modern.

Cover bookcases with same fabric used on sofa

For an interesting effect, cover built-in bookcases with same fabric used to upholster your sofa. Result is a matched unified look that is really eye-catching. Wall area behind sofa becomes a perfect spot for a favorite picture or an art object of some kind. Used here is modern welded metal sculpture, "Matador and Bull," by Syroco. Little tables are also by Syroco. Note use of small screen to shield plant in corner.

Add safari accessories to a sophisticated setting

The look is "Now" . . . . in this sophisticated living room furnished in Drexel's new "Wellington Park" collection. Up-to-date color scheme in burnt orange sets off the subtlety of the menswear plaid covered sofa, crushed velvet chairs, and interesting safari accessories: pillows, animal figures, tapestry, etc. Ideal for apartment living where space is limited, is the oversize cocktail table with pull-out shelves for serving. The bookcases are spacious, add architectural interest and are perfect "show-offs" for accessories.

Living Rooms

In a traditional or contemporary setting, custom urges the use of a major painting over the room's main wall, directly above a sofa. Smaller paintings on either side could have been hung with bottoms of all frames on a single level.

Here the intimate "gallery" treatment turns a tiny hall into pure enchantment. The small crystal chandelier adds glitter to the glamour of the paintings and the mirror at hall-end doubles the effect. This type of grouping may be augmented without rearrangement as paintings are added to your collection.

If you're a painter yourself, show off one of your paintings by placing it on an easel instead of framing it and hanging it on wall. Here, it's placed near a window alcove and becomes an integral part of the room. Sofa here is by Flair and is upholstered in Frontera.

Use paintings as part of your decorating scheme...let them harmonize

How can you hang pictures to do justice to their color and charm and still merge them into your home decoration, make them really share each room's personality? According to Helen Findlay, manager of Wally Findlay Galleries in Chicago, an expert who considers paintings an integral part of home furnishings, you should first relax and remember that paintings are yours to enjoy fully, therefore they should be placed where they can be seen and appreciated every day. There is no false pride about paintings: they may harmonize with furniture, flooring or drapery colors, provide bright accents of color in a room otherwise muted in tone, surprise visitors by appearing as unexpected decorations in unusual areas, such as the back of a door!

Happily, it is acceptable to hang pictures anywhere you wish, in the entrance hall, bathroom, halls, kitchen, dining room or bedroom, as well as in the living room, as shown here.

Keep in mind that certain wall spaces restrict the sizes of pictures. A very narrow wall between windows or next to a door, for example, would do nicely for a series of small pictures hung vertically.

A large unbroken surface, usually the wall against which a sofa or long credenza is placed, is the ideal setting for important paintings or a group of smaller ones. A wall like this offers many opportunities for originality in hanging, although the traditional manner, still very much in favor, indicates one large painting with a smaller one on either side. Variations of this include hanging two smaller ones vertically, one above the other on either side of the major picture; or, place the main picture slightly off center with two or three smaller ones

vertically aligned to the right or left. When hanging such a group, it is advisable to consider it a unit and center it accordingly. Horizontal pictures, whose width sometime measures two or three times the length, may be pleasingly hung either above or below two or three smaller ones, taking care that none wanders too far from normal eye level.

The more contemporary manner to hang pictures is to "bunch" or "mass" a number of paintings to cover most of the wall. Here, there is virtually no limit to the effects that may be achieved. Water colors and oils, ornate frames and plain styles, modern art and traditional works, may all be artfully combined to create an attractive wall. It is, however, more difficult for the amateur to attain striking results than it is to plan the more traditional wall. But, for those willing to experiment, here is a simple way

Bold color takes command, and the Gallic authority in Bernard Buffet's famous paintings assures the onlooker of the importance of this dining bay. In strong agreement are two Orient-inspired red side chairs flanking a black drop-leaf table.

A beloved credenza creates a regal processional from a mere traffic pattern area when you group your paintings above and around it. If you have many paintings, you might change them at various times of the year, practically set up your own art gallery in your own home.

This corner study area is restful in blue and white, a haven of quiet for reading or writing. To add zest to the scene, paintings with bright colors are tripled in the vertical arrangement next to the window. Over a bookcase, two other paintings are placed for an interesting effect.

with furniture, floor or drapery colors, and provide accents of color

to preview the final array. Arrange and rearrange the paintings on the floor along the wall to be decorated. Various combinations may be tried before any nails are sunk. Glassed-in pictures should be hung to avoid sun reflection unless non-flecting glass is used.

Make a "grand entrance" to your home with paintings, even though you have no formal hall or foyer. Over a tiny half-moon table, place a mirror to focus attention on this, your opening gambit in art arrangement. On either side, harmonizing frame designs with the mirror if possible, hang two paintings, preferably but not necessarily by the same artist. Double your winning effect by the simple strategy of hanging the mirror so it reflects the adjacent room setting and, possibly, your triumphant major arrangement in the living room.

Small dining areas, too, gain individuality through adroit use of paintings; Miss Findlay recommends a grouping of paintings by a single artist, similarly framed and placed over a drop-leaf or other extension table, which can give the illusion of setting the area apart even though it is architecturally a part of the living room or kitchen.

Bedrooms offer wonderful possibilities for planning effective placements. The wall over the bed is usually a good-sized, unbroken area that can serve as an intimate gallery of favorites. And the mirror over the dresser can do double duty as it reflects your achievements. In this room it is better, psychologically, to concentrate on softer, less startling subjects than one might use in a living room. But the manner in which the paintings are hung is as open to choice as in any other room. Here, the European custom of hanging pictures on

doors to create the effect of an unbroken wall may be utilized quite effectively. If a closet or cupboard door cuts into a wall at an inconvenient spot, ignore the interruption and incorporate it into the larger wall area when planning picture hanging. Most doors have frames and these add to the impact of a special picture.

The kitchen takes on wonderful airs with its own share of art. Here counter-top work makes it easier to appreciate at close range the very fine details of etchings or lithographs. Or, if you have the space, hang colorful still lifes or a tempting landscape to yearn over.

Trifles or treasures, your own collection of oil paintings, water colors, pencil sketches or precious portraits will make your home a warmer, livelier place to live. Luckily the joy of living with art is a pleasure that grows with time.

For the countless Colonial fanciers—
three new Early American additions

Colonial furniture continues to reign in popularity, and each year manufacturers come up with new variations on the theme. The three shown here are from the "Sugar Hill Pine" collection by Plymwood.

Sailmaker's table is adaptation of table used by sailors in sewing the ship's sails. It has sleigh top with small box-like drawer on one end with removable lid and white porcelain knobs to simulate drawer pulls. One end of table had slight identation on top for placement of lamp.

Two-tiered round cocktail table has revolving Lazy-Susan top that rests on a sturdy pedestal base.

Versatile drop-leaf server has convenient two-door cabinet on bottom to provide additional storage space. Top section of cabinet becomes handy serving shelf. Cabinet doors have raised paneling and antique brass handles. Server is mounted on casters for easy movability.

All three of these pieces come in both antique and honey finish.

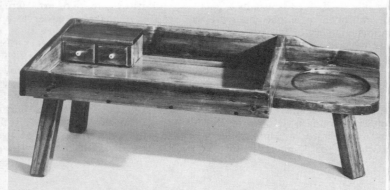

Traditional goes contemporary with today's fabrics and furnishings

A red wall, a white shag rug with black and white swirls, chrome tables and colorful rooster fabric are combined with traditional sofa, settees, a Louis XV reproduction arm chair and a magnificent credenza, to update this traditional room and make it a real "swinger." Wall shelf unit displays art objects, holds books. This room designed by Colby's Home Furnishings, Northbrook, Illinois.

Traditional goes contemporary with one exciting floral pattern

Matching wallpaper and fabric are utilized beautifully to transform a standard traditional room into something that really says "today." Wallpaper was put on ceiling panels. Matching fabric was used to cover window shades, upholster furniture, make pillow and table covering. All are offset by the wood paneling and beams. As you can see, the effect is quite stunning.

117

Sweden has long been known for its exciting innovations in modern design. Newest example is the versatile "Formula" collection introduced by Dux.

In photo left, jewel-colored, bonded nylon knit covers slip over foam cushions set on flexible canvas supports. The chairs turn into multi-unit seating pieces by simply securing their bases with clip devices. Note the neat frames formed of white tubular steel. A matching ottoman and white plastic-laminated tables complete this salute to appealing contemporary design.

In photo above, same furniture in different color is used in another fashion. Added are sling lounge chairs, also by Dux. This room was designed by Colby's Home Furnishings of Northbrook, Illinois.

A classic name and classic carving distinguishes this grouping of sofas and chair. Called "El Greco," it is enriched by lofty Old World-look cut velvet upholstery and dark-stained balustrades and panels.

Deeply-tufted backs and subtle colors in the fabric of the upholstery, reveal the formal side of the Mediterranean heritage. By Howard Parlor.

When the motifs are Mediterranean, look for features such as boldly-scaled furniture that boasts lots of rich carving and grille work. When the background shows textured white walls and the accents are robust reds and oranges, you've caught the essence of the informal Spanish tradition.

Combined to make this room look great are a handsome sofa with black leather end panels, a mammoth three-door display cabinet and an hexagonal cocktail table with wrought iron grille work. All are from Drexel's "Velero" collection.

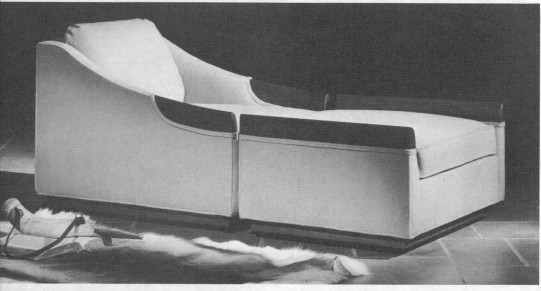

This chair and ottoman combination is for the man of the house

This contemporary, "sleigh-like" design from Flair, is ideal for the man of the house. It's big, comfortable, and is almost a sofa in itself.

It's upholstered in mohair, has wood trim and removable pillows.

Both chair and ottoman are on casters and can easily be moved around the room.

South America: new source of inspiration

The rustic atmosphere of a colonial South American hacienda is recreated in a living room where furnishings copy ancient Peruvian motifs. Authentic Latin American accessories and a rugged background complete the setting.

Occasional pieces, including bar, commode next to sofa and cocktail table, play up Peruvian-look carvings in Inca gold. These details, as rest of furniture, in Andean teak tone, are made in 3M's Tartan Clad. Furniture is by American of Martinsville.

Little touch: turn a trunk into a table

Search the attic or basement for an old wardrobe trunk . . . or find one at a second-hand shop. Give it a good cleaning and a light sanding. Paint hardware gold, wood strips black, and rest of trunk a gay color.

If desired, cover inside of trunk with a colorful wallpaper, Con-Tact, etc. Then set trunk in place and you've got a real conversation piece . . . and a table, too!

Fine French furnishings: the grand era

This charming living room shows a collection of French reproductions that represents the country's finest artistic periods. Designed by Maurice Weir and Yale R. Burge, both N.S.I.D., it features a wormy chestnut Louis XV cabinet, campaign chairs and a Directorie coffee table in steel and brass with a glass top. The traditional color scheme teams beige, off-white, gold and persimmon. Reproductions are combined with antique accessories from Yale R. Burge Accessories & Reproductions of New York.

The open-space California look

Designer Nina Lee, N.S.I.D., shows the California look: uncrowded rooms with lots of space, big windows to let in the light, draperies to keep it out when necessary, and smart, sophisticated furniture. Sofa, chairs and tables were designed by Miss Lee, who also turned a regular square rug into a free-flowing thing by sketching a design on the back, then cutting it out.

The charming Country English look

In spite of a few minor concessions to the modern, such as its glass and metal game table, a gentle Country English air has been captured in this restful living room. A single garden print, sprigged across walls, window and upholstery, lends unity and tranquility. English-isms emphasized include upholstery with deep, downy comfort, open-back bamboo occasional chairs and display space for the family china. By Bloomingdale's.

The compact, small apartment look

A small living room can play many roles if you choose furniture with many functions. For example, the storage unit against wall houses books, hi-fi equipment, TV, clothes, almost anything you'd care to put in it. It also has a foldout table for dining, card games, writing desk, etc.

Storage unit, along with other furniture here, is part of Kroehler's "At Home" collection. Sofas are upholstered with Naugahyde for easy care and cleaning.

New round rugs, new round sofa

"Helios," new round Ege Rya rug from Egetaepper, has colorful sunflower motif, in two sizes: 6'7" or 8'2".

Three semi-circular sofas form circular unit, as shown. Right and left arm sectionals are available as are armless sections with three back pillows. Lazy Susan table rotates for passing food, drinks. Sofa, table from Thayer Coggin.

The lowdown on modern seating

To lounge in a relaxed, informal way, recline on zingy "Calcutta" floor cushions by Regal Rugs. Designed by Lawrence Peabody to spark up today's living rooms, the gay coasters glide along the carpet or floor on big ball casters. Their fluffy sculptured pile covers, which can be removed for washing, are a plush combination of Zefran and nylon. Furniture by Thayer Coggin.

Modern etched in black and white

The latest high fashion "Looks" are blended into one compatible room setting (right). The "Black-and-White Look" is the basic theme, backed up by the "See-Through-Look" of glass table and beadangles room divider; the "Plump Look" of comfortable latex foam cushions, which are weltless (another "look"). The "Shiny Look" is reflected in glass table, Beadangles divider, mirrored globes and the shiny black vinyl upholstery fabric; the "Animal Look" turns up in fake fur, foam rubber throw pillows, the furry daybed, and the ceramic leopard; furniture by Selig shows the "Look" of modern furniture today—big, comfortable, close to the floor, amply cushioned and upholstered, warmer and exciting.

Modern means many textures

One successful way to exemplify the modern mode in a living room is to blend textures as skillfully as colors. Note how it is done in this gracious contemporary setting. The nubby pale upholstery of the sofa and pair of lounge chairs is underscored by the deep rich pile of the dark flokati area rug. Other textural contrasts come from the soft leather and shiny steel of the occasional chair, the gleam of the lacquer finished Parson's table and the smoky glass top of the coffee table. Furniture by Directional.

Create your own modern mural

Lightly, with pencil, sketch a mod-type mural on large
sheet of plywood, heavy cardboard, etc. Then cut black
and white Con-Tact plastic to fit your design and position
pieces. Use strips, circles, triangles, anything you feel expresses today's mod mood.

Nail or hang mural on wall, preferably one painted a
solid color. Add small shelf, held by brackets, under mural.
Put an interesting chair in front of mural, and you'll have
a living room wall unit that really swings!

Focal point of this traditional and elegant living room is the golden graceful sofa featuring deep tufting and gentle curves. Scale and line offer graceful beauty.

The small ladies' pull-up chairs, curvaceous also, with gently tufted backs, are in olive matelassê on off-white background. The olive theme is carried out in a deeper tone in the carpet. Furniture by State of Newburgh.

Gracious living at its best is this living room furnished in pieces of Italian Classic design.

The etageres used together make a focal point in the living room as well as giving an ideal spot for books and art objects.

Softly-rounded features of the exposed-wood trimmed sofa make it a showpiece in the room when used where it can be seen from all sides.

The small hexagonal commode table is just right for the comfy lounge chair by the window, and the high-back occasional chair in red plaid taffeta with olive green welting adds just the right touch, and the fabric is repeated again in the draperies.

Adding accent to the room is the small cocktail table in white on white trimmed in yellow with the wood top. From Drexel's "Livorno" collection, it's a style that will fit in almost any home or apartment today regardless of size.

Display your pictures on posts or moldings

Here's a novel way to show off your favorite pictures. Instead of mounting them to the wall as is usually done, mount them to some fancy wooden posts or moldings you'll find at your local hardware store or lumber yard. Colonial posts shown here come in sections which fit together in various sizes.

Cut poles to size and put them in place. You can nail them directly to the wall or you can position them a few inches away from the wall . . . in which case, you'll either have to toenail them to ceiling and floor, or use rubber disks or doorstop wedges and trim them to provide tension and hold poles in place.

Before positioning poles in place, determine where pictures will hang and put on picture-holding devices.

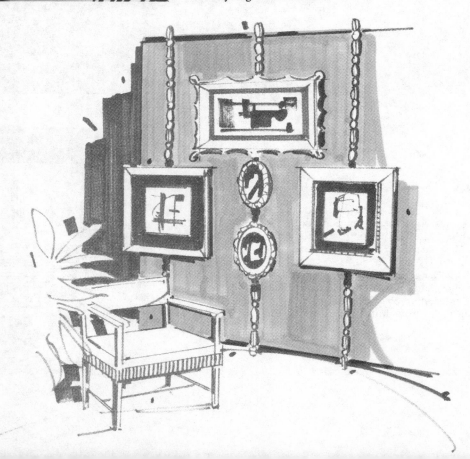

This formal living room has as centerpiece a very
simple fireplace in off-white with off-white panelled
walls to which a pair of gold sconces add a special
grace.

Grace and comfort are also supplied by two
companion sofas flanking the fireplace both in off-
white damask. Gently curving, these comfortable
seating pieces have a low roll-over back even with
the arms, shallow tufted loose back cushions, small
bolsters, plain loose seat cushions and plain tailored
occasionally kick pleated skirt.

Accent chair in bright Melon features curves and
tufting too with convex front and concave sides.
Arms are low gentle roll-over.

All seat cushions are poly dacron and loose pillow back cushions are shredded poly urethane.
Furniture is by State of Newburgh.

The eclectic style: the mixture is the message

More and more today's designers are mixing furniture of one period with furniture of another. Here is a good example of this eclectic style. To emphasize a collection of decorative objects that is largely Oriental, the furnishings of this penthouse apartment have been kept understated. They represent the spirit of several periods. The velvet sofa updates a classic Chesterfield design by combining a contemporary outside shell with traditional biscuit tufting. Chrome and glass tables denote modern while the amusing costumer is a nostalgic reminder of Victorian days. Sofa, chairs and tables by Selig.

Living room for a vacation house

This vacation house living room has a built-in on one wall for TV, hi-fi, and books. Small room divider is filagree hardboard panel set in simple pine frame. Even the coffee table is homemade; it's a large sheet of plywood with smaller pieces nailed on for legs. Furniture is casual. Tile floor is by Armstrong.

Patio can be a living room, too

Partially enclosed porch-patio becomes an outdoor living room by the addition of outdoor carpeting and interesting metal furniture arranged as though it were indoors in living room. Shown here is "Dogwood" collection by Meadowcraft. Cushions are removable as are cushion covers for cleaning.

decorating ideas for
Bedrooms

Make your bedroom a living room in itself

Advance planning can make a bedroom do twenty-four hour duty. Kroehler's "Mandalay" collection features ample vertical storage in chests, bookcases, etc., assuring full use of often-wasted wall space. Comfortable, small-scaled chairs provide place for relaxing and reading. Beds come in all sizes to meet requirements of any bedroom's dimensions.

Include a small dining table as part of the scene

The small luxuries of life can certainly perk up the spirit, and for many the idea of being able to have breakfast in the privacy of their own room, is a true bonus. A round, skirted table, perfect for bedroom dining, is accompanied by bamboo chairs in this multi-functioning bedroom designed by Evelyn LeRoy, NSID, for Dunbar Apartments in Chicago.

Include a useful desk as part of the accessories

A boon to every homemaker is a desk in the bedroom. Here she has a chance to do the marketing lists, write checks and enjoy catching up on personal correspondence. Desk is placed against the window wall for natural light. Quiet serenity is achieved via thick wool rya rug on floor and the new, sound-deadening fabric, "Wallscaping," on the walls. Both are by Lees.

Bedrooms

Do it striped or ruffled

The bedspread is the quick-change artist of the bedroom. Trim, multi-colored stripes give tailored look in top bedroom, while ruffles and flowers combine to create a room of feminine charm in lower bedroom. Bedspreads in both rooms by Desley-Edson, Inc.

Make a headboard

Zebra-striped bedspread by Norman's of Salisbury sets the pace for this bedroom. An additional bedspread creates headboard, was folded around large rectangle of cardboard or plywood, then lightly tacked or taped to the wall and held in place by 4x4-inch wood or fake plastic beams.

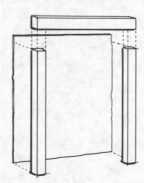

Coordinate bedroom and dressing room

Luxurious-looking fabrics always add an elegant air. In this master bedroom, a colorful harlequin print of sheer Fortrel fabric dresses up the window, bed canopy and bedside tables. Same Celanese fabric is used for dressing table, transforming the closet-dressing room area into a decorative, useful adjunct. White Fortrel polyester carpet covers both areas to fashion a smooth, spacious appearance. Exacting placement of furniture and accessories heighten the individuality of room, plus adding to the illusion of space.

Make individual canopies for twin beds

A canopy can be the crowning glory for a bed. The "Cameo" pattern on mohair satin by McCanless is used in this room for the bedspreads and for the formal, swagged and draped canopies which create an aura of regal elegance.

Make one canopy for twin beds

Same fabric used for bedcovering was also used to make headboard and canopy. Strips of fabric as wide as the bed were drawn taut and stapled to the wall for headboard. (They can be trimmed on edges with tape, if desired.) Then one wide piece of fabric was stapled to the wall, drawn one or two feet over beds, slipped over long curtain rod mounted to ceiling, and allowed to hang as shown. Glue wooden dowel to end of canopy so it hangs straight.

Use one floral pattern for windows, bedspread and table

'Tis true. One smashing print can "make" a room. Norman's of Salisbury selects an overscaled, multi-floral print and uses it for the throw bedspread, the covered headboard, the full-length draperies, lined with a complementary color. Pattern is repeated for the shaped laminated window shade, and even the parsons table is treated to fabric.

Use one floral pattern for walls, canopy and headboard

Pick one print you love, and use it with abandon! An East Indian print of Celanese acetate fabric actually makes this room look larger. Used to cover the cut-to-size plywood window lambrequin, fashioned into a ceiling-hung bonnet canopy and draped headboard, and even on some walls, the colorful fabric practically "decorates" the room. Simplicity in furnishings . . . the chrome/glass-shelved etagere and the straight-lined campaign chests . . . augment the spacious effect.

Bedrooms

Play up existing architecture

Remodeling a century-old farmhouse can offer challenges along with the charm. In this country home, existing plumbing dictated a rather unorthodox position for the master bathroom that meant a jog in the bedroom wall. Cohesion came by choosing U.S. Plywood Weldwood paneling. Not only was it used for all walls, but its extension in two mock-beams across the ceiling gives the impression that the room's odd dimensions were deliberate rather than a necessity.

Consider French provincial

An infinite variety of detail provides a fresh, new approach to that perennial favorite, French Provincial. This commodious, but lightly-scaled triple dresser from the "Monique" collection by Johnson/Carper, is typical of that period in French history when mahogany was a favored cabinet wood and fine brushed finishes were popular. Can't you just see a whole bedroom done in this style?

Bedrooms

BEDROOMS

**Herald the bed with
a handsome headboard**

Twin curlicue iron headboards such as these Italian imports give this Mediterranean bedroom a distinctive look (the imaginative treasure hunter might well find a pair of gold gates to hang behind the king-sized bed). A tall secretary doubles as a night stand on one side. A velvet-skirted table serves the same purpose on the other side. The interesting arrangement over bed includes octagonal painted tole clock and two portraits of real or adopted ancestors. Bedspreads by Nettle Creek.

A shaped plywood panel is mounted behind bed in room papered with waving fronds. Panel highlights a low headboard to show off the ribbon-like cutouts of the bed and to serve as a background for an antique wood carving. The panel is glazed tawny amber to complement the slightly darker fruitwood finish of the furniture. Welting on the golden velvet chair, foreground, is the same paprika red orange as the bedspread, chair and lamps.

A wallpaper mural of Japanese plum blossoms is mounted on a ceiling-high plywood panel to give stature to a very low cane headboard in a combination sleeping-breakfast-sun room. Sliding glass panels separate the sleeping area from the sun room. To increase the feeling of spaciousness, white vinyl tile is laid in both rooms. Two area rugs of equal size are used in the bedroom not side by side but at right angles. A framed Japanese print hung on one of the window panels serves two purposes—decorative and as a sun screen for late sleepers.

BEDROOMS

Built-ins are the answer when a room is shared by two. Here, wall space becomes the decorative focus, as well as the entertainment center. In addition to the normal bookshelves a special unit has been devised that holds TV, turntable, amplifier and speakers. Note the desk and dressing table. Flooring is by Armstrong.

Play with pattern

It's not what you do, but how you do it. Myrtle Todes, NSID, uses pattern with designer know-how for luxury Dunbar Apartments in Chicago. Ceiling sports a chevron wallpaper; settee, a polka dot fabric; window wall, a stripe, all in black and white. Furniture by Tropi-Cal of California.

Cover bureau drawers

An old dresser can find new usefulness with a bit of time and elbow grease. Here, Greeff's "Bee Flowers" fabric is carefully pasted on drawer fronts with slightly diluted Elmer's glue. Same fabric is used for draperies and dust ruffle for bed.

Bedrooms

Build a wall closet

Here's a big project, but worth the time and effort because it provides a wonderful extra closet for all the little things that don't fit in the regular closet. To make it, one whole wall was paneled off, allowing three or four feet for closet area. Then closet was wallpapered and fitted with mirrors, drawers, shelves, etc. This idea from the Western Wood Products.

Build an extra bunk bed

Build a wooden frame to fit into an odd corner, cover it with plywood, use latex foam rubber for mattress, and you have an extra bunk bed. Sheets and pillow cases shown here are "Bali Hai" from Cannon. Extra sheet was wrapped around long wooden board which fits into bottom of bed for co-ordinated decorative touch.

Match spread and shutters

McCanless's Americana print sets design pace for this bedroom. Repetition of print in bedspread and fabric-covered shutters emphasizes theme while providing trim appearance.

Choose a style you like, then create it

Traditional: The well-loved Victorian look is the perfect atmosphere for a serene cup of afternoon tea on a private pie-crust table. The traditional turn-of-the-century floral chintz pattern appears on the bedspread, draperies and cafe curtains.

Mediterranean: A look of liveability is created by combining Mediterranean with modern. The upholstered pieces and the built-in bookcase and storage unit are modern, while the rugged Broyhill furniture is reminiscent of Spanish grandees.

Modern: White walls, polished wooden floors, floor-to-ceiling draperies are perfect background for chrome, leather, glass and simple line furniture, all which say "Today" and say it most beautifully.

a private sanctum that's a leisurely retreat

Use a strong print fabric for bed hangings, bedspread and looped back over curtains as a design counterpoint for the crisscross pattern of trellis panels available at lumberyards and nailed to walls, as shown. To make small canopy section, nail two sides and front piece together, then secure to wall over bed with angle irons.

Co-ordinate with print

Gaily patterned, French accented floral print has sophisticated details to warm the cockles of a young lady's heart. An upholstered headboard and boudoir chair are slip-covered in the same luxuriously hand-quilted fabric of the bed throw—a practical idea for quick-change decorating. Roman shade in same print controls light and privacy. By Nettle Creek.

A trompe l'oeil trick makes a small bedroom look larger. Run coverlet fabric up the wall to end in a small canopy with a matching saw-tooth edge. Side hangings, box-pleated bed skirt and sheer curtains, at the top of window, are an unobtrusive but crisp pale accent. Bottom half of windows are curtained with a matching sheer print hung on bone rings from top.

149

BEDROOMS

Build a book wall

Wall-to-wall bookshelves are the design snapper in an 18th century bed-sitting room. Built around arched, floor length windows curtained in ticking stripes to match the fabric-covered walls, the windows give architectural importance to the room. Wine table does duty for early morning coffee, a spot of tea or late night supper. Designed by Bloomingdale's.

Grow giant blooms indoors

Zingy, overscale poppy print fabric cantilevered over bed, blooms year round. Fabric is easy to hang with cup hooks attached to ceiling on which fabric is hung at corners, then attached to molding to hang straight down behind the headboard. Cartouch over cafe curtains repeats the poppy motif. Secretary has musical motif painted on each panel. The furnishings, Italian in spirit, by Broyhill.

Hang a painting

In the past, major pieces of art were always hung in the foyer or living room. Not today . . . not with everyone being art conscious and decorating being "anything goes" if it works. Here, a lovely painting was hung over the bed on a wood-paneled wall. Painting gives the room a really dramatic look. Bed and commodes in room are by Basic Witz.

Bedrooms

Utilize new campaign furniture

It's good decorating strategy to choose campaign furniture for the bedroom. Uncluttered lines make it a fine choice for schemes from the country-like one pictured to those more urbane. Brass accents the pieces in a way favored by the military 'way back in the 18th century. But today a bright color palette gives you a choice the officers never had. "Brigadier" collection is by Kemp.

Mix interesting patterns

The clever use of more than one pattern is the hallmark of many bedrooms which are young and full of wit. In this example, two mini-geometric patterns, on wall, bed and table, are accented by a pair of Woolmark area rugs by Aldon, one red, one blue, laid on white tile.

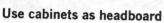

Use cabinets as headboard

When a bedroom is shy of storage space, cabinets, used in place of a conventional headboard, can offer the room you seek. In this handsome setting, cane doors behind the bed open to reveal shelves for magazines, radio and what-have-you. Night tables, instantly there when you flip out drop-lid doors which flank the bed, and a lighted canopy are ingenious touches, too. By Thomasville.

153

Be dramatic with geometric prints

There is nothing plain about the geometry in this zingy setting. The Oriental rugs were long in the family but the dashing spread and kicky wall hanging were made in a few nights with some felt and glue. Campaign furniture is "Brigadier" by Kemp.

Add splashy color with a globe-like chair

Spirited color in a contemporary chair gives verve to the modern bedroom. Base of this chair is polished aluminum; upholstery, vinyl. By Overman USA.

Bedrooms

Co-ordinate with matching fabrics

Garden flowers with a hint of the Art Nouveau influence in their design, blossom (above) on "Felicity," a pattern in pleasing harmony with wicker furniture. "Frost Flowers" (right) pert stylized posies etched against white, play up the one-pattern theme in this modern bedroom. And, updating the belovedly traditional patchwork motif (below) is "Printwork." See how it is an ideal catalyst to an Early American setting. All these coordinated fabrics are by Fieldcrest.

Bedrooms

Match dresser with wallpaper

The chest that was an attic relic or the unfinished piece bought as a budget-stretcher can achieve a custom-like look when treated to a neat covering that echoes the wallpaper. Choose a paper with a washable surface for prime practicality.

Add a swivel chair

This chic chair makes a sleek bedroom fillip. Of rattan and chrome, it boasts two removable seat cushions. By Selig.

Use patterns in closets

A peek into the closets or the dressing room can reveal patterns as pretty as in the bedroom. Here the stylized floral of garment bags and storage boxes, plus the small-scale cane wallpaper, prove that good things come in pairs.

Add a bit of old Spain

Transport the aura of a castle-in-Spain into a bedroom-in-America. Using fake beams, a too-big room was turned into a master chamber with den-dressing room behind a partition of painted plywood. Note how the cathedral headboard comes into elegant focus through this device. Night tables team beauty with utility, while the arm chair adds masculine character. Furniture is Maestro's Spanish Court.

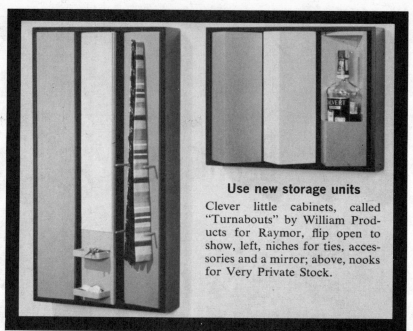

Use new storage units

Clever little cabinets, called "Turnabouts" by William Products for Raymor, flip open to show, left, niches for ties, accessories and a mirror; above, nooks for Very Private Stock.

Bedrooms

Create a fabric headboard

Any halfway handy homemaker can make a fabric headboard. Print in gay treatment at left was eased into place against Arno's Vinyltak, a pressure-sensitive tape. Idea above from Staniford Squire, A.I.D., used six, featherweight, polyurethane "Instant Beams" by Paeco-wood. Beams, which come with their own adhesive, were cut to size, adhered to wall to form canopy. Fabric was stretched between it and pleated into matching side drapes. Below, a modern geometric pattern contrasts with American of Martinsville's tri-panel headboard from their "Preface" group.

Put a laundry room in a corner

With the bulk of the family laundry accumulated in the bed-bath area, it makes good sense to add a laundry wall in the bedroom. This one was designed by Karl Steinhauser, utilizes Maytag washer and dryer. Note the counter for folding laundry and adjacent closet for storage of linens and towels.

Put a laundry under a table

Store portable laundry appliances under a Parsons table. Good for a small family, capacity is about half of standard appliances. Maytag's Porta-Washer rolls to bathroom sink while Porta-Dryer plugs into 115-volt outlet.

IDEAS FOR BEDROOMS

The imposing, aristocratic Spanish tradition

The richness of a 16th century Spanish Renaissance bedroom has been translated into a setting that points up several classic design elements. Its focal point is an elaborate headboard of arched spindles that recalls Hispanic arcades. The latticework on the dresser and chest, the crests on the night tables and even the sturdy, square legs of the desk chair are all typical motifs of the period. From the "Casa Nova" collection of Johnson-Carper.

Victorian-looking brass furniture is really wood

Brass is beautiful, but who wants the chore of polishing it? Drexel's "Barbados" collection takes the escapist's approach. Canopy bed, chair and mirror are all really wood with a tarnish-proof brass metal finish. Storage units emphasize the place-for-everything approach. Drawer chest and double dresser are linked by hanging vanity which shows off decorative bottles, jars.

Valet chair serves a double purpose

Bassett's valet chair, from its "Chalet" collection, comes in Lucerne White and leads a double life: use it to dress sitting down, or to keep wardrobe neat and wrinkle-free. The moulded back holds coats, shirts, or sweaters. The chair rungs are shaped and arranged for shoes.

Other furniture shown is also part of the "Chalet" collection.

Build a writing desk in your bedroom

This novel writing desk extends the full length of these bedroom windows to create a very dramatic effect. It was designed by Nina Lee, N.S.I.D., and was made of solid walnut. You can make a simpler one from a 2x4 frame covered with plywood, masonite, formica, etc.

Build a canopy for your bed

A canopied bed is a reminder of long-gone years when layers of curtains kept drafts away from sleepers. Staniford Squire, A.I.D., created this modern canopy-headboard by applying a new material, polyurethane "Instant Beams" by Paeco-wood. These beams are easily installed with an adhesive. Black and cinnamon plaid fabric was selected for use between the beams and for single panels on each side of the canopy. To complete a strongly masculine color scheme, a candy red bedspread of felt and a matching bolster were added.

Give Fido his own bedroom with a tiny four-poster

Here's a small four poster bed for a lucky Poodle or Persian.

It was designed by Kemp Furniture as a part of their "Montemarte" collection.

Bed is finished in a rich ivory and gold, and will make a delightful addition to any room in the house . . . a real conversation piece.

Unify your bedroom with color

One strong basic color can unify any room. In this instance, we suggest using color as the unifier for a bedroom. As shown here, same color was used in bedspread, chairs, rug accent, lamp shade and picture. Using color as a unifier, you can bring all sorts of odds and ends together into a whole.

Create a four-poster with strings of beads

A switch on formal bed ideas now enjoying renewed popularity is a simulated four-poster created with Beadangles, the unbreakable pre-strung beads which can be bought by the yard. Here, Paul Krauss, A.I.D., designed the shimmering strands to hang from each corner of a simple frame attached to the ceiling and outlined in velvet ribbon. Beadangles can be cut to any length and easily installed by hanging on hollow rods. Crystal strands pick up the bead theme at the window.

163

Curved lines heighten a romantic mystique

In this elegant and romantic bedroom, an abundance of curves captures the essence of femininity. The graceful lines of the period desk and chair are echoed in the turned posts of the canopy bed, the fireplace trim and even the carved angel casually holding a hat box. Arched wooden moldings define the broad expanse of walls. They are covered in Gaslight pattern Naugahyde in a warm shade called butter rum.

Beauty rests in the symmetrical balance

Symmetrical balance gives an air of formal dignity to a room furnished in the classic manner. In this urbane setting designed by Ruben de Saavedra, A.I.D., the twin beds receive cane headboards and tailored spreads topped with bolsters. Cord-hung oval portraits are paired on minutely-striped wallcovering.

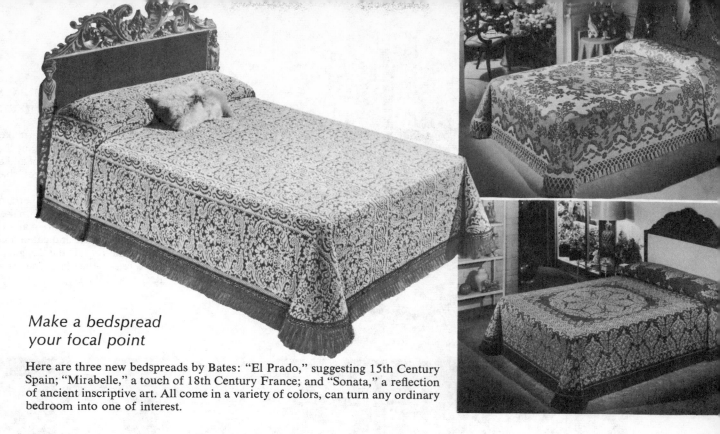

Make a bedspread your focal point

Here are three new bedspreads by Bates: "El Prado," suggesting 15th Century Spain; "Mirabelle," a touch of 18th Century France; and "Sonata," a reflection of ancient inscriptive art. All come in a variety of colors, can turn any ordinary bedroom into one of interest.

Some people like bed linens that are a garden of flowers. Others want to relieve the monotony of plain and pallid colors, but prefer those patterns that are crisp and neat. For them Lady Pepperell shows a handsome yet restrained striped design called "Miralux." It is accented by solid color borders on top sheet and pillow cases. For a mock-canopy effect, a pair of sheets have been sewn together, then draped from two poles extended from the wall.

Stripes turn the trick

A chaise longue makes a bedroom elegant

No piece of furniture makes a bedroom look more elegant than a chaise longue. So why not add one? They now come in all sizes, shapes, colors and patterns.

A few throw pillows, perhaps of a contrasting color, will make the longue seem even more glamorous.

Here, we have indicated a color co-ordination of the longue, the bedspread, the lampshades, the drapes and the rug.

Master bedroom, massive motif

This master bedroom is dominated by a massive Weldwood-paneled wall of exotic East Indian rosewood by U.S. Plywood.

The reverse side of the free-standing unit incorporates generously-sized closets and three-way, floor-length mirrors.

The rosewood bedside cubes include mechanism for drawing the curtains and controlling the lighting for the entire house.

Pink and red cabbage rose-strewn velvet sweeps across the bed and up the arch recessed in the wall. Its rich hues set a color theme repeated in other rooms of the house.

A bedroom for more than just sleeping

Getting more than eight-hour-usefulness from a bedroom requires special strategy in the selection of furniture.

Here, the right components make a haven for sitting and studying as well as for sleeping.

The upholstered chair at right, one and a half times as wide as usual, provides smart design and comfort, too.

The spindle-back headboard offsets the heavy look of the box spring and mattress. Note, too, the living room type occasional tables and the etagere for books and accessories.

Furniture is by Founders.

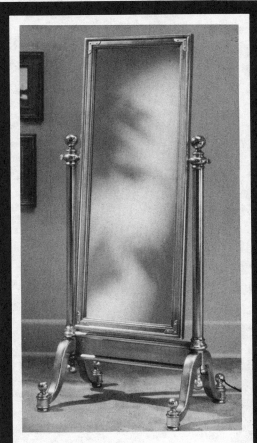

A full-length mirror gives grandeur

A must for every lady of the household is a full-length mirror.

This brass-looking one in Victorian style is from Drexel's "Barbados" collection. It looks like old brass, but is wood with a sprayed-on brass metal finish that won't tarnish.

decorating
Bedrooms

Create a headboard with wallpaper

The walls of this small bedroom were first papered with Stockwell's "Frolic" wall paper. Then directly behind the bed, a panel of Stockwell's "Rhapsody" was placed to create headboard. This is an ideal trick for a small bedroom in which there is no room for a large headboard. Matching "Rhapsody" fabric was used to make bedspread, draperies.

Give the illusion of a canopy in a dormer room

Cover slanted area over bed with floral wallpaper, cover sides with contrasting wallpaper. Cut matching fabric valance, staple or glue to ceiling so it hangs.

Build in a canopy and a storage unit

Scalloped plywood is basis of storage units and canopy built into wall. Matching wallpaper and fabric were used for walls and bedspread. Room by Burlington.

Bedrooms

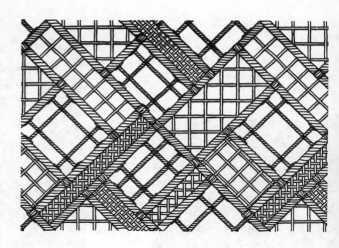

Trim walls and floor with steel strips

Here's a new and interesting idea. Use stainless steel strips on both walls and floor for an interesting architectural effect.

Strips are laid two feet apart on a Woolmark carpet, then are placed two inches apart on the wall. Result is a room of glamor and gleam.

Modern furniture is a perfect complement to today's look of steel. Animal heads, camp chair, and colorful feathers add just the right accent touch.

Do your bedroom in knotty pine

Ponderosa Pine knotty paneling covered with a transparent penetrating stain gives a rich, warm feeling to any bedroom.

Western wood mouldings, applied as panel mouldings over the paneling, increases the decorative effect. A wide crown mould at the top of the paneling and a base mould at the bottom is complemented by a chair rail at chair back height. The louvered doors are of Ponderosa Pine.

**Bring a touch of the islands
with a rattan wall covering**

Starting point for this airy, easy-living bedroom is a new, bold, over-scaled, rattan wall covering from Kirk-Brummel. It's called "Key Largo," comes in matching fabric, and is available in several colors.

Covering was put on all four walls, then matching fabric was used to trim bed cover and to make table covering. A potted plant, some flowers and a few pieces of bamboo furniture were used to complement the wall covering.

A real "fun" feature of the room, and one that really adds that "island feeling" to the room, is an old-style propellor fan which was attached to the ceiling. It can actually function, or just hang there as decoration.

Bedrooms

Use matching bed coverings and draperies for unity and beauty

Lavishing a single dynamic pattern over bedspread and draperies offers a sure-fire way to turn a non-descript bedroom into a dramatic delight. To achieve this exciting look choose a design that's big in scale and colors that are fresh and exuberant. First photo, opposite page: Nettle Creek's "Beacon Hill" pattern puts pink flowers in coverlet, draperies and valance. Second photo: Super-size flowers enliven quilted throw and generously full draperies in Waverly's "Exotica." Third photo: A swirling explosion of orange, hot pink, bronze and mushroom light up Nettle Creek's "Pucello" print. Photo below: A floral print bought by the yard was turned into bedspread. draperies and cushion covers for this exciting bedroom which features furniture from Drexel's new "Wellington Park Collection." Arches of bentwood-shaped headboard and sedan chair are repeated in doors, giving distinction.

Bedrooms

Solve storage problems with a large armoire

Storage can bring distinction and individuality to your bedroom . . . as well as take care of all those things that have to be stored . . . if you'll use the right storage unit. Shown here is a very practical one: Bassett's new armoire from its "Brigitte Collection." In French Provincial, it contains clothes hanger, tray drawers, luxury-sized shelves, etc.

Build a canopy that's really different

If there's a real handyman around the house, you can create the canopies shown below, or make ones similar to them. The first one is built from large sheets of plywood, with thin pieces nailed to edges to give unit bulk. Then whole thing is nailed upright to wall, and unit is papered with same wallpaper used on wall. Other canopy below was assembled from pieces of bamboo bought at auction and variety stores, then nailed together to form unit. Many variations are possible "Bamboo" wallpaper is by Stockwell.

Make this canopy from wood frames and fabric

This canopy was designed for the recent "Rooms of Tomorrow" show and is one that you can build yourself with a little effort.

Materials: 1 1/16x1 1/16-inch square moulding; 1x⅛-inch flat moulding (to determine the amount of moulding, measure the height and width you wish the hardboard to be); 4-penny finishing nails; 1-inch brads; hammer; saw; staple gun; two curtain rod sockets for inside mounting and one curtain rod; fabric.

Directions: Assemble frame as in diagram, use 4-penny nails. Paint desired color and let dry. Place fabric on frame, staple to frame at top, bottom, and then to the sides.

To cover staples, measure height and width of screen, cut 1x⅛-inch flat moulding to that size. Paint with same color used on frame, let dry. Nail moulding to frame, covering staples, and edge of fabric. Make two frames this way.

Remove base from behind bed.

Cut fabric four inches wider than width of bed. Place on wall over bed, staple top, bottom, and then sides of fabric to wall.

Place screens against wall, nail sides to wall. Paneling adhesive may be used instead of nails.

Fasten curtain rod sockets inside of frames, and insert curtain rod. Drape fabric over rod and staple end to wall.

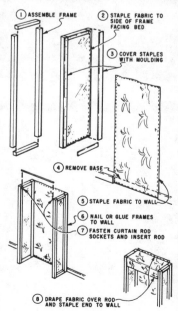

1. ASSEMBLE FRAME
2. STAPLE FABRIC TO SIDE OF FRAME FACING BED
3. COVER STAPLES WITH MOULDING
4. REMOVE BASE
5. STAPLE FABRIC TO WALL
6. NAIL OR GLUE FRAMES TO WALL
7. FASTEN CURTAIN ROD SOCKETS AND INSERT ROD
8. DRAPE FABRIC OVER ROD AND STAPLE END TO WALL

Bedrooms

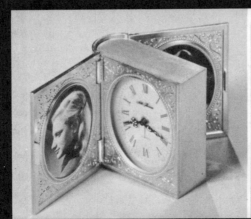

Add a little charm with two small table clocks

These two little time keepers are by Seth Thomas.

On left: "Keepsake," an alarm clock in a bright gold case which opens up and has room for pictures of loved ones on both sides. It's about three inches high.

On right: "Tole Alarm," an alarm clock which looks like a pocket watch, has hand-painted gold scrolls on fruitwood casing.

Make your bedroom a sitting room, too

Just add a couple of chairs and a small table, and you can turn your bedroom into a bedroom-sitting room. Here, the classic Mediterranean mood has been created by using hickory-veneer furniture from the "Casa Nueva Collection" by Hooker. Decorative door inserts and custom hardware add a lively touch to the solid look of heavy drawer mouldings and "flush to the floor" designs.

Turn a closet into a sewing room

Cover closet walls with same fabric used on bedspread, draperies, etc. Cut some shelves from inexpensive pine wood, cover with fabric, install. Do not cover bottom shelf which will be used for sewing machine. Make wall panel with nails or pegs on it to hold spools of thread. Put cup hooks on sides of closet to hold scissors, supplies. Use top shelf for storage of hats, handbags, etc. Use chair small enough to slip inside closet when door is closed.

Re-upholster part of a sectional sofa, use it in the bedroom

Tired of your sectional sofa? Has it outworn its usefulness? Then move part of it into the bedroom. But first, upholster it in an interesting fabric, the same fabric that was used to make window shades, bedspread and drapery trim. In this way you can unify the whole room, give it a very distinctive appearance, and provide your bedroom with a sitting area.

Draperies used here are of a mohair blend; they insulate, sound-deaden and are dust-resistant. Room by designer Robert Caigan.

Children's Rooms

These settings are well organized & decorative

An avid sailor and an American Indian fan are roomates in bedroom above, appropriately keyed to the brothers' hobbies. Kemp bunk beds can accommodate a guest.

Feminine bedroom for a young girl (left) has ample floor space, this accomplished by built-in bed and bookcase walls. Butterfly motif of windowshades and curtains inspired the butterflies painted on floor.

Rich tones of oak furniture by Kemp are counterpointed by lively orange, yellow and green in boy's room (right). Animal theme can easily be changed as pre-schooler matures.

Bouncy floral print is a lively background for girl's room (left). Foam rubber mattresses give bunks a light look. Overhang cut from spread on top bunk makes curtains.

Give your son his own bachelor apartment. Boy's world (right), designed by Kroehler and Masonite, divides a small room into hobby, storage and sleeping areas. Paneling supports adjustable shelves.

Sport equipment is kept conveniently at hand by doubling as decorative accessories in this teenager's room (left). Kemp furniture offers rustic simplicity. Wallpaper matches bedspread fabric.

Give a plain bedspread "flower power" and your daughter a room she'll adore. Felt daisies are easy to make. Sew them on curtains too. Yellow trimmed ivory furniture is by Kemp.

Delectable feminine girl's room (left) is also easy to care for. Eastman Kodel materials are all washable. Printed vinyl-covered hassocks double as tables. Desk and shelves were built-in, as was window seat area.

Children's Rooms

Play with pattern

Three different patterns are at play on the walls of this teen's room. The stripes, floral and graphic are vivid background for Broyhill's "Chapter One" plastic furniture. Bed was placed in corner and turned into a "built-in" by nailing a pole floor-to-ceiling at one corner.

Use a fun motif

Matching wallpaper, window shades and curtains in circus motif adds to the fun of this child's room. To carry out the theme, scalloped molding is attached to the ceiling, repeating the line of the cafe curtains. Easy-to-build open shelves encourages the habit of neatness at a very early age.

Install plywood panels to divide a room for two brothers

One room becomes two with a simple plywood divider that gives each brother his own "room." Divider can be installed in several ways, but basically you build it like this: Locate beams in the ceiling. Nail one 1x2-inch wood strip to beams and nail another at a corresponding point on the floor. Set two ¾-inch plywood panels (cut to height and width desired) against the 1x2-inch strips and nail in place. Nail or glue 1x2-inch strips to other side of panels at top and bottom. Make desks from plywood sheets nailed to tops of small bureaus and to walls with small angle irons.

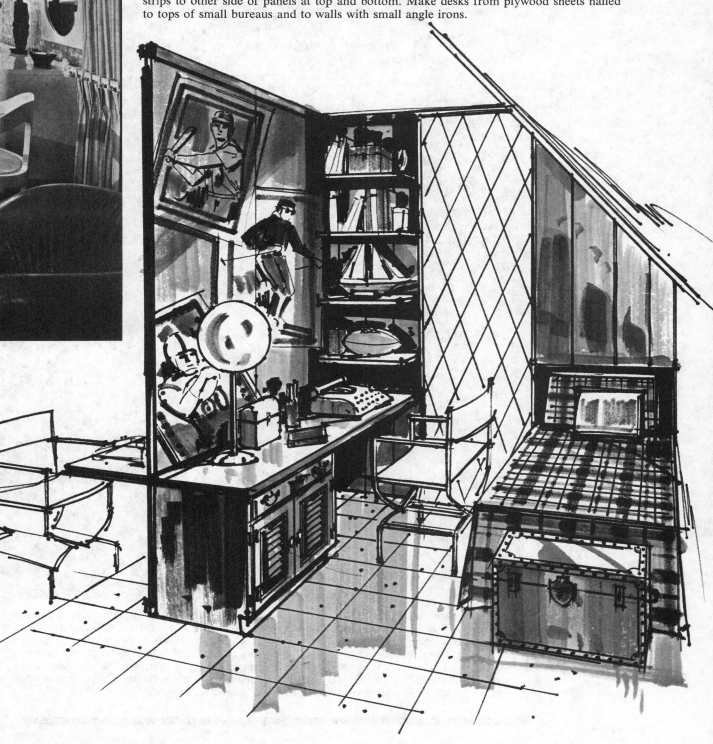

CHILDREN'S ROOMS

This colorful teenage room reflects the personality and tastes of a style-conscious young lady who registers no qualms about mixing solids, stripes and patterns with textured and smooth surfaces to create a total decorating effect. Three walls were covered with Marlite Designer Color Planks, which come tongue-and-grooved in 16x96-inch lengths. A fourth wall gets a colorful paisley fabric, which is also used to make curtains, skirted table and pillows. Built-in bed and ceiling cornice were made from the planking. Colorful area rug and wall hangings add more color, texture and geometric pattern.

Let your Junior Miss have a great time
with wild patterns and go-go accessories

Sizzling colors and contemporary accessories update the look of classic French provincial furniture in this young lady's bedroom. The right-now scene (featuring Kemp's ivory and gold "Montemarte" collection) was designed especially for Debut '72. A sofa by day, sleep space by night, the bed is draped with a simple do-it-yourself canopy, which is made by nailing 1½ inch plywood strips to the bed posts; then an exciting fabric is shirred and stapled to the frame. A secretary desk, topped with a stacking bookcase, serves as a writing table and a display case for personal treasures.

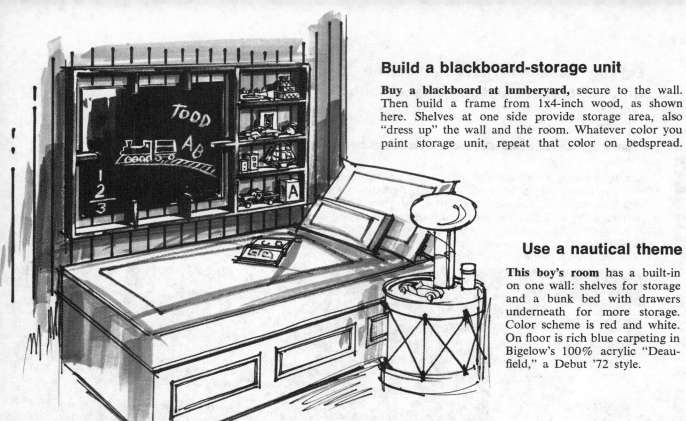

Build a blackboard-storage unit

Buy a blackboard at lumberyard, secure to the wall. Then build a frame from 1x4-inch wood, as shown here. Shelves at one side provide storage area, also "dress up" the wall and the room. Whatever color you paint storage unit, repeat that color on bedspread.

Use a nautical theme

This boy's room has a built-in on one wall: shelves for storage and a bunk bed with drawers underneath for more storage. Color scheme is red and white. On floor is rich blue carpeting in Bigelow's 100% acrylic "Deaufield," a Debut '72 style.

CHILDREN'S ROOMS

Simulate a canopy

At some point during her growing-up years, every girl yearns for the romance of a canopied bed. But room size may not let this dream come true. The next-best-thing is a look which suggests the effect. Here a curved wooden cornice, the kind that ordinarily tops a window, has been treated to pastel paint and nailed to the wall. Extending from it is a ruffled valance and a graceful pair of tied-back side draperies which reach to the floor. The canopy-like treatment and the matching bed covering have both been worked from pretty floral printed bed sheets by WestPoint Pepperell. Sheets also were used to cover one wall. Note interesting storage shelves hung from ceiling on chains.

Make a desk

Needed working space was created in girl's bedroom by painting a long plank white, then placing it over the tops of a chest and a dresser, as shown. Complementing the desk is wonderful window treatment of "Pioneer" window shades and shade topper by Joanna and ready-made curtains trimmed with Conso's tape and fringe, as shown.

Let it be formal and oh-so-elegant

Perfect for any young miss is this room highlighted by matching fabric used on daybed, draperies and crown. Custom-made by Norman's of Salisbury, unit uses their new never-press fabric, "Carousel Check." To make unit, piece of ½-inch plywood was cut in half-oval shape. Underside was covered with fabric. Drapery hooks were screwed into edge of wood, then wood was mounted to wall with two angle irons, as in diagram. Then draperies were hung, and crown was cut from matching fabric, and tacked over top of wood. Choice of accessories can change the look of this room for the age of the girl. Furniture is by Tomlinson.

Girls' Rooms

Build in a window seat, cover it with carpeting

For this ingenious set-up, a storage unit was built in one corner of the room. Unit has pine wood frame and plywood shelves. Next to it, a window seat was built in. Frame was made from 2x4's covered with plywood. This in turn was covered by a large piece of carpeting, glued and stapled in place. Carpeting is same as used on floor, thus providing a unified look to the whole room. For additional comfort, put strip of latex foam rubber on window seat before you carpet it.

Convert an old dresser into a new chest

Have an old dresser in the attic? One you'll never use again? Then why not turn it into a small chest for your little girl's room? To do it you'll need these materials: Varnish remover and brush; scraper; medium and fine sandpaper; plastic wood; hammer; chisel; saw; enamel paint and brush; drawer pulls; decals.

To begin, first remove mirror from dresser. Then remove drawers from chest and remove old-fashioned hardware. Use hammer and chisel to remove any raised ornamentation. Saw off legs un-

til chest rests evenly on floor. Sandpaper bottoms smooth. Remove old finish with a varnish remover and sandpaper—first with a medium sandpaper, then with a fine sandpaper. If drawer pulls are to be replaced in the same position, do not fill in holes with plastic wood. If they are to be moved, fill in all holes, let dry, sandpaper smooth. Paint, add decals and drawer pulls.

Boys' Rooms

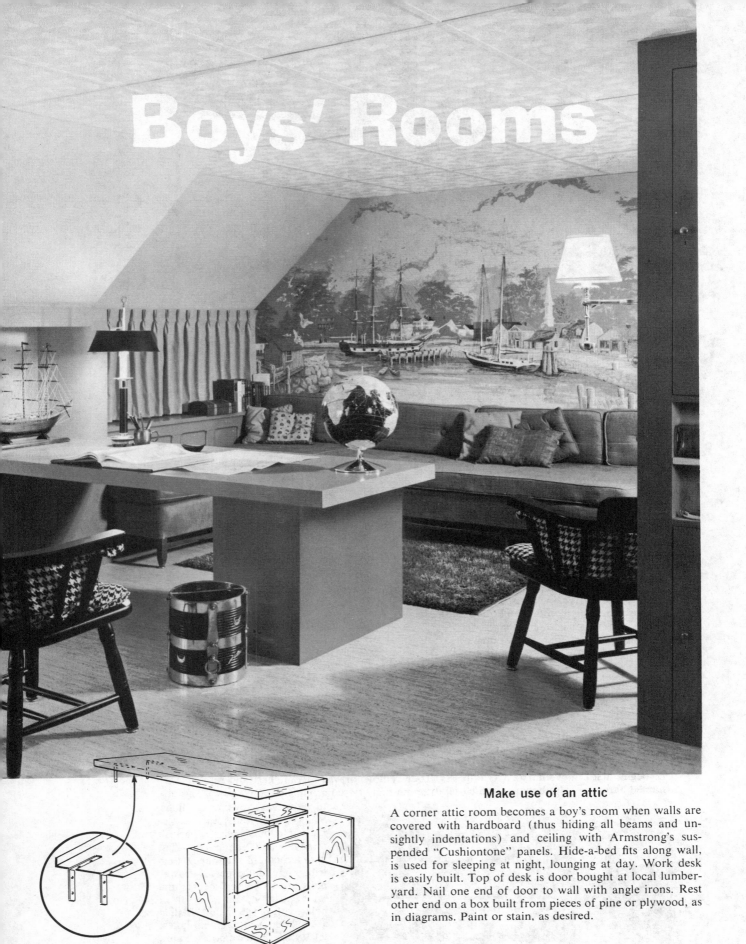

Make use of an attic

A corner attic room becomes a boy's room when walls are covered with hardboard (thus hiding all beams and unsightly indentations) and ceiling with Armstrong's suspended "Cushiontone" panels. Hide-a-bed fits along wall, is used for sleeping at night, lounging at day. Work desk is easily built. Top of desk is door bought at local lumberyard. Nail one end of door to wall with angle irons. Rest other end on a box built from pieces of pine or plywood, as in diagrams. Paint or stain, as desired.

Build bed and storage unit, trim it vividly

Ideal for any active youngster is this bed-storage unit. Bed and lounge are just two narrow, foot-high boxes with slats for storage. Build them from pine or plywood. Use latex foam rubber for mattress, cushions, and bolster. Cover in dazzling striped fabric. Cubes for storage are frames made from 1-inch pine, then covered with squares of Masonite. Use pegboard Masonite for those areas which will show. Paint cubes vivid colors, position them as shown. Small table cube is also pine frame covered with Masonite, and decorated with cutouts of Con-Tact.

Add extra bunks for little friends

If Junior is gregarious, you'll always need space for his little friends who want to sleep over. Here's a good solution: Bassett's new "Bella Vista" bunk bed with an extra bed which rolls out from under when needed.

decorating
ideas for
Children's and
Teenagers' Rooms

Stripe a room for a peppermint effect

Fresh-as-peppermint stripes are colorful, gay and just the right touch for a child's room. The built-in night table is painted plywood nailed in place. It provides a work and hobby area and is inviting for after-school snacks, too. Matching window shade and valance are "Holiday Stripe" by Joanna. Trimmings from Conso.

Use a smashing wallcovering

"Love" covers the wall in a charming young and colorful pattern by Josephson that sets the mood for plush, wearable carpet and painted furniture. Window treatment completes the cozy look using both shutters and Roman striped shade. "Posh" carpeting by Aldon Industries.

Use new "turned-on" furniture

"Plus One" collection by Drexel is new, geared-to-youth bedroom furniture. Two pieces shown here are chest and desk. Other pieces include telephone booth for gab sessions, vanity easel, circular table. All come in brightly-colored vinyl veneer finish to keep the silk-screen designs ship-shape.

193

Utilize new furniture collections

Never have there been so many groups of furniture designed especially for Young America. Here are three! (First photo) American Furniture created this group, complements it with floral fabric. (Second photo) American of Martinsville's "Hombre" will find favor with boys. (Third photo) American of Martinville's "Pizzazz" was designed especially for girls.

Bring dreams to life by turning an attic into a nautical paradise

This wonderful boy's room is really an attic and uses existing wooden beams to set the nautical stage. However, fake beams can turn the trick for any room. Sails of ship were sketched lightly on rear wall, then painted in. Bed is large piece of latex foam rubber fitted into an outline of a ship which was cut from plywood, painted and nailed together. Netting serves as draperies, and nautical furniture finishes off the scene.

Children's and Teenagers' Rooms

Make boutique flowers

They're easy to make, and they look absolutely delightful on a bureau or table. They're really plastic adhesive "Cling Things" bought at local variety stores. Just cut them out, insert a green pipe cleaner between two flower shapes and stick together to form each flower.

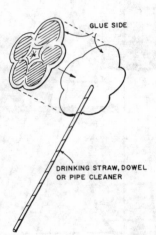

GLUE SIDE

DRINKING STRAW, DOWEL OR PIPE CLEANER

Delight with a jungle motif

Make our easy-to-build boy's bed from 2 x 4's and plywood in the simple box-like construction shown. Use latex foam rubber for mattress. Use "Jungle Junket" bedspread by Bates for bed and for cafe curtains and panels to trim bed. Cover windows with painted wooden dowels and insert toy animals behind "bars." Glue brown felt to corner of room to form "tree." Glue on various shades of green felt "leaves." Staple toy monkey to hang from the ceiling.

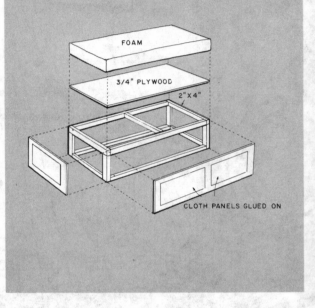

FOAM

3/4" PLYWOOD

2" X 4"

CLOTH PANELS GLUED ON

Paper one wall

For an interesting effect, paper just one wall of a little girl's room with a gay floral print such as "Sunflowers" by Stockwell Wallcovering. Then paint the other three walls a complementary or contrasting color.

Decorate room with lots of little animals. For example, two wooden birds were glued to headboard. An elephant drawing was placed over bed. Small animals were placed atop tables and dresser. A "cage" for animals was built from scrap lumber, wooden dowels, and some scroll work. Unit was painted, then mounted to wall, and filled with stuffed animals.

Have fun with signs

The Younger Set will love these replicas of the various street and road signs one sees all over America. Several companies now manufacture these signs in heavy cardboard or plastic, and you'll find them at local variety stores, boutique shops, etc. Use them on bulletin boards, over a bed, in a corner or arrange them in some interesting border-like arrangement on the wall. For special fun, tack one of the signs to a painted broom handle, secure the handle in a mound of Plaster of Paris, so it looks like a real road sign, and put it in an appropriate, well-traveled area of the room.

Adapt ideas from this bed-play unit

This built-in unit has many ideas a home handyman or carpenter can adapt for a child's room. Unit is built from plywood and pine, is basically one long, wide shelf nailed to wall. Half of it becomes a small bed; other half becomes play area with storage shelves. Small stairs lead up to play area. Toys can be stored under bed. Backdrop for unit is perforated hardboard mounted to wall.

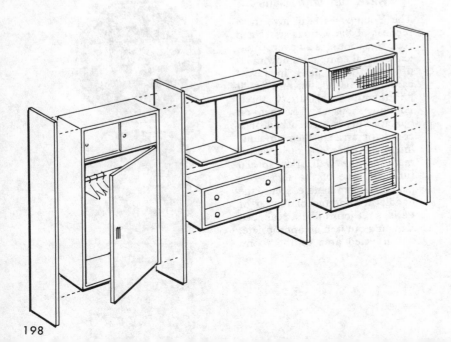

Divide and conquer

The children in this room share an area for games, but can retire to private worlds when the need arises. This is accomplished by room divider made from unpainted, sectional furniture nailed to pine boards to form unit. Arrange furniture so that indentations for desks, storage, etc., on one side can be used for bulletin boards, blackboards, etc., on other side. Note that other unpainted furniture in room was also mounted to pine boards to match divider. Paint furniture desired color.

Used on walls, bed, windows, etc., are "Fiesta Plaid" sheets by Martex, a division of WestPoint Pepperell.

Children's and Teenagers' Rooms

Use a small floral print

This charming little girl's room is decked out with a small, floral wallcovering used not only on the walls, but on the ceiling as well. Also note scalloped frame over bed area. This was cut from plywood, trimmed with molding, then mounted to ceiling and wall. Molding was continued down both sides to form special area for bed. Tile on floor is by Armstrong.

decorating
Children's and Teenagers' Rooms

Include storage for teenage boys

Divide sleeping and study areas with a desk, if there's room. Provide a room-length counter with storage below and bookcases above for all those things teenagers collect. For daylight plus privacy, hang a cafe curtain low on window. For greater privacy, add a window shade that pulls up from sill.

Provide a big table for teenage boys

Corner your sons' beds against a built-in bookcase to leave floorspace for an all-purpose table which can be used for studying, games, etc. It will be a welcome addition. Tailored spreads and bolsters, sturdy hardboard paneling, and uncluttered window make a statement of masculinity in this bedroom.

Little girls need storage space, too

Surprise your child with a sophisticated look. Little girls love elegance like this flower-covered daybed with its French curves. Build a complete wall of cupboards —you'll never miss the floor space and you'll love the storage space forever and so will she.

Children's and Teenagers' Rooms

Use closet for baby's "changing" room

Transform a small closet into a storage area for baby's bath, changing pad, diapers, etc. Install small shelves to hold supplies. Paint closet a solid color to contrast with rest of nursery. Put folding doors on closet for easy access to supplies. Rest of room is gaily papered, has Armstrong tile on floor.

Keep children's room simple, gay and practical

Cover walls and shade with a "fun" print. Tile the floor for easy cleaning (Armstrong pattern used here), and keep the room relatively simple for easy flow of traffic. Attach long drapery rod to wall, hang baskets from it to hold dolls. Build in two low shelves to hold additional toys and books. Use large wicker basket to hold clothing. Add table and chair for games.

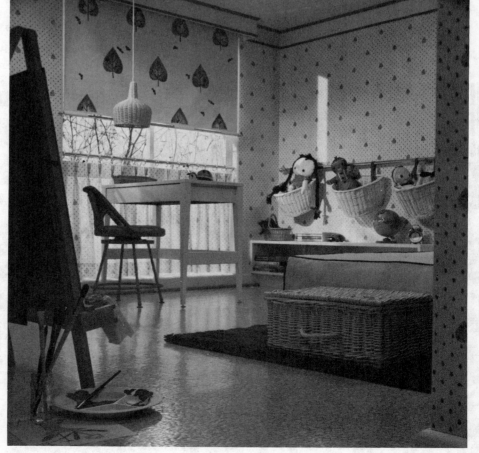

Use storage wall to keep boy's room tidy

Designer Albert Herbert, A.I.D., provides an incentive to tidiness with wall storage by Royal Systems, which provides all the stuff-away and show-off any boy could need. Unit can be moved about easily.

Decorate a boy's room with a vivid stripe

A striking stripe pattern (wallpaper, fabric, etc.) will hit any young boy's fancy, give ·his room a really dramatic appearance and be the focal point of the room. Furniture is by Johnson-Carper.

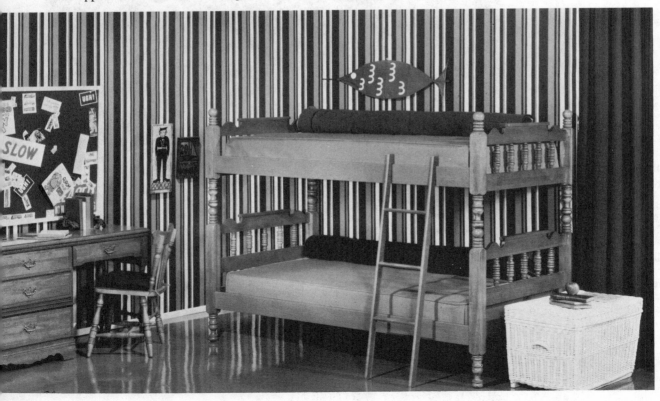

Make storage units from cardboard boxes for child's room

Gather a collection of same-sized, heavy cardboard boxes. Cover them with solid-colored plastic adhesive, such as Con-Tact. Divide some in half with cardboard fillers. Group them in interesting fashion in front of a colorful, striped wallpaper and hanging valance of same wallpaper mounted on cardboard.

*Children will love
this playroom with
its winding road,
toy house
and bunnies
everywhere!*

To make this charming playroom, first cover floor with Armstrong tile with "winding road" pattern.

Build "house" from plywood, nail in place over closet area and paint bright colors. Use "house" to store toys or play in.

Nail white picket fence around lower wall. Entwine fence with paper flowers.

Paint "sun" on cardboard, nail to wall.

Make "scarecrow" from scrap lumber and fabric, nail in place.

Cut chair seats from pine. Attach store-bought wooden legs to seat.

Sketch bunny bodies on pine, cut out. Attach bodies to seat with screws and glue. Attach angle iron in back for additional support. ("Tail" will cover angle iron when it's put on later.)

Paint chairs desired color.

Paint on facial features, as shown.

Glue or tack on fluffy tails and ears cut from felt.

Add bow at neck.

Use any appropriate table, painted same color as chairs. Add tulip trim cut from plywood.

Build a pretty playpen in the corner

Playpen was assembled from two French doors with plexiglas windows, plywood base piece and railing, and curved molding on ceiling with bent curtain rod to hold draperies. "Fence" is trimmed with felt flowers. Floor by Armstrong. Shades hang on doors as trim, and mobile hangs from ceiling.

Add special features for a future ballerina

Here's a bedroom to carry the ballet beginner to a tour de force. A full-length mirror is accented with decorative ballet position cutouts on wall to serve as reminders in doing exercises at brass ballet barre. Stage is set with Kemp's ivory-finished furniture with its delicate flower trim.

Fun wallpapers brighten a room

From cheerleading to hobby horse, from rope-skipping to playing with boy's best friend —and even including a bit of youthful courting, Classic Wallcoverings Connoisseur's new "Bambini" design is winsome and mischievous. On shiny white patent vinyl, it comes in several color patterns.

Friendly fauna—the long-necked giraffe, handsomely plumed ostrich, cheery chimpanzee swinging on his elephant friend's proboscis, and of course the lordly lion— bring new fun to walls in Classic's "Fauna."

For teenage boy: poster wall panels from felt and wrought-iron drapery rods

To make panels, cut felt to desired size, wrap around sheet of heavy cardboard or homosote. Nail to wall. Trim with two long wrought-iron drapery rods which come with brackets to hold them in place. Use push-pins to position banners, flags, notes, etc., to the cardboard-covered panels.

Using same felt, make matching cover for bed.

A future headliner will love this Academy Award winner

This bedroom would certainly attract any stage-struck young miss! It's filled with sheer drama from the brightly-lighted dressing room mirror to the rich shaggy "Zanzibar" rug by Cabin Crafts.

Even the seating offers a touch of the dramatic: she sits on a Cleopatra stool to comb her hair and in an Indian basket chair to study the script of her high school play.

For teenage girl: window trim and name panel from felt and wrought-iron drapery rods

To make window trim, cut strips of felt as shown. Position wrought-iron drapery rod over window, then pin or glue felt strips in place.

To make name panel, mount rods to wall, cut piece of felt. Cut letters from contrasting felt or from braid and glue or sew in place. Then wrap panel around rods, gluing or pinning on underside. Rods by Gould.

A future scientist will appreciate hobby-study area

This all-business small room was outfitted with wide shelves for electrical equipment, smaller shelves for books and typewriter, and a large, high table for the future scientist to work at.

Middle of floor was kept wide-open. Telescope was placed at window for stargazing.

Room is from a Tarry Hill model home at Tarrytown, N.Y.

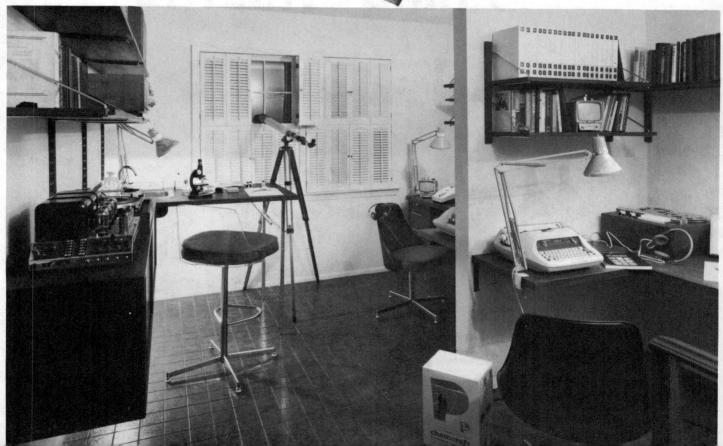

Do your dining in the modern manner

Modern design plays up curves as well as angles in dining room furniture. In this slick setting, the palomino-toned table top is set on a circular pedestal that separates, as here, when leaves are added. More pleasing curves appear in the contours of the buffet and upholstered swivel chairs. From "New Concept II," a collection by Milo Baughman for Thayer Coggin.

Dining Rooms

Turn a desk into a table

When you are pinched for space, a standard extension-type table that turns into a desk expands your horizons. Above, leaves down, it provides room for correspondence. At right, leaves up, there is an ample facility for guests when the furniture is rearranged in the room. Flooring is Armstrong's Vinyl Corlon.

Create a Spanish-style dining room

No hacienda? Do your thing the Spanish way! Trim the ceiling with mock-wood, dark-stained beams. Cover the floor with a hard-surface material in a tile-type motif. Choose furniture such as this trestle table, credenza and leather chairs by Maestro.

No wine cellar? Then add a wine rack

The wine lover who doesn't have a crawl space, let alone a cellar, needn't be without a place to store his bounty. Here are two fine wine racks, no wider than a chair. The jumbo, six feet high, holds 67 bottles; the junior, 39. Both are by Raymor.

211

Dining Rooms

Let your rug be the focal point

Texture underfoot can do it! When, as here, a setting is dominated by smooth wood surfaces, sumptuous contrast is called for. That's why a room-size, super-deep white shag rug was chosen as the foil to the mellow painted finishes of White of Mebane's stunning French Provincial "Lorraine IV" collection.

Co-ordinate your table with a window

When you are lucky enough to have a window that looks out on a cityscape instead of a fire escape, put your table where you can reap the benefits. Taking advantage of a window treated to a sun-filtering shade and topper of printed shantung-like Ceylon by Joanna, is a smart little rectangle of thick wood resembling a butcher block. Store-bought legs hold it upright.

Dress up dining room windows

Blah little windows can reach high fashion status even when they are poorly placed, as in this apartment. The unique tapestry-type effect is actually crewel embroidery on linen which covers shutter panel frames. This window idea and the furniture were designed by Nina Lee, N.S.I.D.

Cover one wall and the ceiling with mirror squares

To achieve this distinctive effect, room was first painted a dark color. Then mirror squares (from mirror kits bought at local hardware or department stores) were mounted checker-board style, on one wall and on ceiling. This gives illusion that whole wall and ceiling have been mirrored. Add mod-style furniture and you're 1970!

Use a colorful wallcovering

A room that is just a room can be turned into something special when its walls are lavished in a gay profusion of flowers. United's wallpaper sets off the convenient "floating" wall server and "Renaissance" party table and chairs by American of Martinsville.

DINING ROOMS

Engineer a pass-through and conquer inner space

Lucky is the home-owner who can open up both the kitchen and dining area with a pass-through. This dining area gives guests the opportunity of either kitchen or foyer watching! Decorative shutters will screen the view when necessary. The use of Armstrong floor tile in all areas gives an all-important unity.

A lover of Scandinavian modern defines the dining area with an area rug, repeating the round lines of table and chairs. Shoji screens and paneled walls are subtle background contrast.

Skirting a table is the way to carry through a Moorish mood. The high lamp draws the eye upwards to the arched lambrequin, created with the same fabric as the table covering.

A thoughtful window treatment and a carefully-tended planter turn apartment dining into an outdoor adventure. Window shades and matching cafe curtains hide an "unappetizing" view.

Dramatize your dining background

Nature creates the best background for alfresco dining. Wicker, rattan or bamboo are the natural, low-key furnishings that complement the ever-changing, ever-interesting decor.

Add new dining aids

Bassett's new mobile server from "Urbanite" collection has drop leaves for cooking and serving areas, can be rolled right to the table. General Electric's new, dining room refrigerator puts cold drinks and food, but seconds away from the table.

Do it up really grand!

Buy bamboo poles or split bamboo poles from lumber-yard or oriental specialty shops (or cut bamboo poles from bamboo-patterned wallpaper) and attach to walls, as shown. Mount bookcase in center wall with two long mirrors on either side. Carpet floors with carpeting running up the sides. Make seating units to serve as "doorway" to room. Each unit is a box built from 2x4's, covered with plywood, then with carpeting. Foam rubber cushions sit atop units.

Build a folding screen

Use it as backdrop for your dining room table, or as divider to separate dining room from living room. Screen is six pieces of pine or plywood, each painted or covered with squares of fabric and then outlined with strips of black tape. When each panel is finished, hinge the entire group together for this dramatic effect.

Dining Rooms

Magnify space with mirrors and see-through furniture

Double your dining area with solar bronze glass mirrors covering dominant wall. Wall is echoed in matching glass tabletop set on stainless steel saw horses. The designer, Roz Mallin, N.S.I.D., covered other walls and ceiling in floating flame fabric by Elenhank. Captain's chairs are plexiglas. Room designed for new Dunbar building in Chicago.

Add charm with a chandelier

Current Mediterranean styling is featured with this 5-light candelabra by the "Kwik-Lite" Division of Geringer. The fixture is available in 2 finishes in matte black with matching wood or avocado green with country oak wood.

Add grandeur with an alcove

When an apartment lacks a separate dining room false beams, columns and curtains can create an interesting facsimile.

Here a drapery-plus-shade arrangement divides a large foyer into an entrance way and intimate little dining area.

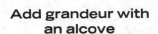

Let your floor set the mood

Apple green walls and draperies form a cool background against the black slate and white marble checkered floor in this lovely dining room.

Victorian chandelier, Queen Anne chairs, mahogany table and sideboard add elegance to room.

Be "with it", go wildly modern!

This mod dining room was designed by Neil Stevens, N.S.I.D., for the new Dunbar apartment house on Chicago's famed Gold Coast. On the focal wall, covered in a Florentine-finish silver paper, stands a handsome, stainless steel, X-frame sideboard which features a glass top. The wall itself is dominated by an abstract painting in a silver frame. At each end of the wall stands a three-panel screen covered in bamboo-printed silver paper. In the center of the room, under a solar bronze lucite grid light, a chocolate-lacquered, parsons-type table is used for dining. The teak dining chairs are imported from Japan. Floor to ceiling brown linen drapery covers the door window leading to the patio. A zebra rug defines the central dining area.

Create a dining room by dividing a large living room in two with a large cabinet . . . and turn the back of the cabinet into a buffet serving board

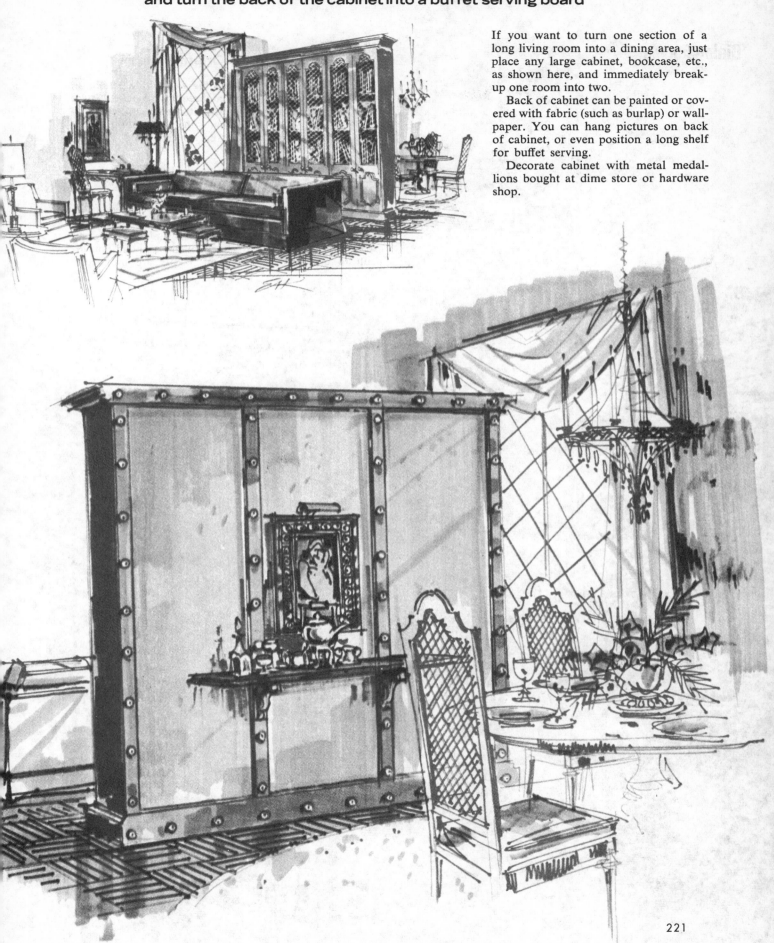

If you want to turn one section of a long living room into a dining area, just place any large cabinet, bookcase, etc., as shown here, and immediately break-up one room into two.

Back of cabinet can be painted or covered with fabric (such as burlap) or wallpaper. You can hang pictures on back of cabinet, or even position a long shelf for buffet serving.

Decorate cabinet with metal medallions bought at dime store or hardware shop.

Dining Rooms

Conjure up an Oriental motif

Defy tradition, go Oriental in a big way with a Mandarin motif cut into ceiling-high lambrequins to reveal silky white draperies and a Chinese potted palm. Cut lambrequin from plywood or masonite, then paint or paper it to suit your decor. Trim cut edges with braid or gimp.

Use wallpaper on wallpaper for an unusual effect

Cover walls with Stockwell's "Swiss Miss." Then, using their "Heidi Stripe", cut strips and attach to wall, creating design shown. Use matching fabrics for table covering and create similar design. Really very imaginative and not difficult to do, either. For accent, chairs are in checks.

Use a dazzling wall covering

Stir up a storm of wild patterns in co-ordinated colors and you'll find you have a dining room for young moderns, especially if the wall is covered in Jack Denst's new "Ode to the Morse Code, Baby," wallpaper.

Wall covering comes in cerise, brown, dark red, gray or bright red. Carpet is bóld plaid, and chairs of distressed white wood are upholstered in flamestitch fabric.

Final fillip is red fox throw on bench.

Use a wallpaper mural

Hang a wide-screen wall covering over your buffet and let art dominate your dining. This new Tapestry panel from Jack Denst's "Environment 15 Collection" is called "Ode to a Wild Carrot," and is printed in rust, orange and brown on white linen.

Oriental influence is felt in Baker furniture and accessories by C.D. Peacock.

223

Dining Rooms

Use a folding table for a small dining room

If space is a difficulty, here's an attractive modern Danish table by Hampden that may solve your problem. Open up this walnut-grained, vinyl table and you have a dining area of 72x30 inches. Fold down or remove the leaves and you have a compact 30x36-inch incidental piece. Or fold up the legs, put it in closet.

Create a dining room with a round rug

Let outdoor carpeting set the stage for an outdoor dining room

The room outdoors will have a more tailored look this year. Outdoor carpet has made extension of indoor elegance both practical and desirable. These new fade-free, weatherproof carpets come in literally hundreds of colors, patterns, and textures. Some are needle-punched (to look like felt). Still others are tufted or flocked (to look like real carpet).

This one is "Bright Forecast," one of a family of three outdoor carpets made by Lees. It's made of Acrylic pile yarns tufted through a solid sheet of polypropylene.

A good way to set off a dining area in a larger room is to place table on an attractive round rug, as was done in this one-room vacation house designed by Barbara Dorn, A.I.D. Focal point of the room is the circular fireplace designed so that it can be enjoyed from all areas of room. Royal vinyl carpet used in living room, vinyl slate flooring on rest of room.

Create a dining room using a wall-hung storage unit

Space, convenience and good looks were the chief considerations when Albert Herbert, A.I.D., designed this kitchen as a room to be used for more than just cooking. Wall-hung furniture by Royal Systems provides plenty of vertical storage and dining table with drop-leaf extension. Glass-fronted cabinets displaying china and glass have colorful wall interest as well as the more practical function, while the lower cabinets and chests store silver and linens in addition to giving extra serving surfaces.

IDEAS
FOR
DINING ROOMS

Give dining room windows a formal look

Formal, traditional, and thoroughly delightful is this easy-care window treatment featuring "Roman Lamp," a screen-printed roller shade from Joanna's Prestige Prints collection (above left).

Lambrequin around window was cut from plywood, nailed in place, painted white to match woodwork, and then trimmed with Conso's wide scroll braid.

Give dining area a floral look

Let flowers bloom year round in your dining area by laminating a shade with a floral print. Used here is Stauffer's heat-sensitive, adhesive-coated Tontine shade cloth which comes in two types, opaque Tri-Lam for room-darkening and Tran-Lam for a controlled amount of translucent light. Both come in widths to 68 inches and can be readily bonded to most fabrics with a warm iron.

Bands of self-adhering, nylon velvet ribbon frame the window and become the matching shade border. The same trimming edges the short white organdy cloth topping the patterned table covering.

Give whole dining room a floral look

Matching wallpaper and fabric combine to create this room of floral fancy. Scalloped lambrequin was cut from plywood, covered with fabric, nailed in place. Cafe curtains were cut from same fabric, put in place. Then, top of lambrequin and bottom of shade were trimmed with Joanna's new press-on fringe. Same fringe also trims the white topper on table to accent underskirt underneath.

Observe the formalities...

Children behave better and friends are flattered when dinner is served in a formal dining room like that above.

"Royal Tribune" furniture by American of Martinsville combines elm burl with walnut veneers and pecan solids to produce a warm, rich effect. There's lots of storage space for dining needs in the glass-doored china cabinet, server and buffet.

Note lambrequin around window. It was cut from plywood, nailed in place, then painted with rest of room.

...or go wildly modern!

Modern is more than a simple design description. It also means the application of materials that are up-to-the-minute. Both concepts blend together in a compact dining group set in a little alcove (left).

The oval table top, of black melamine plastic, is paired with a base of polished chrome on cast aluminum. Both surfaces come under the easy-care category. "Tiger skin" cloth covers the inner contours of the gleaming pedestal-base chairs. Their backs are of black vinyl. Furniture is by Chromcraft.

Small table suits small room

Furniture manufacturers are coping brilliantly with today's larger people and smaller rooms by providing solid, but scaled-down pieces like this dining group for a small room by Directional. Glass-top table is just 44 inches in diameter and the right height for comfortable molded walnut swivel chairs.

Dramatic lambrequin dramatizes twin-windowed room

Stately and sumptuous, yet contemporary as a moon flight, is this dining area. Modern furniture with a strong architectural look, gains added impact when displayed against twin windows dramatically united by a single floor-to-ceiling lambrequin. Build lambrequin from plywood, paint desired color, trim with fringe, braid, etc.

An opulent crystal chandelier brings dazzle to any dining room

For real elegance in a dining room nothing can be more effective than a dazzling chandelier.

Shown here is the charisma of crystal in a new cast bronze lighting design of grandeur from Lightolier. The blazing jewels invite, ignite and intensify an aura of romance and radiance. The antique gold finish gleams with Old World artistry.

No dining room? Invent one!

Small alcove area becomes dining room when treated as shown in photo left.

A ceiling-high mural gives outdoor air to indoor aerie for eating.

Small table fits in place on snowcap white Olefin carpet.

Note use of tile trim on steps.

Slick prefab fireplace is just right for area like this.

For sip-ins and snacks

The furniture is functional and so is the floor in this distinctly "today" dining corner for informal gatherings (above right).

Vivid pillows around a low pedestal table add to the color and comfort of the magenta Imperial Court carpeting by Evans-Black.

Munch around a maypole

Knees never knock table legs in this family room dining area.

The table is slung from a central pole, required for support when a basement bearing wall was removed. If pole cannot be removed, build table in pieces, fit around pole, secure together underneath.

Comfortable wicker chairs double for dining and relaxing.

Tile floor is by Armstrong.

Put it all on one wall

The one-wall kitchen has been most often seen in efficiency apartments or small homes, but because it adapts so well, it is becoming increasingly popular in new home construction. Here, we see the one-wall kitchen placed against a brick wall of a vacation house. Appliances (here, they're by Hotpoint) are accented by a wild collection of wall trims which help to create a whole exciting unit.

Create a KITCHEN
which has a space
and a place for everything

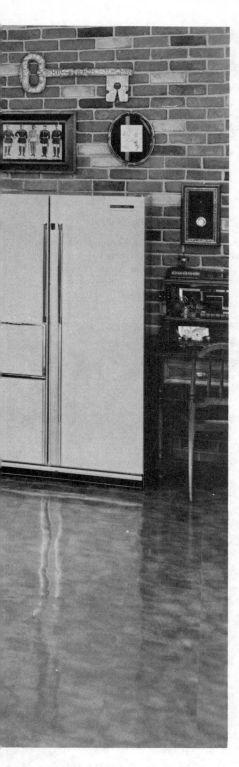

Use carpeting on floor and for splashboard

For unity, same carpeting used on floor ("Abstractions" by Viking) was also used to cover splashboard in this simple, smart-looking country kitchen. Carpeting in kitchen makes for easy cleanup, comfort underfoot, less noise and less breakage of glassware.

Build storage unit

Make your kitchen window a decorating focal point by surrounding it with a series of simple wooden shelves to be filled with colorful, everyday utensils. Unit will also serve to display a patterned window shade, covered with the same material used on the walls.

Have fun with animal high chairs

"Mr. Frog" and "Mr. Bear" were designed by Bassett Industries to introduce the Sesame St. generation to the world of animals and to encourage good eating habits at the same time . . . "Mr. Frog," for example, does not hop around at mealtime and "Mr. Bear" is president of the "Lick Your Plate Clean" club. Chairs are sturdy, have removable trays.

Laminate shades with same wall pattern

The charm of this kitchen comes from a decorating trick that always works. Cover walls and ceiling with an interesting wallcovering, then use matching fabric to cover shades, thereby unifying the room. You can even make a table covering of the same material . . . or cover a canister set . . . or a bulletin board . . . all of which results in a neat custom-made look.

Angle a sink, use a mural for a window

This kitchen design gives the sink a new dimension. By setting the sink at an angle, additional counter space is available for food preparation. You can also set up an "assembly line" to polish off the evening dishes in record time. Another design feature is the Marlite mural panel behind the sink. The pictorial scene takes the place of a window on this inside wall. Like all Marlite, this plastic-finished mural is highly resistant to heat and moisture. It can be damp-wiped clean; never requires refinishing. The mural is ⅛″ thick plastic-finished hardboard. It can be installed over any solid backing with wallboard adhesive.

"Cook's Island" is located in center of this modern ceramic tiled kitchen. Two sets of four burners are easily accessible and are set in a tile countertop, eliminating the need for chopping boards or the use of trivets or asbestos pads. Rim of the "island" is raised to prevent liquid spillage or utensils rolling to the floor. Around the sink area and adjacent to the twin freezer-refrigerator, counter-tops and walls are also surfaced in tile. Its heat resistance and easy cleaning make it excellent for the indoor bar-be-que grille. Floor is quarry tile in a complementary tone to set off the kitchen color scheme.

Work wonders with beautiful, easy-to-clean tile

Here's a kitchen for today that has everything including decorative, durable ceramic tile. This one has a beautiful serving counter/breakfast bar in colorful mosaics, heavy-duty glazed tiles for work counters and durable quarry tiles for the floor. It's a kitchen you can be assured will look as fresh, new and fashionable as the day it was installed.

The spacious age comes to today's modern ceramic tiled kitchens that are bright, cheerful, easy to clean and have an abundance of counters and storage space. These custom designed drawer and door units boast ceramic tile sides and edges for added durability and decorative unity. Note unique built-in kitchen desk for homemaker's convenience. Tiled counters that are heat, scratch, stain and moisture proof are ideal for sink and stove areas. All kitchens here designed by the Tile Council of America.

Include a desk and chair . . . and a modern painting

Since the kitchen is the hub of the home, make it visually pleasing and comfortably practical. Here, modular chair and simple shelf provide a "pause" area, while painting gives wall decorative impact. Note the plentiful storage space provided by the Tappan cabinets, the doors of which can easily adjust to left or right hand swing.

Add a battery-operated clock with Southern charm

Every kitchen needs a clock, but why settle for just an ordinary-looking one when Seth Thomas makes one that looks like wall art? Gracefully curved, in antique green or blue, no cords or outlets are needed for this battery-operated wall fashion.

Utilize new 12-foot-wide vinyl flooring

Do-it-yourselfers take note! Sheet vinyl flooring in new 12 foot width enables you to install most floors in one continuous piece. Made by Armstrong, the cushioned flooring needs no adhesive and can be put over most resilient floors. Simply purchase a piece cut to the approximate dimensions of the room, lay it in place. Then trim to size along wall edges with a sharp knife or heavy shears.

Add a small counter in front of window

Typical of today's small apartments, this diminutive kitchen gains counter space suitable for food preparation and mini-meals, merely by fitting a shelf into the recessed window area. Note how textured window shade ("Spice" by Breneman) echoes the floral motif of the cafes, via simple cut-out paste-on trims. Adhesive bonds the appliques in place, remaining flexible enough to roll up and down with shade. Sprayed with clear Krylon, the paste-ons end up washable as the vinyl-impregnated shade. Old fashioned ice cream parlor chair, cushioned in lime green, is perfect working height.

Dramatize cabinets with wood molding

Contrasting molding used on doors and drawers can take kitchen cabinets out of the realm of the ordinary and give a personalized look to the kitchen. Here, the red painted molding accentuates the grain of the pale wood and blends with the brick wall and Armstrong's "Castilian" vinyl flooring.

Divide and conquer space

See-thru divider, which separates kitchen cooking area from the counter dining and sewing areas, retains airiness of room while pinpointing the various functions. Octagonal linoleum by Armstrong suits Early American theme.

KITCHENS

Use a colorful, vinyl wallcovering

Minimum maintenance is one of the bonus features of vinyl wallcovering in the kitchen. Even the white background shown here in one of the new Tarry Hill homes in Tarrytown, N.Y., wipes up in a jiffy. Avocado Caloric range and dishwasher pick up color of the topiary tree.

Build your own kitchen table

This kitchen has built-in cabinets, shelves, and kitchen table. Table top is thick block of wood from lumberyard. One end is nailed into existing wall structure. Other end is nailed to an oblong wooden box built from pine or plywood, with one shelf to hold cookbooks, magazines, etc. Table top can be covered with piece of Formica, bought and cut to size at local lumberyard, then cemented in place.

KITCHENS

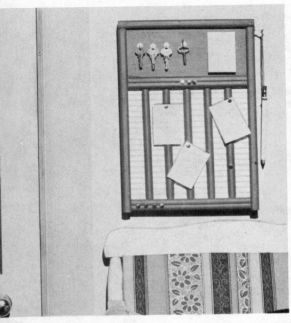

Make bulletin board from washboard

Family notes can become a decorative adjunct to your room. Sherwin Williams Paint Company suggests you buy or find a wooden washboard. Cut off the legs, painting the wooden part one color and the metal part another. Cut half-round moulding strips to fit over metal part. Paint them the same color as the wooden part of washboard. When dry, nail them to metal part of the washboard in a vertical pattern.

Instead of a table, build in a serving counter

A kitchen serving counter can save time and effort for the homemaker. Here, ceramic mosaic tile counter is merely a step away from island cooking surface and sink, facilitating both serving and clean-up chores. Tile Council of America also recommends use of tile for floors and walls of work areas for complete practicality.

Build a counter island with a range and dining facilities

Eating/cooking island makes excellent use of often unused kitchen space. Topped with practical ceramic tile, it wisks clean with a damp sponge, and even the newly designed grout remains unaffected by stains. Uncurtained windows give day-long view of outdoors. Suspended mobile swings gracefully in breeze from open door. Tile Council of America.

Match canister sets with wallpaper

Personalized touches give your room the "Total Look." Here, ordinary metal canisters, recipe file, note book, etc. are covered with coordinating wallpaper and wallpaper cut-outs to perkily coordinate with the walls. Idea from The Wallcovering Council.

243

KITCHENS

Have fun with wallcoverings

Color and pattern are basic ingredients for a pretty kitchen. Today's bright new wallcoverings can practically do the decorating job for you! Top right illustrates a dining area given a provincial flavor via the Waverly wallpaper and companion fabric used for laminated window shade and shutters. (From Window Shade Mfgrs. Assoc.) Top left spells elegance, with large-scaled colorful tile patterned wallpaper and textured Viking carpet on the floor. Mini-kitchen shown, bottom left, spotlights brilliant paisley fabric of Celanese fiber on walls and Bigelow's "Weather-Tuff" on floor. Stylized floral fabric wallcovering of Celanese fiber and window shades team with Bigelow carpeting, in right bottom room, to fashion a lively atmosphere.

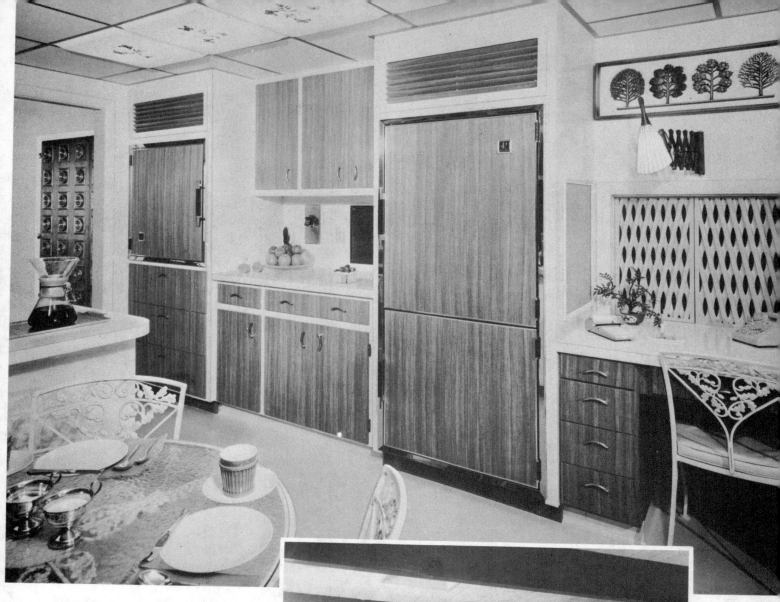

Include an office area

Put kitchen space to maximum use. A built-in desk area will let you do double-duty. While the cake bakes, you can write the checks and organize the marketing list. Here, adjustable lighting fixture gives best light where you need it. Bulletin board is conveniently placed for reminder notes. The use of a glass-topped table and painted wrought iron chairs preserves airy look in the room.

Make it sleek and modern

The uncluttered look of contemporary is kitchen-perfect. The beauty of the wood cabinets is spotlighted with simple round door-pulls and straight stainless steel legs on the base units. White Formica used for countertop extends out into room to provide eating area. Thin black vent hood over cooking surface looks almost like wall art, while beams and skylight add interest to the ceiling. Small-scaled roll-about chairs slide easily over the American Olean "Murray" quarry tile.

decorating ideas for Kitchens

Exciting print adds drama to room

Decorating with co-ordinates assures pattern and color harmony the easy way. Here, a wall design called "Daniella" by Canadian Wallpaper is teamed up with a co-ordinated soffit border, and the window is draped with a matching fabric. Wallcovering is vinyl coated, washable, and ready pasted for easy application.

Be formal

If you'd like to get away from the "kitcheny" look, why not use a more formal treatment on your windows? Here, Norman's of Salisbury uses a custom Show Shade (laminated roller shade) with a valance and a hem style with added charm by use of tassels. Homemakers can choose from the many hem styles available these days, or they can design their own. There's a great variety of braids, tassels, pulls, poles and hold backs available in addition to the hundreds of fabrics suitable for laminating.

Mix wallcoverings for interesting effect

Consider mixing prints. Try integrating textures and combining colors. The effects will delight you and create a completely personal look for your handsome kitchen, as shown here. New self-cleaning ovens are available in a wealth of colors (white to avocado, coppertone or harvest) from General Electric.

Put a lovely dining room in your kitchen

If there's room for even a small dining area in your kitchen, make use of it and make it grand. Here, a small area is made to seem bigger by placing small round table on a slightly larger round rug. Fabric used to make table covering and seat cushions was glued to walls to outline windows and ceiling, and to plywood cutouts that fit into the windows.

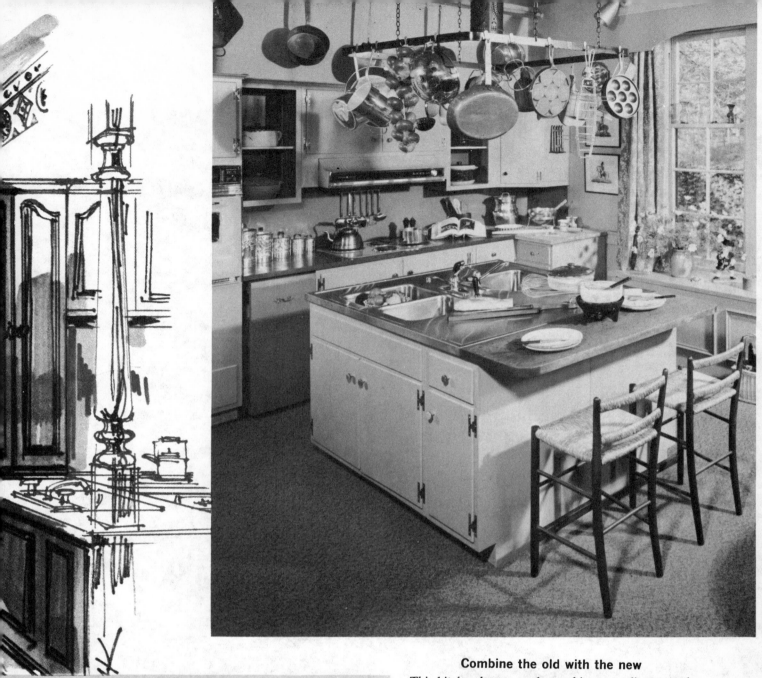

Combine the old with the new

This kitchen boasts modern cabinets, appliances and soil-resistant Lees carpet alongside old-fashioned accessories: butter molds, pie tins, whisks, a wicker wine tote, etc. The result is quite charming. Note extra serving area at custom-built kitchen island.

Trim with Decorounds

Add charm and color to kitchen bulletin boards, areas over sink, etc., with round wall plaques which are merely hung in place. The ones shown here are by Art Fair, 80 Fourth Ave., NY, NY. They come in a variety of styles on rigid metal frames, are protected with washable plastic lamination.

Kitchens

Blend practicality with good looks in the kitchen

The glamorous kitchen with the decorator look can be as efficient as it is handsome.
Here, a trio of rooms offer imaginative ideas which you can adapt. The kitchen above
with its peninsula sink, proves that we've escaped from the mania of always putting
the sink under the windows. In this arrangement, the sink not only is a room divider,
but a vantage point from which one can keep an eye on the small fry. In another
unique placement (photo top right) a versatile mixing center takes a center island
location. This creative planning allows for lots of storage and work space and even
the convenience of a surface outlet for plug-in appliances. Those who like country
qualities will appreciate (photo bottom right) a room with charming aged brick on the
wall and the use of details such as hammered hardware and old lanterns. All kitchen
cabinetry by Marvell Kitchens.

Streamline your kitchen for efficiency and beauty

All of these kitchens are skeek, modern and easy to take of. Reason: All cabinets, tabletops, counters, etc., are covered with Formica, which comes in many colors and patterns and which resists spots, stains, scratches, etc. Note the many different ways Formica can be used. Most interesting is the kitchen with the serving counter which separates the kitchen and the dining room.

Bring beauty into the kitchen with an art gallery on one wall

Put your pictures where you live . . . kitchen included. Even the rustic look of barnsiding can be an exciting field for a fine collection of prints and reproductions hung side by side with pots and pans. The pictures shown here are all from the new SyrocoArt Collection which contains over 250 prints, brush-stroke reproductions and a Boutique group of original miniature oil paintings all framed and matted.

Hang a cutting board clock on the wall

Early Americana clock design is transistorized, is 12 inches high. Comes in Woodtone or Avacado hand-rubbed antique finished. Clock is made by Westclox.

decorating
Kitchens

Adapt ideas from these custom-built kitchens

Three kitchens with ideas: Big old-fashioned room (above) solves awkward architectural problem with corner oven accessible from both sides. The charm of an all-wood country kitchen, (top right) has dark-stained, soil-resistant finish. A row of cool blue and white Dutch tiles are a decorative foil. Note handy "office" tucked in corner. For purists, sleek contemporary kitchen (right) free of ornamentation but with endless opportunities for experimenting with color and lighting techniques. Cabinetry in all kitchens by Marvell Kitchens, Inc.

Kitchens

Make it modern

Sleek as a laboratory is this plastic-oriented kitchen. Cabinets, furniture and see-through shelving damp-wipe. Shelves are by Raymor. Magee's Herculon olefin carpet, "Alfresco", cleans easily.

Carpet the floor

Add dimension and warmth to curio-filled, already ideal kitchen with an Antron nylon carpet. The bright Moorish-tile inspired design is called "Barbizon" by Monarch.

Use a gay rug

Tasseled area rug is lush and plush for kitchen use. Practical, too, as it is made of Herculon olefin, a stain and moisture resistant fiber. Also mildew proof. "The Chevron" is by Regal.

Make pot'n pan rack

A folding hat rack painted a bright color moves into kitchen to hold pots and pans. Kitchen spoon holder is made from coffee can painted to match. Idea from Sherwin Williams.

Trim a wall

Hang a clock ensemble low over a counter to enjoy the colorful honey blossom and bumblebee design. Clock runs on flashlight battery. Made by Arabesque. Companion wall pieces also available.

Kitchens

Trim with plates

Old-fashioned plate rail holds row of pretty, antique plates to decorate an all-wood kitchen that could be from the '90's. The acoustical, textured ceiling by Armstrong is welcome modern touch insuring blissful quiet.

Paper a window area

Harlequin-patterned paper decorates area around ponderosa pine casement windows without masking view. One hand opens weathertight windows with pivot for ease in cleaning both surfaces from inside.

Use a great print

A floor of sassy posies running rampant on Congoleum's vinyl Cushionfloor, "Light 'n Lively" is the magic catalyst that pulls this room, with odd corners, bad angles and unrelated furnishings, together.

Build an extension

"Stretch" a kitchen without materially changing it. Install sliding glass doors opening on wood plank deck. Add cupboard facilities, outdoor table and chairs for warm weather dining spot.

Panel the room

Cabinets, refrigerator doors and divider wall are made of Marlite's textured wormy chestnut woodgrain paneling. Divider creates cooking area, dining area, and relaxation area for chatting and reading while dinner cooks.

Match with wallpaper

Using a matching wallpaper in a sleek General Electric kitchen and in an adjoining cosy dining area is a professional decorator's trick to coordinate two different areas with one important design motif.

Turn your kitchen into a strawberry patch

Total integration of this kitchen's ceiling and wall are accomplished by covering ceiling and upper wall with a strawberry pattern called "Summer Holiday" by Stockwell, and by covering lower part of wall with companion "Grille." Actually, lower portion is put on first, then upper portion is cut with scissors (as desired) and fitted onto grille pattern. In this way you can place flowers wherever you wish and can work out many interesting patterns.

Kitchens

Co-ordinate with wall covering

The impact of a strong black and white, cane-patterned wall covering on the ceiling, walls and window shade lends dimension to a narrow galley-kitchen. "Invincible," Viking's woven nylon kitchen carpet has sponge rubber back for underfoot comfort. Framed, wall-hung cabinet stores glasses and dishes. Folding, hinged shelf and metal vegetable bin under sill are handy.

Match wall covering and window shades

Paisley-patterned wall covering is repeated in shades on four narrow windows in fashion-wise kitchen. Decorative ceramic tile in complementary colors adds functional and textural interest. Well-planned lighting plot by Moe Light ensures adequate illumination over table, sink and counter. The large ceiling dome provides room with general light when necessary.

IDEAS FOR KITCHENS

Three custom-built kitchens, each with its own personality

A kitchen can be full of lace and frills and still be fully functional, as is the very feminine one above. The oval working area has a step-saving plan plus plenty of counter and storage space. Novel table hung from pole is a useful space saver.

In a more modern mood, the kitchen (top right) reflects the same careful planning, but a different personality.

Cabinets are sleek, clutter is minimal, yet hospitality is evident in the bar corner and soffit murals above cabinets.

Another contrast is the neo-Colonial kitchen (below right) with its hammered hardware, V-groove doors and drawers, and big, brick "fireplace"—actually a gas grill. Cabinetry in each of these highly individualistic kitchens is by Marvell Kitchens, Inc.

CHARMING KITCHENS

They're serviceable, good-looking and well-planned

Handsome molding enriches appliance doors as well as cabinets of spacious kitchen (above) by Armstrong Cork Co. Molding can be bought in all sizes and shapes at your local lumber yard, and easily nailed and glued in place. Molding can completely change the look of any room.

Cooking island sets off attractive breakfast area. Note fascinating collection of old jars and accessories scattered around the room.

Define your breakfast area and provide additional storage with a floor-to-ceiling room divider made from plywood or pine. Simple divider, such as that sketched above, can be a home handyman's project. Or have your carpenter make it, then paint or finish it yourself in a gay color.

Season your kitchen with a bold accent rug. Geometric design by Regal Rugs, (right) is stain-repellent, moisture-resistant Herculon fiber. Barbecue unit and ovens are installed in wall paved with old bricks.

Stylized wallpaper enlivens walls and soffits of spacious kitchen (below) from a Tarry Hill model home at Tarrytown, New York.

Caloric dishwasher and double-decker gas range are used with beautifully grained oak cabinets.

Flooring is brick-like sheeting.

CHARMING KITCHENS

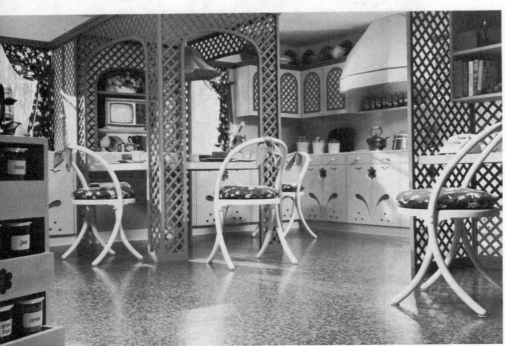

Decorative trellises set apart the various other activities, aside from cooking, that go on in delightful kitchen at left.

A handy do-it-yourselfer could find the materials for such a trellis in the local lumberyard.

To carry out the idea, walls and upper cabinets are treated to trellis wallpaper print.

Note clever cut-out design of lower cabinet doors.

Flooring by Armstrong Cork Co.

Be adventurous in your kitchen. Give cabinet doors and walls a spectacular style treatment as in kitchen below. Large floral prints are glued in place, covered with a clear lacquer and framed with lumber yard molding. By Armstrong Cork Co.

For a light look in a very large kitchen, base cabinets are suspended from the floor (above). Upper cabinets are wide but short so as not to block fabulous view of ceiling high windows. Tree coming through floor was cemented in place and suspended breakfast bar was built around it. Vinyl flooring is by Armstrong Cork Co.

To add elegance to your kitchen, attach a pair of brass, decorative sculptured drapery holdbacks or tiebacks as towel holders. Use those that measure 3½ inches across, screw them onto a wooden cabinet of same kind.

BATHROOMS

Combine paneling, tiling and carpeting for today's modern appearance

Beautiful wood paneling, hexagonal terra cotta tiles and luxurious carpeting are the highlights of this stunning bathroom. Carpeting is Barwick's "Soft Approach" which covers the two-level scheme and extends up the side of the tub, integrating this fixture into a unified decor. Twin basins with ample counter space and a mirror with theatrical lighting are added features. Also note use of plants and modern art in this bathroom by J. Frederic Lohman, A.I.D.

An old-style sink becomes a wall unit when covered with a plywood shelf, which hides pipes and bowl. To make shelf, cut long piece of plywood for top. Cover with Formica, if desired. Cut hole in top to match sink, nail to walls. Cut front of shelf from another piece of plywood, scallop with saw as shown, nail in place. Paint shelf to contrast with wall. Empire bench, framed mirror, sconces and old-fashioned towel tree carry out the antique feeling.

BATH

THE SECLUDED WORLD OF THE

Let a shower curtain reign supreme

Create a graceful swag: Buy an extra shower curtain, trim one edge with fringe or braid, then loop curtain through large drapery ring attached to ceiling. Tape or tack ends of curtain to walls, as shown.

Co-ordinate with windows: Buy matching shower curtains and draperies, or make draperies from an extra shower curtain. Use tiebacks on both for unified effect.

Match with dressing table: Buy an extra shower curtain, cut into two parts, cover dressing table (here it's nothing more than a piece of plywood fitted on top of a radiator). Tack or staple large piece of curtain in place, then the smaller piece. Cover tacks or staples by gluing on strips of fringe or braid.

Mirror one wall to double the size of a bathroom

Simplest way to enlarge a bathroom (or any room for that matter) is to put a large mirror on any of the walls. Here, a mirror was mounted over cabinets and wash basin, thus appearing to mirror the whole wall and seeming larger than it really is. Colorful tile on walls reappears doubly beautiful in mirror. Tile on walls and floor is by American Olean.

Bathrooms and Dressing Rooms

Work wonders with windows

Handsome window treatments can happen overnight with new, easy-to-work-with vinyl wallcoverings and laminated shades. At right, bold red and white "Romany Stripe" shade by Connaisance is mixed with bright blue and white polka dot walls. Window shade and walls are vinyl. Blue trim covers window and mirror frame.

For a sun-filled bath, the window treatment below is fashioned of a translucent boucle shade ("Claybourne" by Breneman), platinum rod and rose braid trim that matches the terry towels. The shade was chosen to combine privacy and natural sunlight.

Across page, this made-to-order look was accomplished by combining Norman's of Salisbury shade and matching swag, sparked with decorative brass holders. The built-in storage unit adds a decorative touch, too, when ivy and colorful collection of glass is mixed among the shelves.

Add glamor and gleam with accessories

Ancient Romans used cupids to decorate baths; modern homemakers can do same with new ensemble from Arabesque. Musical cherubs flank ribbon-wreath dial of battery-powered wall clock, while their twins ornament solid brass towel rings.

Re-do and re-new with matching wallcovering and fabric

The dramatic transformation that wallcovering and correlated fabrics can make is vividly illustrated in these "before and after" shots of a small bath. The decorator has imaginatively used an airy "Poppy" wallcovering by Stockwell with its matching fabric for shower curtains. This over-all effect visually enlarges the room and gives it a feeling of soft elegance. All was accomplished with a minimum of construction, too.

Do it up Colonial style

Give your bathroom an Early American look by installing fake beams of urethane. Ones shown here are by Williams Products, are lightweight and simply glued in place. Colonial cabinets, lighting fixtures, etc., are easily installed. Use mirror kits (squares of glass) to mirror area over sink. Use flagstone kits (squares of flagstone) to cover floor. You'll find kits in hardware or department stores. Small photo gives an idea of the variety of urethane beams and architectural components now available.

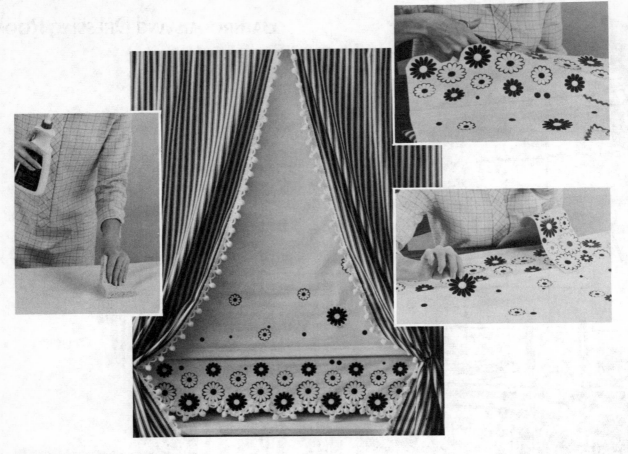

Make an old shade new
with pretty flowers

Start with your old vinyl shade. Remove it from brackets, roll it out on a flat surface and spray clean with Fantastik. Wipe away dust and grime with a damp sponge.

Remove wooden stick. Cut shade just over the sewn hemline. Make a new casing about six-inches above the bottom, making sure the stick will fit easily, and sew across either by hand or machine.

Decorate with packages of stick-on vinyl flowers from dime store; position them along the bottom edge, creating a scallop-like design. Place them quite close together at the bottom, scattering them lightly all over the shade to create a magical, all-over print effect.

When you've finished flower sticking, cut carefully around the bottom flowers, making scallops. Be sure to use a light pencil outline before you start.

Trim the scalloped edge with ball fringe to match your draperies, sewing it by hand or machine.

Create your own Roman bath with a sunken tub and luxurious carpeting

"Villa Antiqua" carpeting by WestPoint Pepperell's Cabin Crafts with its Mediterranean tile pattern, is perfect complement to sunken tub of modern day Roman bath. Martex "Geometrix" towels are elegant touches, too. Sliding door leads to patio sunbath.

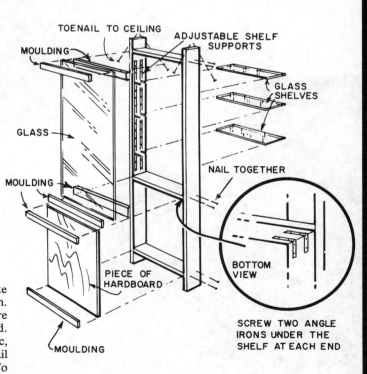

Build a room divider with storage shelves

Measure width of cabinet and height of ceiling to estimate 1x6-inch pine needed. Cut basic pieces, nail as in diagram. Attach metal adjustable shelf brackets from hardware store. Measure inside of frame for colored glass needed. (Libbey-Owens-Ford makes stippled, texture doric, surf, hammered colored glass.) Position frame, nail to walls and cabinet, toe-nail to ceiling and floor. To secure glass, nail molding to inside top and bottom of shelves. Position glass. Nail two other pieces of molding top and bottom, securing glass in place. Position hardboard. Have glass shelves cut to width of divider.

277

Use an easy-dry chair in bath or dressing room

Sturdy, but not massive, this "Butterfly" chair by Burris Industries is a functional addition for bath/dressing room. Smartly covered with "wet look" urethane upholstery, it is breathable and will wipe-clean.

Shape tub and shower area in interesting fashion

Pre-planned to take advantage of alcove area, a rounded sunken tub becomes "conversation piece" of the home. Tiled walls and floor by American Olean are complemented with wallpaper border at ceiling. Sculpture and living plants add to scene.

Adapt remodeling ideas from these "before and after" examples

"Before and after" photos on this page are a good indication of what can be done to improve almost any bathroom. Both "before" photos show old-style bathrooms that sorely need modernizing. Updated bathroom (top) and powder room (below) now utilize space, color, and fixtures to best advantage, giving both decorative cohesiveness.

Note the vanity in the bathroom, with its ample storage space and spacious tile top. Visually-enlarging mirror runs complete length of cabinet and up to ceiling, thereby making room seem much bigger than it is.

The black, contoured marble counter top in the powder room sparks a contemporary look. Shiny silver wallpaper runs up the wall onto the ceiling. Accessories are notable for scale and decorativeness.

Tile in both of these rooms is by American Olean.

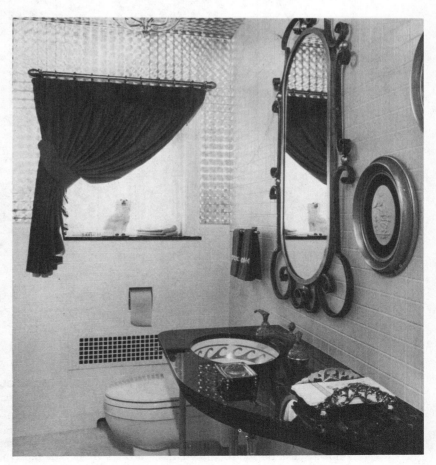

decorating
Bathrooms and Dressing Rooms

Scatter flowers around the room

To get effect shown here, use a flowered wallpaper, plastic adhesive or fabric. Build plywood base around sink, cover with flowered pattern. Cover large sheet of wood with flower pattern, glue mirror to it, mount unit to wall. Add extra "window" by buying a colored Masonite translucent decorator panel at local lumberyard, then mount it to wooden frame and nail to wall. Fix a small light behind panel, and it'll look like a window. Finish off the room by cutting flowers from your pattern. Put some on the wall, others on the ceiling, and a whole group around top of wall as border.

Use the French manner for m'lady's dressing room

A French hand-blocked drapery frieze ("Guirlande et Tulle" by J. B. Reveillon) and a matching wallpaper are inspiration here.

Between windows is dressing table with double skirt of ivory taffeta and embroidered tulle, over which is antique Louis XVI gold framed mirror.

Floor is rosewood vinyl in parquet pattern. Rug is a V'Soske hand-carved beige. Chandelier of crystal casts soft glow of light over all.

Use the African motif for his dressing room

Designed by Paul Krauss, A.I.D., this room houses all the necessary grooming aids for today's meticulous male. It even includes an over-the-sink sunlamp for healthful relaxation.

GAF's new Luran Airtred "Cork" sheet-vinyl flooring was used on floor and walls around the sink area.

Closets and other surfaces were paved with GAF's royal blue felt, and mottled brown, stain-resistant, leopard-spotted, vinyl wall covering. Brilliant red towels punctuate this tasteful masculine pallete.

Bathrooms and Dressing Rooms

Do it up grand

In photo left, elegant wall paneling is combined with lush carpeting. Mirrored wall doubles width of narrow room, and recessed lighting adds final note of elegance.

Carpet with a stunning pattern

The prettiest bathroom ideas begin with carpeted floors, as shown below. Impact of colorful "American Style" pattern by Ozite, mixed with textured walls, dresses up what would have been a bland room.

Bathrooms and Dressing Rooms

Add vibrant new vanity

New for bathrooms is "Scandia," a frosty, sun-streaked, blond finish for vanities and cabinets. It's a subtle tone that lends itself to almost every color scheme. Choose hardware accents in white-streaked gold with matching marble-like tops. From Williams Products.

Use an exciting washable wallpaper

Washable vinyl wallpapers sparkle with color and imaginative designs. They are also durable, easy to clean, and a good choice for bathrooms. This "Sunflower" pattern is from Stockwell.

Use a striking Roman stripe

"Horizon," a variation on the classic Roman stripe, with wavering lines providing a dramatic new look, is a new vinyl upholstery fabric just introduced by Durawall. Comes in a variety of colorways.

Wrap your bathroom in beautiful tile

Beautiful tile is combined with tropical greenery. Tile by American Olean is used on both walls and floor to dramatize sunken tub. Note built-in pebble garden and interesting lighting fixtures.

Use a see-through shower curtain

Designed for Fieldcrest by famed designer, Yves Saint-Laurent, is this see-through shower curtain of seamless, polished vinyl. It's called "Vision" and comes in six different colors.

Also available are matching tailored window drapes, and a vinyl bath rug, tuft-patterned in a contrasting nylon pile.

Paint a pattern on tile

Custom tile in the bathroom adds a note of elegance, but may be quite expensive. You can, however, paint a pattern on tile with a paint brush and Sherwin-Williams Epoxy Enamel.

Just plan a simple pattern, using the squares as a guide, and then paint it in! Here, pattern matched a pattern on window shades.

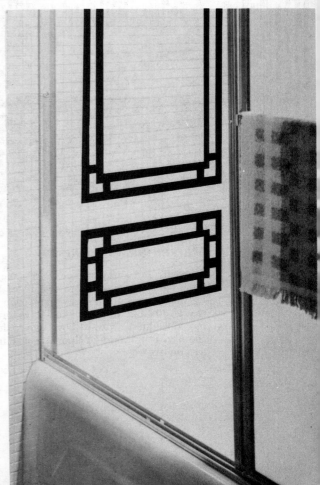

IDEAS
FOR
BATHROOMS

Marvelous for makeup

Seashells and shiny striped wallpaper set the scene for a lamp-lighted powder room ensemble. The marbelized vanity-sink with built-in drawers is one of Marvell's many ready-to-install cabinets that solve problems such as the one this family faced: how to provide a pretty powder room in a minimum of floor space. This alcove installation was the answer.

Give an old bathroom new elegance

Here's how to bring elegance to a standard bathroom: Nail painted wooden molding to the walls, as shown. Position long mirror in center of one panel. Sew fancy fringe to edge of shower curtains. Add color co-ordinated rug, seat pillow, towels, etc.

New wood for old feeling

Early American yet comfortably contemporary, this bathroom features the warmth of wood—knotty pine cabinetry and movable louvers. Colors of Lady Pepperell "Rose Lea" towels, both plain and patterned, coordinate with rug.

Accessories control clutter

A fine way to avoid clutter in your new bathroom is to use wall accessories that are both decorative and useful. Here, Lady Syroco mirror, towel racks, shelf, toothbrush cabinet, waste basket, magazine rack, clock organize items.

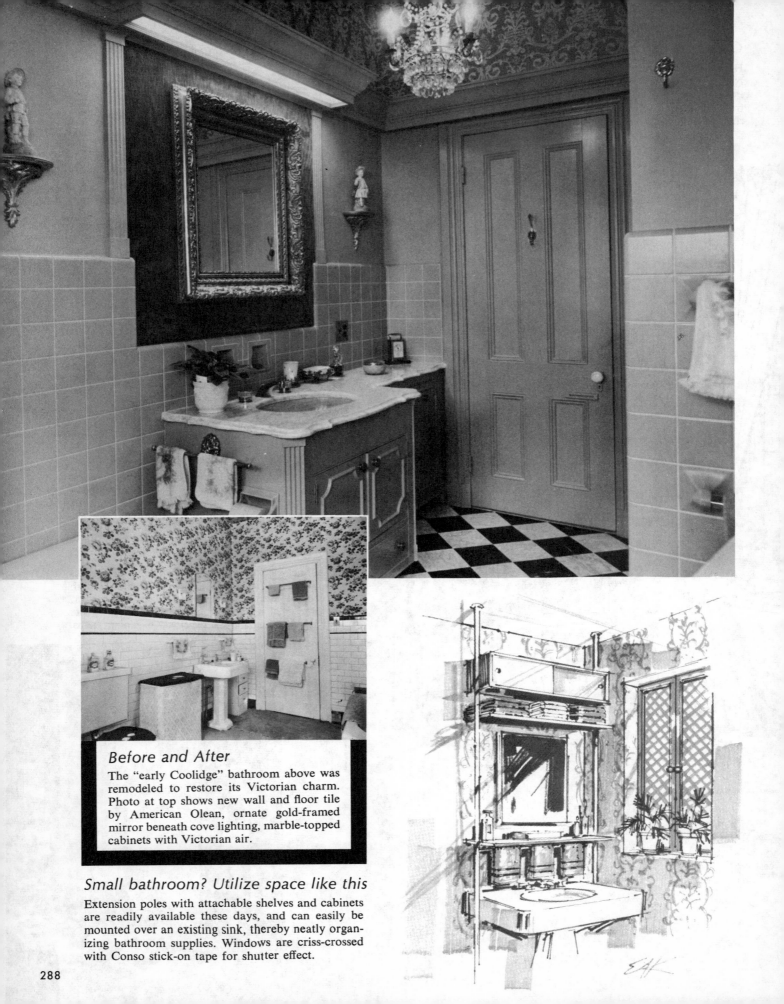

Before and After

The "early Coolidge" bathroom above was remodeled to restore its Victorian charm. Photo at top shows new wall and floor tile by American Olean, ornate gold-framed mirror beneath cove lighting, marble-topped cabinets with Victorian air.

Small bathroom? Utilize space like this

Extension poles with attachable shelves and cabinets are readily available these days, and can easily be mounted over an existing sink, thereby neatly organizing bathroom supplies. Windows are criss-crossed with Conso stick-on tape for shutter effect.

Bathe in a flower bower

Houseplants thrive in the humidity of a bathroom. Here, a live plant grows in a bower of colorful fake blossoms. Dressing room walls are covered with Scotchgard-treated "Clipper Cloth" by McCanless Custom Fabrics, Inc., to match the tied-back shower curtains.

Yesterday's charm, today's comfort

Bright daylight is filtered through louver shutters and ruffled organdy curtains in the dressing room alcove (below) of the remodeled Victorian bath shown at left. Flocked wallpaper and fringed moire shower curtain emphasize the turn-of-the-century decor. American Olean tile and modern carpeting accent contemporary comfort.

decorating ideas for Family Rooms

Let paneling set the stage

This open floor plan, accented by an imaginative decor, provides versatile living space for a modern family. The family room adjacent to the kitchen will be in use all through the day—by Mom in the morning for her coffee break . . . as a lunch time relaxing area for the kids . . . as a play area in the afternoon for toddlers . . . and as a home office in the evening for Dad. Easy maintenance was assured by using washable Marlite paneling on the walls and ceiling. Included in this unusual decorative treatment are two textured panels—travertine on the main family room wall and tapestry on the entrance wall in the foreground. Plastic-finished Marlite can be installed over old walls or new framing, does not require refinishing.

Enliven wall with game plaques

Glue checkers, dominoes, playing cards in interesting fashion to heavy, colored cardboard. Glue painted wood moldings around edges. Hang on wall. Color combination of white, black and red fits perfectly with black and red checkered tablecloth.

Use Mediterranean here, too

This popular style can go into the family room as easily as the living room. Here, Spanish-type furniture and an open beam ceiling are highlighted by Moorish chandeliers made by Thomas.

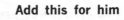

Add this for him

For comfort, this contour chair and ottoman by Waynline. Exposed walnut frame is upholstered in Rucaire, a new, washable fabric with the look and hand of top-grade leather. Recently introduced to the home furnishing world, Rucaire is made by Hooker Chemical.

Use Swedish modern for adult family rooms

Adult family rooms look new and very modern with big-enough-for-two lounge chairs. Plush, smooth leather or bold, bright fabrics complement the sleek Swedish designs. Note two-tone walls which create a sense of greater space and provide an interesting back-drop for the abstract art and storage unit. Furniture by Dux.

Co-ordinate carpet and bench

For interesting, co-ordinated effect, cover seat and back of a tall winged-chair bench with same carpeting used on the floor, in this case, "Multiflor" by Monarch. Glue or tack carpeting in place. Add a few charming accessories, and this corner of your family room really comes to life!

Show off family treasures

This "show-off" wall design is nothing but a collection of 4x4-inch beams, painted any desired color, then nailed to the wall in any arrangement you wish. Areas created are filled with pictures, photos, knickknacks, etc.

Family Rooms

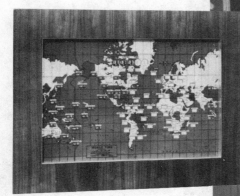

Put "fun" clock on wall

"World Time Clock" tells you what time things are happening all over the world. Designed by Howard Miller Clock Co. of Zeeland, Michigan, it's an illustrated map which registers the time for 70 key locations in the world. Clock automatically compensates for daylight savings, also indicates daylight and night around world.

Transform a basement into attractive, fun-and-work quarters

With space at a premium in many of today's homes, it is frequently necessary to devise clever schemes to make rooms do double duty.

This was the situation faced by one young married couple, who needed a place for their youngsters to conduct Cub Scout activities and a place of their own to entertain casually. The one rule they set for themselves was that the room had to be completely convertible.

The couple agreed that the children would feel inhibited in a room too obviously designed for the needs of grown-ups, and their adult friends would hardly feel comfortable in a nursery.

In meeting the challenge, a portion of the unfinished basement in their Colonial two-story home was transformed into a cozy family room which could be switched from pack meetings to parties with the ease of a chameleon changing colors.

The size of the job staggered them at first. Cinder block walls, concrete floors, bare rafters, steel I-beam, jutting across the ceiling, exposed support column, uncovered steps—the pair surveyed the site of their family room-to-be with great concern.

Later, many of the obstacles proved to be blessings in disguise. To a large degree, these obstacles narrowed down the number of ways the room could be handled and eventually dictated some of the solutions.

For instance, the steps formed a natural boundary for the interior wall. (The rest of the basement is now a storage-utilities area.)

The I-beam and support column begged for concealment. After boxing in the steel beam with plywood, parallel plywood beams were added on both sides for decorative consistency.

The side beams were then carried down the wall to flank the brick fireplace and provide a focal point for the room which previously had been lacking. On the opposite side of the room, the three beams were stopped by a false wall erected to enclose the support column and hide the underside of the steps.

The paneling presented no difficulties. The couple selected 4' x 8' sheets in a medium wood shade with a chipped surface like the axe markings on hand-hewn planks. The sheets were nailed onto 2" x 4" studs after insulating over the cinder block.

For the ceiling, the couple picked Armstrong acoustical ceiling tiles for sound absorption and ease of installation. The tiles were stapled onto furring strips which had been nailed to the rafters.

At spots where lighting was desired (in storage, activity, and entry areas), the husband merely substituted tile-size lighting fixtures which he obtained at the

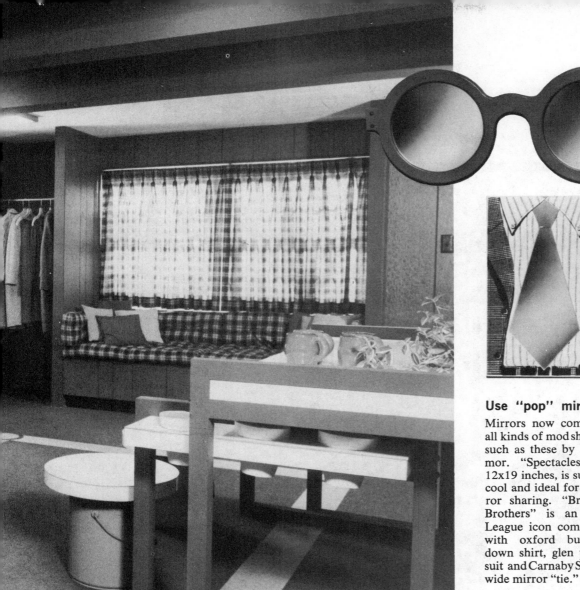

Use "pop" mirrors

Mirrors now come in all kinds of mod shapes such as these by Raymor. "Spectacles" is 12x19 inches, is supercool and ideal for mirror sharing. "Brooks Brothers" is an Ivy League icon complete with oxford buttondown shirt, glen plaid suit and Carnaby Street wide mirror "tie."

same store. Since the fixtures were prewired at the factory, an electrician's help was not required.

For the floor, another Armstrong product, was used: Wearathon indoor-outdoor carpet which is made by an exclusive Durabond process to withstand strong wear and tear. Its olefin fibers resist moisture, and the carpeting can easily be installed with minimum effort.

At this point, the project was far enough along that the two could begin thinking of expressing the dual themes of the room. Therefore, they chose blue for the carpet and inserted a border of gold with the aid of a metal ruler and sharp knife.

The blue and gold introduced the scouting colors into the decor and the custom effect of the border struck a note of informal grace.

Next to be considered was storage and display space. Toward this end, a row of cabinets was added on the fireplace wall.

Above the cabinets went standard shelving which was then finished with a simple front to resemble birdhouses. In these cubbyholes went the family's collection of ceramic birds and owls.

The cabinet tops double as handy counters for late-night buffet dining. The whole ensemble received coats of blue and gold paint.

More storage space was built into a window seat. At the same time, wall partitions at either end of the seat create the illusion of a stylish bay window and provide a nook for an open coat closet in the corner of the room nearest the outside door.

Now luck took a hand. The couple had a mental picture of a pair of tables of basically simple construction that could accommodate a brace of scouts for craft periods or meetings, or could be used alternatively for card parties or suppers. When not needed, one table would fit under the other and both could be pushed over to the side of the room, out of the way.

The only slight problem: no tables like these existed that they knew of. Fortunately, a good neighbor was a carpenter and he decided to join the creative building team. Thus, the promised tables arrived in short course, fulfilling all of the particulars and with the added dividend of a protective surface covering of plastic laminate.

Thus inspired, the couple fashioned companion stools out of empty 10-gallon paint cans and gave them matching laminate tops. The final steps consisted of a wash of vivid red paint for the stools and door, and dressing up the room with accessories.

decorating
Family Rooms

Do it with nostalgia

To create this nostalgic family room, first the floor and parts of the wall were covered with ceramic tile. Then walls were decked with Stockwell's "Bittersweet" wall paper and two "Nostalgia" panels, which embrace the charm of our early landscapists. Panels could be joined to portray a continuous mural, if desired. Furniture and accessories are traditional. Iron coal stove mounted on tiled base was painted gay colors.

Add a party table

Party tables serve dual purposes (games and food), are becoming more and more popular in family rooms. Shown here is Bassett's new model from its "Conquest Collection." It's designed in Moorish oak for today's Mediterranean look, is low in height to accommodate all ages.

Comfort with foam

Galeota lounge chair by Moreddi is made entirely of molded foam rubber, is a three-position design that easily converts to a chaise and is also available as a two-seat sofa. Comes in a variety of colors. Furniture of this type, while designed mainly for living rooms, is also "at home" in family rooms, too.

Round it out nicely

A bright, colorful rug is a perfect addition to any family room, particularly a small one like this. Here, a brilliant sunflower-burst of color creates an inviting circle of warmth on this new round Ege Rya rug by Egetaepper. Rug is element around which entire room revolves.

Light it correctly

Necessary for a successful game room is a high level of illumination. Here, plaid walls are offset by reflectant white panels using Moe Light's aluminum accent strips. Ceiling-mounted fluorescent fixtures are 2 feet square, feature walnut frames with brass trim.

Add a wonderful rocking chair

Since color and more color is the great trend in decorating these days, even the lowly rocking chair has been effected. This Early American model by Tell City not only comes in the blue shown, but in green, red or yellow! Comes in other styles, too.

Have fun Early-American style

This family room features furniture by Buckstaff which is arranged for flexible entertaining. Table for two has flip-top for party expansion needs. Game table is also used for dining. "Windows" are really clear plastic, gold sheeting in wood frame with long light bulb behind it.

Family Rooms

Be ultra-modern

If you live in an apartment and have limited space, find a nook or a small room and turn it into a modern-type family room. Here, a brightly-colored, geometric rug, Magee's Woolmark "Rampage," sets the mood. Chairs are the latest thing in mod colors.

With a minimum amount of accessories (sculptured plant and painting), the room achieves a casual formality.

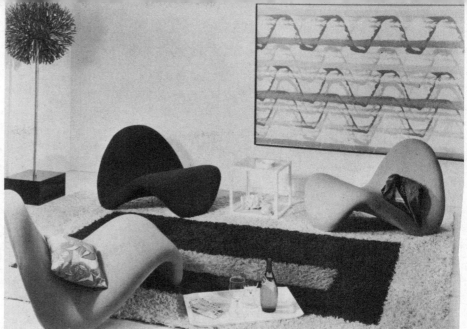

Add a vibrating chair

Vibrating lounge chairs are a welcome addition to any family room. Shown here is new model by Niagara Therapy. Chair has a cycle massage motor which provides exhilarating or relaxing massage and helps stimulate blood circulation. Two knobs on lower right arm regulate movement.

If desired, chair can be ordered with special built-in heating element for additional relaxation.

A two-way reclining action allows chair to be positioned for viewing TV or for full reclining. Comes in vinyl, in a variety of colors.

Use outdoor carpeting

Outdoor carpeting is ideal for a family room where there's a lot of traffic underfoot. It'll stand the gaff and resist stains.

Shown here is one of the new, foam-backed, printed carpets by Armstrong. Because of the foam-backing, these carpets can be "loose laid" or simply taped down, thereby eliminating padding or installation fees.

Note use of easy-to-clean plastic furniture.

Family Rooms

Say it in French

To create French-styled family room, cover wall with appropriate wall paper, windows with wooden shutters, and use wire furniture.

Kiosk was built from large, round, cardboard packing tube with shelving and papier maché top added. Ceiling is covered with Armstrong acoustical tile.

Say it casual

Contemporary furniture, interestingly arranged, brings life to this casual family room.

Also noteworthy are the built-ins on both sides of the piano. Built-ins can house dozens of family supplies (TV set, books, hobby equipment, etc.). Armstrong tile used on floor.

Build a simple bar, divide family room into a corner for conversation and a corner for games

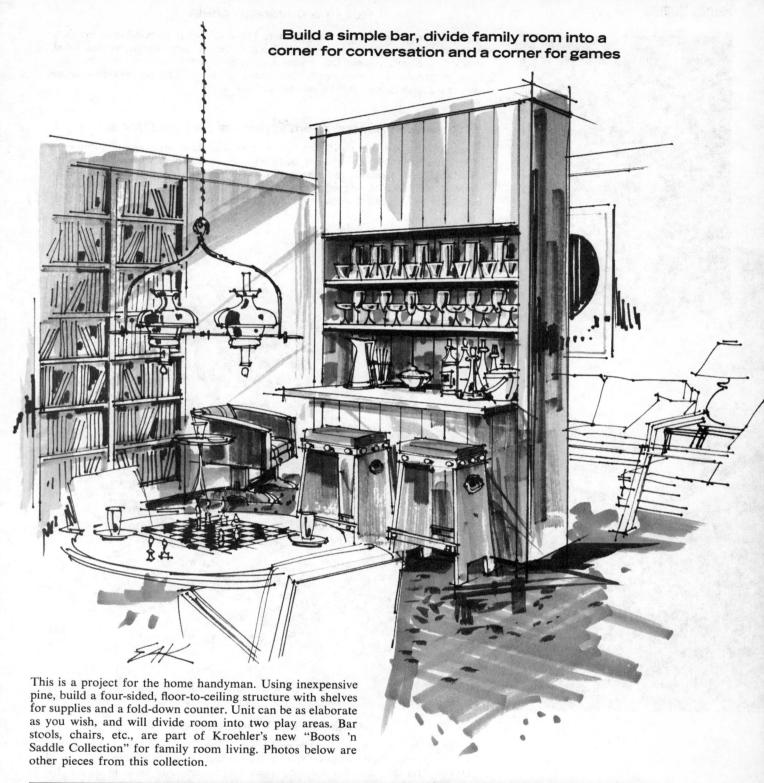

This is a project for the home handyman. Using inexpensive pine, build a four-sided, floor-to-ceiling structure with shelves for supplies and a fold-down counter. Unit can be as elaborate as you wish, and will divide room into two play areas. Bar stools, chairs, etc., are part of Kroehler's new "Boots 'n Saddle Collection" for family room living. Photos below are other pieces from this collection.

Family Rooms

Roll in a beverage chest

If you'd like a bar in your family room, but don't want to build one, here's a possible solution: A beverage chest from Lane. A new design, it has fitted racks and compartments for bottles and glasses. Both sides of the split top open to provide two Formica-covered work surfaces. The rosewood-veneered unit is on casters and can be moved about easily.

Make your fun room luxurious and traditional

In photo right, we see traditional furniture grouped and arranged to form very interesting family room. Highlight of room is big desk-table and red leather wing chair placed in front of arch book cases. Inviting bridge players to action is square table set off to one side, leaving rest of room available for conversational fun. Note that beautiful wood floors are left uncovered for all to see and admire.

Make it sleek and modern

Far from "homey" in the usual manner, but still great fun to have fun in, is this high-rise family room with two long sofas for seating, zebra rug on wall-to-wall carpeting for dramatic impact, bookcases for storage, and table in corner for games. Note interesting arrangement of pictures on wall.

Make it comfy and Country English

Country English is alive and well in the jet age, as photo right proves. Room is dominated by a large sofa around which are gathered love seat, wing chair and occasional chair on a large, rough shag rug. Also prominent are the severe black and white stripes of the fireplace hood, and hutch-writing desk. This room, and all others on this page, by Colby's of suburban Chicago.

IDEAS FOR FAMILY ROOMS

New chairs for a group get-together

Designed in Sweden, "Lotus" chair from Dux has low-slung tub shell of rigid polystyrene in glossy white finish. Squashy shirred slipcover-cushion of bold printed cotton adds color.

An unused basement now exudes country charm

Once upon a time the room below was just a dusty basement, but a good paint job, some acoustical tile on ceiling and some vinyl tile on floor (both by Armstrong) completely changed the room. Added to this was an interesting collection of country-style furniture and accessories. Note interesting built-in units and how stove is set into wall.

An unused basement now makes a swinging scene

Major overhaul of this basement resulted in a spectacular family room. Floor was tiled with black and white tiles, brick area was put in as backdrop for modern fireplace, and rest of room was painted white.

Wall covering used here is called "Zebra" and was designed by Columbus Coated Fabrics as part of their Satinesque, Foil, Flock and Fashion collection of Wall-Tex. It comes in black and white and in brown and white in the currently popular wet-look vinyl. As you can see, zebra-like panels can highlight both painted and brick walls.

To give color contrast to the room, the modern stool-chairs are in orange and red, as are the pillows and other accessories.

Table was made from a round block of wood which was nailed to four pieces of wood, then painted.

Family rooms can be wildly mod like this one...

Here's an environment room for activists who love their graphics big and swinging and their hard rock music taped and amplified. Designed by Milo Baughman for Thayer Coggin, the room is built around an entertainment center housed in four cubes lacquered red/orange and chrome yellow. These house hi-fi, record storage, tape storage, amplifiers and bar fixings. The facing sofa composed of urethane foam slabs is covered in chrome yellow corduroy. The chair at the right is upholstered in an orange basket weave and the chairs supported within a "fence" of chrome finished steel tubing are covered in scarlet corduroy. The cube lamp pedestals are lacquered in red/orange. Walls are painted in curved shapes of red, orange, yellow and white.

...or they can be more traditional like this one

Here's another basement salvaged from clutter and turned into a delightful family room. Floor was covered with Armstrong tile. Built-in sink and stove unit were installed, as were "riverboat" doors and trim. Room was painted white with green trim. Then bamboo-cane furniture was added, along with interesting accessories.

Sun God on wallpaper mural keeps an eye on this family room

A massive Sun God, "Hyperion," is an affable witness to fun and games in a family room. This new, large-scale design is among the "Tapestry" Panels of The Jack Denst Designs, Inc., "Environment 15" collection of murals. Panels may be mounted to wall, hang free tapestry-fashion against the wall, or be suspended as room dividers. Their scale permits them to dominate a room's decorative scheme, offering a theme to guide furnishings. Printed on supported linen, this two-panel mural comes in two shades of red with a red overprint.

Handsome table and chairs by Jens Risom Design Inc. are contemporary in mood but acquiescent to the traditional design of the sun god. Also in a traditional vein: pewter porringers and engraved pewter mugs.

Dormer room becomes family hideaway

It makes sense to plan a family retreat in an extra upstairs room away from all the hustle and bustle, such as this cosy area with carpeting by Evans-Black. Note built-in cabinet for books, hi-fi, etc.

A splendid setting for fun and games

Look what's happened to bridge tables

Textured vinyl flooring by Armstrong Cork Co., makes base for family-hobby-entertainment room (above).

Note sofa-lounge made from wooden door placed on wooden storage boxes. Put foam rubber cushion on top.

Bookcase wall unit was built-in, was designed to coincide with ceiling beams.

New game tables depart from the conventional look and shape, as exemplified (left) in table and chair designs by Stendig, Inc.

Finely detailed table joins top, apron and legs into an unbroken curved framework. Lift-out insert top reverses from white plastic to green or tan felt.

Chair seats are of handwoven cane. Furniture is available in black or white lacquer or red aniline finishes.

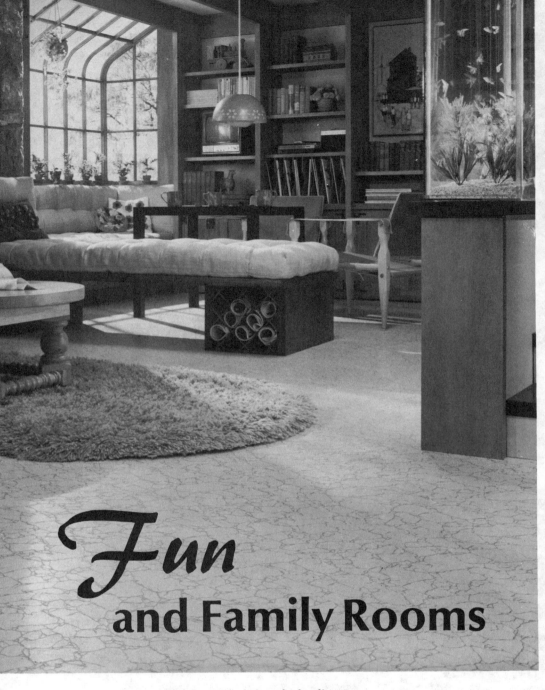

Fun
and Family Rooms

Mini-loveseats belong in family rooms

Entertaining lamps

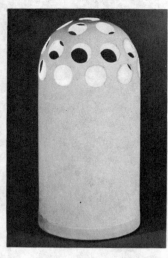

Circular die-cut perforations make the design and release the illumination of metal dome lamp designed by Terrence Conran for Quartite Creative Corp.

Adjustable spot globe (above) is handy to have in an all-purpose room. Metal lamp, like the style above it, comes in assorted bold colors. By Quartite.

For lounging in a big way try one of the new mini-loveseats (left). These wide, wide comfortable chairs were designed by Kipp Stewart for Directional.

Plump pillow back and bolsters enhance comfort of design far left, while other version boasts the decorative impact of open wood or chromium frames. Side of frames are filled with cane mesh panels.

Fun **and Family Rooms**

Two-level room for work and play

To divide large family room (above) into separate activity areas, a platform was built to create a second level for lounging and music appreciation. Lower level contains home office, dining area and floor space for fun and games. Designed by Armstrong Cork Co.

Corner setup for younger set

Enchanting play and storage units set off corner for the small fry in spacious basement family room (above, left), designed by Armstrong Cork Co. Units are built from plywood, cut out, painted and assembled.

Turn your attic into sitting-sewing room

The often-neglected, out-of-the-way dormer room or attic can be put to good use as a sewing room or as a quiet retreat for the lady of the house. Room (left) from Tarry Hill model home in Tarrytown, New York, accomplishes these purposes.

Stackable cubes do double duty

Shiny fiberglass cubes from Italy do double duty. With vinyl cushions they're seats, without, they're snack tables. Extra bonus—they stack up when not needed. By Raymor.

311

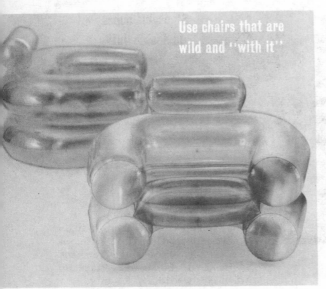

Use chairs that are wild and "with it"

Intriguing sausage-shaped chair (left) is inflated vinyl. Imported from Italy, chair comes in yellow, red or clear. Can be inflated by a cylinder of compressed air. By Selig.

Gyro chair (right, top) is of molded, reinforced fiberglass. An amusing addition to any room, it is also comfortable.

Fascinating Hyaline chair (right, bottom) has frame of tempered plate glass. Sausage rolls, upholstered in glove leather and connected by adjustable leather straps, are attached to frame by steel bars. This chair and Gyro by Stendig.

Plan a discotheque party room in your basement. Two versions are seen below and left, both by Armstrong Cork Co. In setting left, bold striped and paisley wallpaper and striped corlon flooring set the scene for action.

Room below also centers around easy-to-make cage (diagram and directions below.) Smaller area has polka dot paper chairs. Both rooms feature extensive built-in wall storage of all kinds.

Transform your basement playroom into a modern discotheque...with a lighted "Go-Go Cage" in the center!

2"X2" NOTCHED CROSSPIECES

STAPLE SMALL LIGHTS TO WOOD STRIPS OR MAKE SLOTS FOR WIRES

3/4" PLYWOOD TOP

1/4" PLYWOOD SIDES

2"X2" CUT TO HEIGHT OF ROOM

2"X4"

To make "Go-go Cage", cut four sides and one top piece from plywood or scrap lumber. Nail them together, forming stage, using 2x4-inch framework inside box for support. Paint sides one color and top another color.

Then cut four 2x2-inch wood strips to correct height for your room. Also cut two notched crosspieces for top of "cage". Paint all of these same color as top of stage. Nail or screw all strips together and to stage. Also use glue for additional support of the unit.

Staple strands of small lights onto wood strips. If desired, you can make small slots in strips before placing them, and then slip the light wires into them.

Fun and **Family Rooms**

decorating
Guest Rooms

Plan accommodations for two

Tuck two guests comfortably in a corner of this all-purpose den designed by Colby's of suburban Chicago. Mix contemporary storage units with a classic bentwood chair. Use the warmth of an Icelandic sheepskin rug to pull a cool room together, and play space tricks with see-through plastic tables. Color it all black and white with orange accents in the wall hanging and parsons table.

Let it be small, but so nice

A guest room does not have to be large to be effective. It merely has to be tidy, interesting and functional . . . as is this one. Against a gay floral wall print, there's a comfortable daybed with bolsters, writing table, chairs, and a large lounge pillow. Small accent rug and clever shelf arrangement completes the room. Designed by Comfy Pillows.

Make it a full-fledged bedroom

Give your guests a full-fledged bedroom, if there's space. Guests love the luxury of a private bed-sitting room with desk, armchairs, and carefully coordinated decor, as shown here. Fresh flowers are a loving touch.

Guest Rooms

Make it smashing!

Pamper your guest. Even if space is tight, taste and hospitality needn't be skimped. This replica of a Directoire daybed is nice for naps and super-satisfying for reading and sleeping. Add a campaign table for writing or face painting, and a tigerskin rug for Pow!

Put a guest room in the corner

Put a guest in a corner cupboard. The one behind this bright blue Naugahyde sofa holds a fold-out bed and also provides shelf space for storage. This wall bed unit by Kroehler (from their "At Home Collection").

Bed your guests in a garden

Use a very gay, very floral patterned bedspread, such as "Poppy Dot" by Field-crest. Carry through with matching blanket and sheets. You might even make draperies from sheets. Strew more poppies in the guest bath . . . there's a matching shower curtain, even matching towels and aprons. And cut out some flowers, glue them to floor, shellac and varnish them to protect from wear.

Try something new in a guest corner

Here's something new for your guest room corner . . . an all-purpose daybed from Dux with a sleek frame of tubular steel. Resilient polyurethane makes a comfortable seat-cum-mattress, and fat cylindrical bolsters provide eye-appeal as well as reclining ease. Can be ensembled with matching laminated-topped tables and seating pieces.

Departmentalize to save time and effort

This delightful utility room was designed to serve a range of related needs. Great care has been taken to provide an ample and appropriate place for sewing and mending, the care of clothing and special projects from gift-wrapping to making paper dolls. Each departmentalized area can be used in tandem. Storage space is keyed to each area. Multi-colored furnishings and built-ins call for a soft subtle floor covering. Acoustical tile and tile on floor are by Armstrong.

Use folding doors for easy access

Folding doors save space and allow easy access to mechanical equipment. This plan offers efficient use of space in a pretty room that makes routine work sheer delight. Sewing machine is right at hand for quick mending and back-to-school projects. Appliances by Westinghouse.

Make it "happy" with flowers

Cut imaginative, even extravagant flowers from wallpaper, plastic adhesive, or fabric and glue them to wall in interesting fashion. Use green tape for stems and leaves. This simple trick will turn any drab utility room into one that is absolutely exciting and fun to work in. Note small shelf attached to wall for sewing machine.

Provide good lighting

Select lighting fixtures that not only match the color scheme but provide proper lighting for close work or reading in a cozy corner. A special recessed eyeball fixture spotlights sewing machine. The recessed ceiling fixtures by Moe Light have emerald-blue trim to match the gayly-colored cabinets. Built-in cabinets and drawer-lined wall hold a multitude of supplies.

Enhance and co-ordinate with a "fun" wallpaper

Combine imagination and efficiency in a home laundry center that fits conveniently into a hallway, a guest room or wherever there's plumbing. A sweep of counters provides a work top area and compartments for all storage needs. Louvered doors open to a gay burst of colorful, carefree wallpaper. Appliances are by Maytag.

Use small corner for hobby area

The variety of space you find and define throughout your home can be exhilarating and add a new dimension to each day.

Here, tucked into a corner, is a private hobby area for sketching, sculpture or whatever.

Around the hobby corner is a clean sweep of automatic appliances in a utility room sparked with personal paintings. Appliances by General Electric.

Build a fold-out sewing-storage unit

Made of standard western woods, this built-in, fold-up sewing center holds all wherewithal, including shelves for fabric and drawers for patterns, thread, scissors and sewing essentials.

Table top may be folded away in an instant. "Legs" become bulletin board when unit folds into wall.

Use perforated hardboard for supplies

Peg boards as pretty as wallpaper also provide a practical background for this utility room.

Shelves are organized in tiers to hold laundry essentials.

Once again, louvered doors matching the cabinets conceal this efficient area when it's not in use.

Appliances are by Maytag. Note three-section tilt bin for soiled clothes.

decorating ideas for Utility Rooms

Make it plain or fancy

Plain or fancy, creative planning for utility rooms will alter the look and maintain efficiency. Above, the style is rustic with wallpaper and matching fabric over cupboards with brick-pattern vinyl floor tile. Below, the high-fashion look is set with stained-glass cupboards and sleek cabinets. Appliances by Maytag.

Make room for your hobbies

A practical room for household chores and a pretty setting for hobbies, keeping accounts, writing letters or finishing an interrupted chapter. Shelves spaced for storage can make every corner count. Note the wicker totes and baskets used to hide-away washable fabrics. Underfoot the carpet is decorative and practical "Carve Craft" by Barwick. General Electric appliances.

Make big use of small space

When space is small, think big. Below left, wall-hung clothes dryer is used above Maytag washer, just a step away from kitchen area. By combining these two work areas, plumbing expenses are reduced. The same L-shaped counter can be used in larger kitchens, too. Below right, automatic washer and dryer are placed against wall with colorful wallpaper mural as an interesting backdrop.

Utility Rooms

Use a closet

If you have a closet to spare, convert it into a laundry center. Adjustable clothing rack is a handy hang-up for permanent press garments just after drying. And overhead shelf stores laundry aids and extra pillows. Appliances by Maytag.

Be ultra modern

Located at one end of a family recreation room, this laundry center offers the homemaker a pleasant area in which to work and accents her interest in oriental art objects. Elevating the Maytag dryer provides a special convenience for tall homemakers. The 15-inch platform conceals a storage bin for bedding and other bulky items. Between the washer and dryer, is a cabinet which is separated into three tilt bins that serve as storage for sorting soiled laundry.

Grow real and fanciful flowers to brighten your work room

Plastic-backed adhesives, such as Con-Tact, provide a charming atmosphere for work area when hung like wallpaper and applied to appliances for a beautiful built-in look. Overhead, valance is cut from plywood, covered, and nailed in place. Cut out individual flowers, stick on wall and ceiling to finish off this colorful corner. Note use of glass shelves in front of window to hold real flowers.

IDEAS FOR SITTING ROOMS

Some well-rounded conversation around some beautifully-rounded wicker furniture

Subtle textural contrasts are highlighted in a restful room which emphasizes natural tones and materials. Cane appears in matching chaise longue, settee and tub chair. Two wicker storage chests are backed by grasscloth wallcovering. Even the lacy area rug is of a natural fiber. Interlacings of colored wool embellish the bamboo Roman shades. Stronger accent comes via orange-y Japanese Tansu chest, floral table skirt and verdant foliage. By Bloomingdale's.

Love seats belong in this kind of room

Love seats are now available in many shapes and colors. Shown here is charming pillow-back model designed by Kipp Stewart for Directional. Love seats work well individually or in pairs.

For him: a masculine, den-like setting

A small room with a fireplace and paneled walls immediately suggested the masculine to this homemaker, so she added the necessary red couches, the zebra skin rug, the heavy writing desk and all the accessories needed to turn this room into a man's sitting room.

Tete-A-Tete chairs are ideal for sitting room

This chair ensemble is an interesting addition to any room and can turn any corner into a sitting room. Designed by Selig, the chairs have pleated backs, come in a variety of colors and fabrics.

Wicker again sets the stage for conversation

Wicker is now a year-round choice for informal rooms. Lacquered in white, it is an ideal foil for the red, white and blue colors of Regal's area rug of Herculon olefin fiber. Lacquered in red, wicker reappears in an amusing elephant-shaped lamp table and Oriental desk chair. Striped wallpaper and checked upholstery fabric complete the patriotic scheme.

A sitting room of silver and gleam

"Love in Bloom" wallpaper by The Jack Denst Designs, Inc., is printed in red and cerise enamel inks, complements the stainless steel floor, coffee table, lamp, and accessories. Couch is red, chair is blue.

A sitting room of glass and floral finery

Two love seats are separated by an interesting floral table. One wall was painted a dark color, another fitted with glass shelves for glassware. One-of-a-kind iron stove, cube end tables are added touches. By Abraham & Straus.

Special Rooms

Combine wild mural, juke box and dance floor for swinging family room

A pop-art mural, "Faces and Trees," from Pandora Productions, set the pace here. Equally imaginative are juke box from antique shop and vinyl dance floor bordered by wall-to-wall carpeting. Rest of room is rather formal, offers nice contrast. Clean-lined furniture is from Crossroads of California's "Design 9" collection, combines solid oak with Tartan-Clad veneer to resist stains and scratches.

Paint straight-line super graphics in a sitting room

Super graphics are total environment, surrounding a room with modern art. Super graphics are also bold colors, and a freedom from restraint. This sitting room, hard-edge and bold, is black, white and bright kelly green. The chairs are green and the Woolmark carpet by Custom Floor Covering is a black and white checkerboard. Walls and table carry out the exercise in geometry.

Remodel a small basement area into a lounge

Ideal for teenage parties, after PTA meetings, etc., is this small basement area turned into a lounge. Walls were covered with Masonite paneling, floor with vinyl tile. Then fireplace, brick wall and hearth were installed. Then one long piece of wood was positioned along one side of room for seating.

Special Rooms

Love seats are perfect additions

Studio, reading, sewing or sitting rooms are perfect places to use love seats which are small, compact, pretty, and give a living room appearance to any room. Today they come in all sizes, shapes, color. This one is from Directional's "Sedgefield" collection.

Create a garden-workshop for yourself

He has his den or workshop, so why shouldn't you create a room that matches your interests and personality? This garden-workroom with the butcher-block table, handy pegboard, and space-saving wall unit is ideal for a lady with a green thumb. "Wallmaker" unit from David Page has Tartan-Clad vinyl veneer, making it resistant to stains and scratches. Indoor-outdoor carpet by Barwick makes for easy cleanups, too. Room designed by Peg Walker, A.I.D.

Make a garden room

Ideal for year-round use is this small garden room. At windows are McCanless Custom Fabric's "Fabriganza" draperies with heavy casement sheers underneath. Inexpensive rattan furniture from furniture-in-the-raw stores was painted pastel colors. Highlight of room is small "garden," which is really a plywood box fitted with a piece of galvanized steel, as shown in diagram. Potted plants fit into unit, which is adorned with small statue-like figure.

Make a little lounge

Turn a large hallway or a little room into a lounge with a colorful area rug, some modern furniture, and a painted graphic on the wall. Here, windows boast "Riviera" venetian blinds by Levolor Lorentzen. Outlining them is lambrequin made from plywood. Parsons table and chairs are perfect foil.

Revamp an unused bedroom into a mini-office

For a woman of many interests, here is a charming home office. Clutter is concealed within the vest pocket workspace in the former closet. Clean-line furnishings, bright splashes of matching pattern on doors and windows and "Look Sharp," polyester shag carpeting by Lees, complete this feminine retreat.

Special Rooms

Whip up an easy-care dressing room

Lucky is the woman whose home boasts a dressing room next to her bedroom. She may not be Mme. Recamier but she can lounge on her white wicker chaise without worry about housework as she knows that this room was designed for easy upkeep. The furniture requires but occasional dusting and the carpet, Monarch's "Casual Tile" pattern, is of sturdy miracle-age fibers.

Add a daybed to complement a study

This study where one can take a nap as well as read, do needlepoint, or have a quiet conversation, boasts a comfortable daybed. Here "The Pad" by Simmons is made of quilted layer of foam topped by white vinyl which looks like leather. When it is time to sit rather than sleep, bolsters provide needed back support. Casters add mobility.

Spark a sun room with outdoor elements

This sun room, set directly off the patio, offers the appeal of nature with indoor practicality. Its flooring, a leisure type dubbed "Topside" by Lees, looks elegant but can easily be sponged free of muddy footprints. Lawn furniture by Woodard is topped in a blue and white garden-look floral. The potted yucca and fresh posies continue the indoor-outdoor theme.

Style a feminine yet frill-free sitting room

A pair of laminated shades, plus companion wallpaper, set the pace for a charming sitting room designed by Sue Morris. The shades act as focal point for the treatment, updating old-fashioned windows and are framed by full, tie-back white curtains. The pattern then flows onto the walls, concealing unattractive beams. For snap, Miss Morris chose a yellow wicker settee, white bamboo chair and snakeskin coffee table. The wood floor was stained the brilliant green of the floral print.

Special Rooms

Update a pantry into a cozy reading nook

An outmoded pantry escapes the tick of time by being modernized into a nook off of the kitchen in which one can look up recipes and plan menus. Storage space for cookbooks is within the interior of a pin dry sink from Kemp's "American Settler" collection. The wall is treated to a gay striping of stylized cutouts which echo the orange of the carpet and window shade. The captain's chair take a seat pad of clear yellow.

Make a little lounge in a large hallway

Wake up a box-like hallway with a spectacular wallcovering like this Jack Denst design, "Where the Air Is Rarified," a contemporary melange of purple, red and plum with a hint of Middle Eastern minarets in its motif. With such a powerful wall treatment, furnishings should be kept on the simple side. Here they are sinuously modern. Together, the wild wallcovering and the wire furniture transforms a hallway area into a charming extra living or sitting room.

Use black and white to spark up a home office

A crisp black and white theme is played out in large and small scale patterns for lively and interesting looking sitting room that also serves as a home office. Wall paper is a composition of old handbills, an amusing background idea. For proper lighting over table-desk, twin fixtures are used instead of lamps. Idea from Wall Covering Council.

Paper a hobby-sitting room with one delightful print

Enchanting hobby-sitting room has contemporary version of the clos lit (French alcove bed). Sparkling, feminine sitting room is pulled together by the all-over use of small scale leaf printed wallpaper. From the Wall Covering Council.

IDEAS FOR SPECIAL ROOMS

Safari room for the adventurous-minded

Here's a room designed for those who want to get away from it all! It's done in wood, canvas and cane, and gives the illusion of the outdoor world.

Lightweight campaign chairs of natural canvas and wood, a foldable cot and stools, are all sleek and simple. The big table is versatile, too. It can switch its role from desk to dining spot to server right on demand. For the bliss of pure relaxation a porter's chair of cane and canvas is padded out with a bouncy cushion and added ottoman. By Bloomingdale's.

For good listening, music wall curves to form baffle in this elaborate music room by Vladimir Kagan, A.I.D. Built-in hi-fi system is constructed of U.S. Plywood's ¾-inch Brazilian rosewood, as is elliptical cocktail table. English brown oak Flexwood sheaths the curved wall and lines niche for records and tapes. Flexwood, thin wood veneer laminated to a cloth backing, is designed to cover round, curved or flat surfaces.

Two rooms for music lovers

Turn a small attic into a music room by building a foot-high, wooden seating unit on which to place cushion seats and hi-fi speakers. Phono stereo system by Scott sits on table. Four cushions on homemade wooden box provide additional seating.

Here are two ways to do something special with a small room: turn it into a potting shed or into an office. Here's how:

Potting shed: The built-in cabinet and sink under the window is about nine feet long, is used for re-potting, taking cuttings, general care of plants.

Open, built-in shelves display plants, potting materials, additional clay pots, peat moss, etc., in attractive con-

A swank office-library for the family secretary-treasurer

tainers. Shelves can be fitted with artificial lights if desired.

Plants also hang from ceiling in clay pots in baskets on chains. Garden hand tools hang in center wall area.

Floors and walls are covered with Ozite foam rubber-backed carpet tiles which come in 12-inch squares in a variety of colors. Instructions for installation are on package; photo here shows basic installation. Carpet tiles are practical underfoot in a garden area since they are im-pervious to mildew and fungus, and are very easy to clean.

Office-library: Built-in unit under window is now covered by a thick, comfortable foam rubber slab and bolsters in gay, upholstered fabric.

Storage shelves now hold books, papers, records, etc. Typewriter can be stored on shelf when not in use.

Carpet tiles on floor and wall have acoustical properties, help quiet noise of typewriter.

A studio and art gallery for someone who paints

A spare bedroom was painted white, the ceiling a dark blue, and light fixtures were added to make this interesting artist's studio and gallery.

Paintings and sculpture are displayed around the room, while an easel holds the work in progress. An art table stands nearby for pencil sketching.

This idea from a Tarry Hill model home at Tarrytown, New York.

A workable utility room for the lady of the house

Extensive work was done on this basement to turn it into a charming, practical utility room.

Ceiling was covered with Armstrong acoustical tile, floor with Armstrong tile, and entire room was fitted with wall cabinets and shelf areas over the washer, drier, etc.

Most interesting is the work table which was built around an existing post in the basement.

Room was painted bright pastel colors.

A study-library for the world traveler

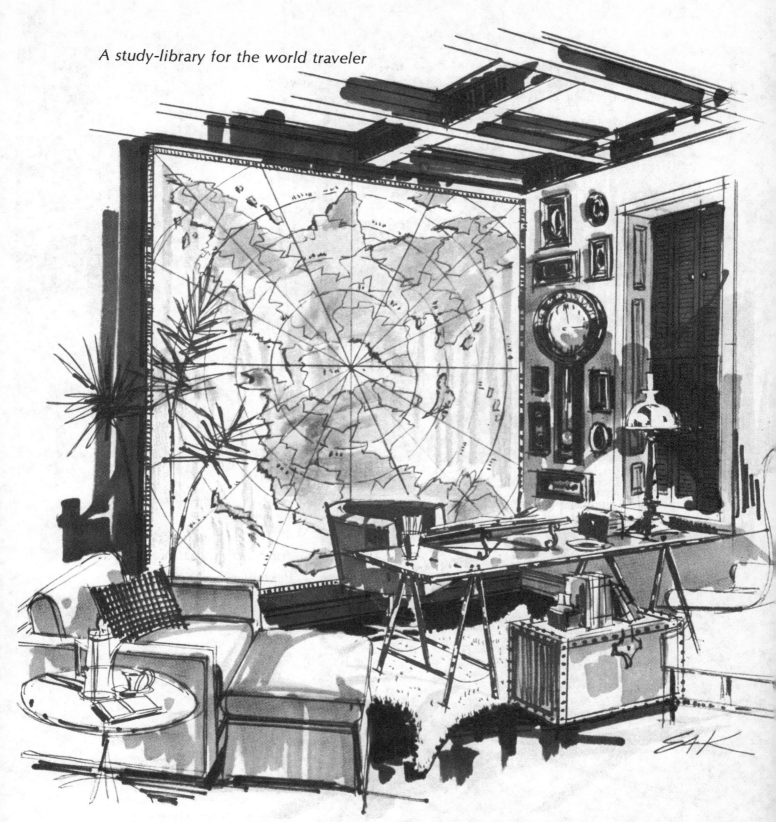

A spare room or one end of a bedroom can be transformed into this fascinating study-library for a real or would-be world traveler. Highlight of the room is a huge map which is framed and mounted to wall, as shown. Add some interesting furniture and lots of accessories that suggest travel and far-off places. This is the kind of a room any man will love.

A hobby-work center for Mr. and Mrs.

Desk by Khoury Brothers becomes mother's sewing center. Father's work area is several chests, various shelves and piece of pegboard, all joined together, painted same color. Seating unit has storage drawers.

An indoor gazebo for outdoor people

Hand-painted wall murals depict view from a gazebo with blue sky, bamboo fretwork and palm fronds.

Englander's Del Prado Da-Bed provides the major seating.

Bamboo chairs, felt-draped table, Tiffany lamp, bird cage carry out garden atmosphere.

An attic hideaway for the whole family

This attic was finished off beautifully with Armstrong tile on floor, knotty pine on walls, wooden shutters on windows. Even sofas are home-made with foam cushions for seats.

Highlight of room is wooden totem pole in front of window. If you can't find the real thing, make one out of papier mache.

A bedroom-storage room for the family golfer

To keep him from waking up the whole house on Sunday morning, provide the family golfer with a room of his own. Paper walls with golf motif of some kind. Used here: pages from a golfing book, obtained from a printing plant.

The gleam of metal and glass — so popular for contemporary settings — gives vitality to feminine bedroom (above) framed in walls of white moire fabric.

Another modern (and practical) note is the use of soft vinyl leather on two pull-up chairs and for window-shades. Room designed by Stern Bros.

Elegant grandeur of French drawing room (left) derives from walls of ivory colored silk and handsome painted and wood-finished Louis XVI and Directoire reproductions.

Daybed contains a modern secret: mattress pulls up and out for sleeping. Fabrics in Bloomingdale's room are silk and velvet.

*Beautiful interiors reflect
a variety of periods*

Traditional rooms for Today

A room of white stucco walls and random plank flooring is
appropriately furnished in a potpourri of country French and Spanish
reproductions. Quilted fabric is a contemporary print, painting
a modern abstract. By Bloomingdale's

Traditional rooms for Today

Wide choice and variety exist within the traditional idiom, an observation clearly demonstrated by the Bloomingdale's room across the page, shown in two strikingly different traditional poses.

In setting top, English Chippendale furniture is grouped, contemporary fashion, around square cocktail table and area rug. Thai influence of red stained walls and windows is echoed in choice of silk fabrics, porcelains and wooden temple fragments.

Second version of room shows another furniture arrangement worked out in an eclectic interplay of French and modern furniture.

Sunny shades of lemon and orange luminate this handsome bedroom furnished with Louis XVI reproductions. Cornice shape of canopy bed is restated in the drapery cornice. Painted furniture is mixed with wood finished pieces. By Bloomingdales.

Today's traditional room can be an elaborate composition, slavishly authentic to a specific period, or a less serious, freewheeling arrangement that makes outright concessions to contemporary ideas. Rooms displayed in this section show the enormous variety possible within the framework of the traditional label.

Pale colors, and the extensive use of white, are especially favored for many traditional settings (and for modern ones, too.) Stain-repellent fabric finishes and the use of vinyl upholstery are ways of dealing with the practical aspects of the pale look. Another way to win the battle is choosing an effective cleaning process. Duraclean is one of the excellent professional cleaning agencies available—their method not only removes soil but leaves furnishings in a more soil-resistant state.

The eclectic style, a currently favored theme, is expressed (above) in a cosmopolitan mix of English, French, Italian and Spanish designs.

Tuxedo sofa, tufted in natural cowhide, and glass-topped metal table introduce two contemporary elements.

Zingy background of brick and papered walls and beamed ceiling doubles the impact of mingled periods. Bloomingdale's.

Traditional rooms for Today

French country furniture is chosen for a room framed by stucco walls and decoratively placed beams.

Capturing the mood of the setting is Cabin Crafts area rug, Belle Tapis, a simplified version of a provincial design.

Room has been planned as a quiet sitting area, or for such activities as reading or letter writing.

Rug is all acrilan.

The traditional look gets a contemporary translation in Stern Bros. setting (right).

Almost all the furniture, with the exception of the modern coffee table, are simplified adaptations of traditional styles.

Note the use of half-round columns to frame shaded windows.

Oval area rug defines the conversation grouping.

Floor is vinyl tile.

Foyers

Create one with beads

Separating without losing the view is the special asset which Beadangles bring to decorating. The unbreakable strands of pre-strung beads can be bought by the yard and cut to fit any length required. Here, they were utilized by Paul Krauss, AID, to create a small foyer which can still share the light and air from the living room. The Beadangles are hung on flexible vinyl tape with pre-punched holes which accept the top bead of each strand.

Be sleek and simple

Decorate a small foyer or hallway with slim, slender furniture, such as these two pieces from Brueton Industries. One is their combination shelf-console and mirror. The other is their half-round console with mirror. Both are made of shiny hardware and gleaming glass, and will bring a modern elegance to any foyer.

Hang an office in your foyer
It's easy to build, a delight to use, and makes any foyer distinctive. It's really just a large box built from pine with several small shelves added to hold various necessities. Dress it up with some modern art. Then put an interesting chair in front of the unit, and you're in business.

FOYERS

Panel your hallway, make it into a small room

Here, one wall of a small foyer was covered with Brazilian Rosewood Weldwood paneling by U. S. Plywood, after small built-in bench was erected on wall. Small sofa lines other wall. Modern painting, cushions, etc., adorn bench. Accent rug "Stonehenge" by Bigelow sparks up the whole area. Modern chair and large plant are the finishing touches, which help make this foyer into a small room.

Hang wallcovering as carpet

No, that's not a carpet hanging on the wall in the foyer at the left. It's "Abracadabra," a colorful tapestry wallcovering from Jack Denst Designs. This single panel mural can be hung tapestry-fashion or stretched gallery-fashion. It looks great either way. It comes in several colorways.

Do it up Mediterranean-style

In this Mediterranean-style foyer, a simple area rug is a perfect complement to Spanish tile, furniture and stained-glass windows. The tile is by Armstrong, and the final result of the whole foyer is one of grandeur and graciousness—a perfect setting for greeting your guests.

FOYERS

Console: By Heritage, it's from their "Tour de France" collection, a Debut '72 feature. Here, it's flanked by chair and two square pictures.

Cabinet: Use one to fill a niche. Here, it's a Mediterranean version on Spanish-style floor tile by American Olean. Painting is in same mood.

Settee: Chamé, the Naugahyde fabric with a French accent, covers this settee as naturally as whipped cream, and gives this foyer a look of elegance.

Storage-wall: Perfect to hold phone, books, magazines, art treasures, etc., this modern storage unit and wicker stools set on tile floor, "Navara", by Congoleum.

Credenza: Mediterranean-style, it sets mood for foyer which is accented with antique wall hangings, baroque candlesticks, etc. By Kemp furniture.

Play up one important element

Area rug: Hang a colorful area rug on the wall, allowing a small part of the rug to cover the floor, as shown. Place small table and mirror to complete this arrangement.

ideas for Windows

Frame with bookcase: A series of simple pine shelves frame a wide picture window and becomes a backdrop for beautiful draperies and a wide shade trimmed with Joanna's press-on looped fringe.

Frame with cornice: Here's another way to treat the same window. Cut a cornice from plywood, cover with the same shade cloth used for the shade. Trim both with looped fringe.

Play up the architecture: A series of small laminated shades emphasize the many small windows of this room, at the same time unifying them into a whole. Furniture is by Lane.

Unify with fabric: Here's a window niche with a different look. Instead of placing a long sofa into the alcove, use a comfortable loveseat, covered in a tree-of-life design and set a spacious table beside it. Cover valance over window with matching fabric. The hand-woven look of the shades, which have brass-banded borders, contribute light-and-privacy control.

Match lambrequin with shade: Handsome striped fabric was laminated to Joanna's "Exlite" shade cloth, which was also used to cover the lambrequin.

Outline with molding: Extra wood molding outlines ordinary, double-hung window (below, left) creating interesting to-the-floor effect. "Sunchex" shade is finished with Joanna's Self-Adhesive fringe.

Stripe it up: Add flavor and light control with "Carousel Stripe" shades by Breneman. Extra yardage of shade cloth covers pair of tall screens to add breadth without deviating from the "straight and narrow" theme. Braid outlines the whole, adding linear definition.

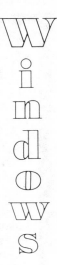

Make a glimmering window wall: High spot of this room is two tall mirrored screens, which stand between windows fitted with aluminum venetian blinds. Together they make whole wall gleam. Modern furniture sits on bold area rug by Egetaepper.

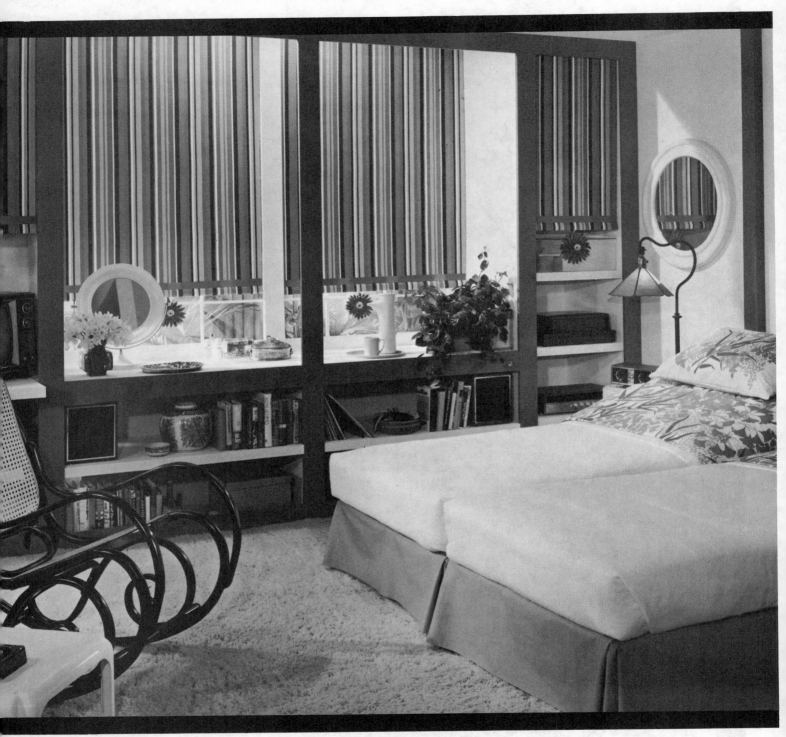

Build storage-utility unit around windows: Just a minimal amount of space produces a clean-lined, lightly-scaled wall-to-wall treatment that contains decorative light control for later sleepers; a TV viewing center cleverly angled to the bed; hi-fi, bookshelf and storage space—and even dressing table surface where it benefits most from daylight. The "working wall," smartly outlined with 1x4s in teal blue, frames a series of window shades designed not only to add black-out service at the windows, but to pull down over electronic equipment when it's not in use. Variegated striped fabric ("Emotions" by Bloomcraft, of cotton and Fortrel) was laminated to Tontine Tri-Lam window shade cloth by Stauffer. (If you'd like a detailed booklet on how to laminate shades, write The Window Shade Manufacturer's Association, 230 Park Ave., NY, NY). A compact headboard was produced with a series of painted 2x4s, positioned as shown. Simmons Adjusto-Beds operate electrically, can be raised or lowered.

Trim with tape: Trim window shade and valance ("Kashmir" by Joanna, here) with strips of Conso's stick-on tape. Then position tape around edge of ceiling and run down the wall, as shown, to create a very interesting window wall. This is a great, inexpensive way to dress up a room.

Use folding shutters: Ideal for bathroom windows are hinged shutters with cutouts in panels. Cover cutouts in back with curtains made from towels and mounted on small curtain rods. Small valance goes across top of window. American Olean Tile was used on the walls and the floor.

Windows

Brighten a corner: Do it with shutters painted white to match the woodwork and positioned as shown. Makes a perfect place to display two colorful burlap shades by Joanna.

Match furniture: In this room (right) racing stripe trim used on Schoolfield Industries' "Indianapolis 500" collection, is used to frame window and bedeck floor. Stripes are really pieces of Con-Tact plastic tape in matching colors. Furniture features scratch resistant 3-M Tartan-Clad vinyl veneer.

Dress up beams: Cover beams between windows with same fabric used to make draperies, then show off some beautiful shades. These are custom laminated by Norman's of Salisbury.

Spotlight a garden: This city homeowner (right) bricked-up an unsightly view and created a small garden, which can be seen through windows and almost becomes part of the living room. Furniture is from Broyhill's "Showcase" collection.

Include door in window treatment: This window wall alternates panels of striped sheer draperies with complimentary window shades and unifies three diverse elements—large picture window, smaller one, and glass-fronted terrace door. Tontine translucent "Colony" shades are in textured beige, with Conso fringe trim matching drapery stripes. Beam above windows, covered in same beige hemp which "wallpapers" entire room, gives effect of cornice.

Let slim blinds set the pace: First, paint the walls red. Then cover floor with a red plaid carpet ("Highland Red" by Barwick, here) Instead of curtains use red, slim "Riviera" blinds by Levelor. Use red checked bedspread. Furniture is from American of Martinsville's "Hombre" collection, finished with Tartan-Clad vinyl veneer in dark oak, which resists stains and scratches. A card table covered with black felt for a game table, leaves the desk free for study equipment.

Accent window wall with floral print: Here's dinner à deux in an appetizing pink plus red plus white setting. The window wall frames a round table which opens for guests, goes way out for parties. Ceiling-to-floor ready-made print draperies by Tilbury are tied back to show sheer, washable ninon undercurtains by Karpel. The deep, braid-trimmed hems are nice dressmaker touch. A lipstick-red Fortrel carpet lends character to faintly pink ceiling and walls. Fabrics and floorcoverings made of Celanese fibers. Photographed at Ivey's, Charlotte, N.C.

Use bamboo blinds: This modern dining corner is trimmed with three inexpensive roll-up bamboo blinds. Most unusual thing about this window wall is window box nailed to beams separating windows. Area rug ("Helios" by Egetaepper) underscores the color scheme.

Windows

Unify with color: Black and green patterned draperies frame these windows (at left). White "Colony" shade cloth valance and shades by Tontine repeat the point in their trimming and shade pull. As contrast to the strong horizontal lines of the window, furniture by Directional is nicely rounded.

Decorate with storage shelves: This teenager's bedroom features a simple built-in that provides storage for all kinds of daily necessities. The wide shade and shade cloth valance ("Calcutta" by Illinois Shade) are trimmed with bands of fringe.

Build corner window seat: Make basic frame from 2x4s, cover with plywood, paint to match rest of room. Make pillows from latex foam rubber to fit window seat. Slim "Riviera" venetian blinds by Levolor fit windows. Note use of paintings on walls.

WINDOW SHADE WIZARDRY

Some ingenious treatments for windows of all kinds

Sunflowers spill over onto shade

Dot it with polka dots

Give a small bedroom great flair. Here it's done quickly and easily by adorning a plain windowshade with sunflower cut-outs from same material used on draperies and bed spread.

Dotted window design looks complicated, but is a simple do-it-yourself idea. Off-white shade and matching topper get scallop-shaped fabric border, all garnished with remnant cut-outs.

FABRIC APPLIQUES FOR WINDOW SHADES

Motifs cut from closely woven fabrics, such as polished cotton, chintz and percale, are best for applique. To keep raw edges from raveling, paint the cutting line, on the back, with colorless nail polish before cutting. If large areas are to be done, spray the back of the fabric with a clear acrylic spray, such as Krylon, or press iron-on Pelomite onto the back of the applique. When using nail polish or Krylon, test first because some fibers, such as acetate, will dissolve.

Cut out carefully with small, sharp scissors and arrange pieces as a complete design on the shade. Then apply glue to the reverse side, one cut-out at a time, making sure the entire surface is covered before pressing it on to the shade. Smooth it out carefully, checking that all the edges are attached securely, and that no air bubbles remain. (If fabric is sheer, the glue can be spread on the shade cloth.) After the pasting is completed and the adhesive has dried, the face of the fabric may be protected by an additional coating of spray.

Cut a bow from gay checks

Design your own cut-out from a plain or checked fabric, using same material used for making draperies. Paul Krauss gave blue windowshade above a blue and white checked bow. Pattern was first drawn on paper, than traced on fabric.

A ceiling-high window wall is turned into a decorative focal point in room above. Painted wooden frames divide one window into six. Printed leopard vinyl window shades fill in the frames, provide individual light and privacy control. Acrylic carpeting of charming den is from Bigelow.

WINDOW SHADE WIZARDRY

Lambrequin and matching window shade are winning combination for a tall skinny window. This treatment makes the window appear wider, it also adds architectural character to the setting.

Lambrequin or frame can be easily made of plywood, then covered with paper or fabric and then nailed to wall. Window shade has been laminated with the same print used on frame.

Other ideas: Shape of window can be almost completely obscured by covering the wall and even the ceiling with the matching pattern. Vary the shape of the lambrequin — make it scalloped, give it a more dominant shadow box shape. Put braid or fringe along the inside and/or outside of the frame.

Tall, skinny windows? Try one of these solutions.

Horizontal lines of white fringe trimming on windowshade and shade topper flatter the tall narrow window of bed sitting room above.

Here a narrow window becomes more dramatic by using fringed valance and by outlining window frame with braid also used to band shade.

For the nursery, colorful cutouts

Simple border design of colorful cutouts enlivens plain white windowshade, relates it to sill-length draperies. Circles were cut from drapery print.

Adapt a pattern, paint it on

Floral motif of crewel fabric was enlarged and stencilled on solid blue shade. Edmund Motyka used this technique to personalize this window.

One wide shade provides a clean, uninterrupted line at the window of kitchen dining area. Invisibly vinyl-coated, shade is ornamented by braid trim.

One for three

The authority of a lambrequin-framed window is easily emulated by the skillful use of a wide braid for double window. Solid shades get tassel trim.

Use tapes for lambrequin look

Shade accents "kicky" idea for a teenager

Checked dado captures the spirit of a young environment. Sketch (left) shows how it's used on opposite wall at door. Braid which trims wallpaper also makes shade border and tie-backs for draperies. Note picture frames use room wallpaper for backing.

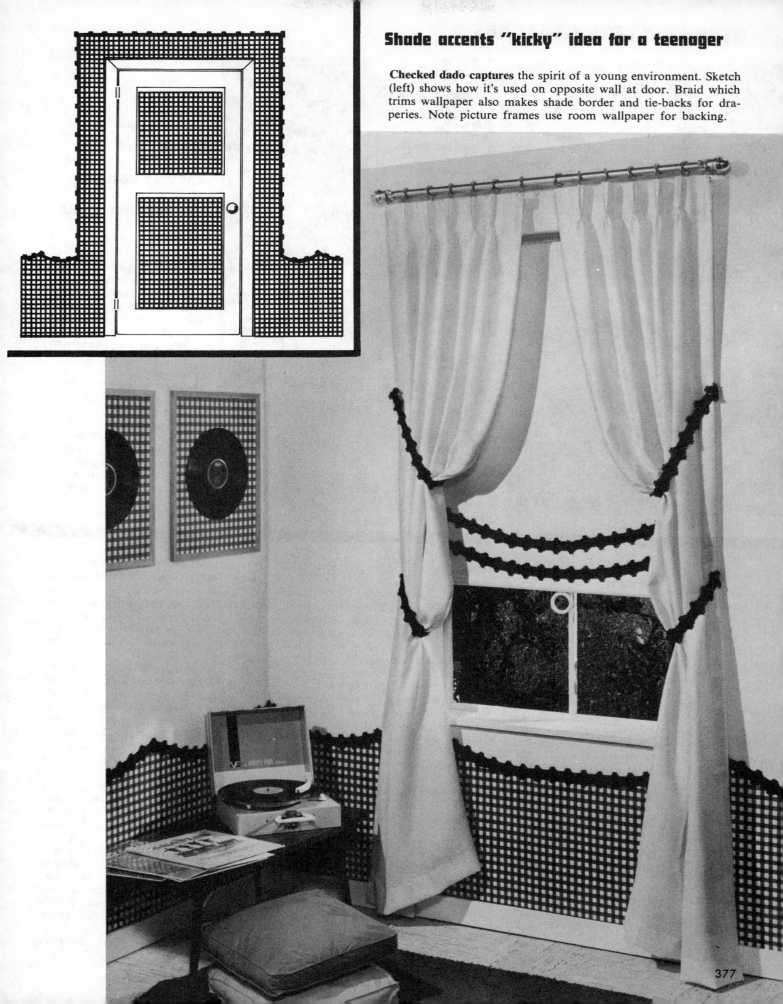

WINDOW SHADE WIZARDRY

Shades add another pattern to patterned room

Window shades make sense from a practical as well as decorative standpoint in a room whose architecture permits a broad view of the outdoors.

Walnut-framed floor to ceiling windows in living room (left), open to a large patio. Shades can be pulled up to quickly reveal the view.

Note that patterned shades were chosen for a room already filled with pattern. This mingling of motifs lends animation to the sleek, modern furnishings.

GETTING WINDOW SHADES IN TRIM

Teamed together, shades and trimmings contribute an important new dimension in shade decoration. A look at the trimming department's wide selection will suggest many exciting ways of adding a custom look to a room. Types of trimming are infinite, their versatility limited only by the imagination. The classic list includes fringes, braids, gimp, and tape, in hundreds of colors.

Braid and fringe, used together in mix-match combinations, add handsome, definitive flavor by virtue of the small, but effective, change of pace from one type of trim to another. And all of these trimmings can be used for interesting coordination of upholstery and slipcovers with curtains and shades.

In addition to the standard trimmings, there are all sorts of design opportunities. Ribbons, in grosgrain, velvet, or novelty weaves, eyelet edging, rick rack, and other braids, are all available in fashion, notions, or ribbon departments. Printed borders obtainable from decorative fabric firms offer interesting treatment ideas as well. Other attractive ways to dress up your windows include the use of decorative shade pulls and shade cloth valances.

Standard trimmings. Each shade manufacturer offers a complete line of standard hem shapes and trimmings which can be ordered from actual samples, or from photographs. In addition, many department stores and shade shops have their own lines of hem shapes and trimmings from which to choose.

Custom selections. If a desired style or color of trimming is not available at your local shade shop or department, any trimming may be purchased elsewhere and sent to the factory or workroom with your shade order.

In department stores, trimming departments usually adjoin the shade department, making it easy to obtain the trimming and order shades at the same time.

How to Order: When purchasing custom trimming for standard shade hem shapes, allow one and a half times the width of the shade—more for very deep scallops, less for the very narrow.

Specify exactly where you want the trimming placed on the shade—on the edge, over the stitching of the hem, etc. Also mention the number of rows of trimming, if more than one; whether they are to touch, be separated, or overlapped. In the last two cases, indicate the amount of space between rows, or the amount of overlap desired. Remember that it is best to keep trimmings near the bottom of the shade, in the area not ordinarily rolled up.

When ordering a custom hem shape, take a full size paper pattern of it to the shop. Keep the shape fairly simple and remember to choose a trimming that is flexible enough to conform to the hem properly. This is important, because not all trimmings have enough "give" to curve. Some can be used in straight rows only.

Standard shade hem shapes are now available in many decorative moods. They may be straight, with trimming on the surface of the shade; shaped in any of a variety of scallops, or cut out.

Straight hems have pockets that hold the slat (an essential part of any window shade) at the very bottom of the shade. Trimmings can be added at the edge, on the hem seam (about one and a half inches from the bottom) or in rows above it.

Shaped or scalloped shades have an

Stencil your own design

Make them match

Perk up your bedroom with a matching windowshade. Here's an easy way to give some kind of interest to a small, neglected bedroom. Buy a strongly patterned fabric. Make the spread. Laminate the shade yourself or have it done professionally.

Stenciling, a time-honored craft dating from the 18th Century, can produce exciting custom effects today. In setting at right, the unusual accordian-fold pattern of the floor, by Bishop and Lord, is restated as a border design on the window shades. In both instances, stenciling did the trick. Design was cut on stencil paper bought at art store.

"apron" that hangs below the slat. There are deep and shallow aprons; formal and provincial shapes. All aprons, however, must be edged with a trimming to hang correctly.

An extra wide hem may be cut out to form loops which support a rod that doubles as slat and shade pull. The number, size, and shape of the cut-out sections can be varied, as can the rod or pole, which can range from the ordinary wooden shade slat, painted, through cafe curtain rods, to metal, wood, or bamboo poles. The edges of these cut-outs may be left plain or trimmed with narrow braid.

DECORATIVE PULLS

Standard shade pulls are crocheted rings, silken tassels, brass rings in many styles and sizes, and, for an almost invisible contemporary look, slide-on plastic grips. Manufacturers also offer a great variety of brass, plastic and tasseled types to complement almost any period furnishings.

Custom Pulls. Furniture hardware stores offer handsome choices. Curtain rings, wood or brass, make ideal pulls—the wooden ones can be painted to match

the shade. For special effect one can use matching drawer pulls on the shades. Costume jewelry departments, accessory stores (or even toy stores!) often yield unusual and attractive items. Just be sure the chosen pull is not too heavy for the shade.

Do-it-yourself shade pulls. The yarn department offers wool in pretty colors, solid or multi-color, from which to make tassels, or little "yarn doll" pulls. Trimming, wrapped around a curtain ring, is effective, too. Many people who enjoy carving have whittled their own wood pulls. The possibilities for individual and personal effects are infinite!

SHADE CLOTH VALANCES

These are available in every standard shade cloth, and hem shape, and can be installed easily on curtain rods. They can be ordered with the shade and offer an enormous variety of mix-match combinations for valances and shades. Hems can be trimmed to match or contrast with the shade.

GENERAL HINTS

Many of the decorative effects discussed here can be duplicated at home on

plain shades. Some can be copied outright, others adapted to suit one's personal taste and specific needs.

It is possible, too, to create your own hem shape. You can order a shade with an unfinished apron below the slat, and cut it to your own pattern. The apron can be obtained in any desired length. When ordering, specify whether you want the slat hem roomside or streetside. The shade pull is attached there so, frequently, the type of pull will determine which way the hem should face.

Keep trimmings fairly near the bottom, in the area not ordinarily rolled up. Also, when you work with an apron, the unfinished edge must be trimmed.

Do not attempt to sew trimmings to a shade yourself — either by hand or machine. Shade factories and workrooms have special equipment for this purpose, which protects the shade from wrinkles. However, trimmings can be applied easily, and permanently, with an adhesive such as Bond's No. 6793. This adhesive will remain flexible when dry so that the trimmed area can be rolled up with the rest of the shade when necessary. The paste-on method is also used by many professional shade shops.

WINDOW SHADE WIZARDRY

Garden trim for garden room

Windows rephrase the pervading garden theme of handsome sitting room, designed by Reuben de Saavedra, A.I.D.

Round poles reminiscent of rattan are used as pulls and attached to the shades by looped tape, the same tape which also trims the striped shades. Shades like these are an excellent solution to a multi-windowed room.

When painted shades pull down at night they reveal same scene you'd see during day

Paint or tape your own border design

A dark shade trimmed with a contrasting design is a vigorous decorating agent in a room which uses a great deal of white. Handsome white border of blueberry shade was traced on with white oil paint.

To make the window more important, tall white shutters were used to frame it.

Floor was lacquered same blueberry color of shade.

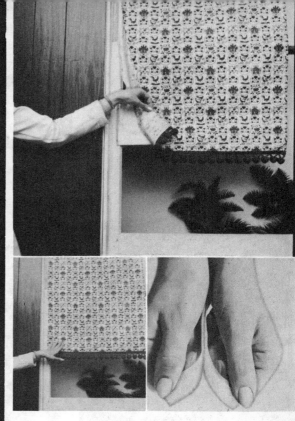

Window unit offers seating and storage

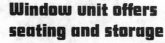

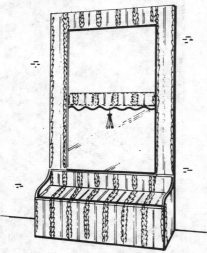

Make extra storage a part of your window design, as in sketch above.

Build a window frame and box-like window seat from plywood and scrap lumber. Cover with wallpaper or adhesive patterned paper and nail to wall.

Use plain windowshade and add a border of the patterned paper.

Nighttime view, identical to the daytime scene, is served up by window shades that are a painted mural of the surrounding landscape.

Lucille Corcas painted this scene on windowshades of glass-walled room and solved the problem of too much blackness revealed at night.

Most of the window shade ideas discussed here are from the Window Shade Manufacturer's Association.

Using tape and fabric, redo old or inexpensive shade

A new method of making decorated shades is to use Dritz Velcro, a versatile, lightweight, sure-grip nylon fastener which is composed of two narrow tapes that adhere to each other and made to be ripped apart and re-adhered countless times for laundering and other purposes.

Cut fabric one inch wider than width of shade and three inches longer. Unwind the shade on a flat surface for easy and accurate measurements.

Position the "hook" tape (Dritz Velcro has a hook and a pile tape that adhere to each other) to the top across the width of the shade, just below the roller and stitch it to the shade along both edges of the tape.

Remove the slat from the bottom of the shade, position another strip of "hook" tape just above the hem and stitch along both edges of the tape.

Now make a ¼″ hem on both long edges of fabric piece, and along top and bottom edges (previously measured to coincide with dimensions of shade), hemming this and applying the "pile" velcro so it positions exactly facing the "hook" tape.

That's all there is, and you've finished a decorative shade with fabric that you can remove for changes of season decorating and for laundering.

IDEAS FOR DOORS

Instead of a door, use strings of beads

For something different, hang strings of glass or wooden beads in doorway. Here they are a perfect foil for mod room featuring Thayer Coggin furniture, all of it sheathed in the new skin-tight anodized, silver-toned metal veneer. Sofa and loveseat rest on sheathed platforms. Rectangular box is an entertainment center containing space for tapes, records, etc., as well as bar supplies.

Tips on louver doors

Louver doors may be the answer to a surprising number of home problems.

For example: a hallway, foyer, dressing room or bath has sufficient wall space for a closet, but not enough floor clearance for a conventional closet door. Folding or sliding wood louver doors are the answer. The former, which fold back upon themselves like an accordion, need only minimal floor clearance. The latter, which slide open and closed on ceiling or floor tracks, need no clearance at all. Both styles are available in stock sizes of ponderosa pine at local lumber dealers.

Or: a decorative connecting door is needed between the kitchen and dining room; bedroom and dressing room; or dressing room and bath. Wood louver doors in folding, sliding or "cafe" styles are ideal. The unique slat design provides privacy and hides clutter, while admitting light and air. Their classic slim-like look makes louver doors appropriate for any decor—such as a streamlined kitchen on one side and an elegant dining room on the other.

Folding louver doors of ponderosa pine, hinged together in a series, make effective—and beautiful—room dividers or privacy screens. The natural richness of wood, plus the deeply-sculptured louver lines, make these dividers an elegant room accent—like fine furniture or handsome wall paneling. Unlike metal units, wood louver doors can be stained or varnished to highlight the natural grain, or painted to suit.

Use louver doors to solve space problems

Use of folding louver doors of ponderosa pine permitted installation of spacious closets in this narrow hallway. Regular closet doors would not work because they would be too large. The handsome louver design also added visual interest to the walls.

Cover one wall with panel doors to give room architectural interest

Wall-to-wall stock panel doors of ponderosa pine (matching entrance door) can be nailed to a living room wall to duplicate the richness of custom-made sculptured paneling at very little expense. If desired you can build shelves against wall, nail doors in place and have hidden storage space. One door can be cut in half to produce the decorative panel over the fireplace.

Raised panel doors, like fine furniture, are dramatic; they have dimension in depth, cast deep shadowlines that break up an otherwise flat, monotonous surface.

DOORS

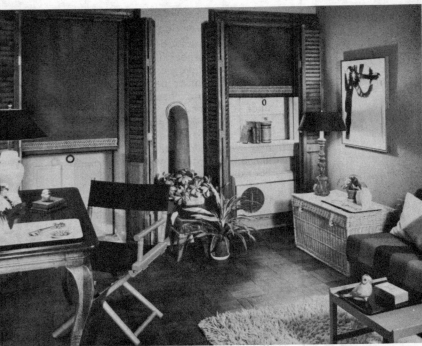

Create unity with similar treatment for window and door

When a room suffers from poor placement of windows and doors, a similar treatment of both gives a sense of unity. This inexpensive solution is easily duplicated. Shutters were attached to both, then stained walnut to match the floor and trim. "Commander" shades by Joanna were trimmed with braid and hung to equal length on window, door.

Dramatize a French door with a period shade

A French door brings inside the romantic look of the garden beyond. Instead of the traditional sheer curtains, this cozy sitting room sports a soft, swagged shade by Joanna, that is in keeping with the room's eighteenth-century quality.

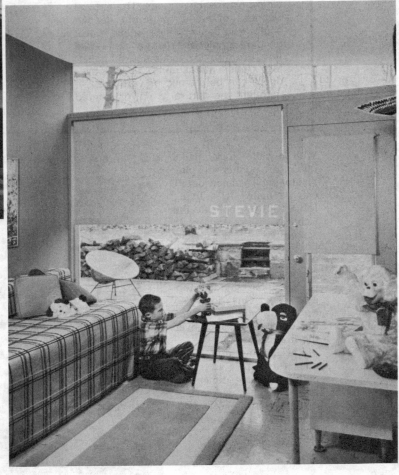

Match window shade to wall color

One of the easiest ways to create the feeling of space in a small room is to keep doors the same color as the walls. The decorator of this modern home used cocoa-colored walls and matching "Regalite" shades on both window and louvered door.

Include door as part of window wall

You can increase the height of a room by drawing the eye up with strong vertical lines. This family room uses floor-to-ceiling beams between the windows and door and on an adjoining storage wall. Vertical stripe on laminated shades accentuates the point.

Include door as part of architectural frame

An easy-to-duplicate built-in minimizes the imbalance of a wall in this teen's bedroom. The unit features a dressing table and desk, plus a window and door that are masked by laminated window shades to give privacy yet look like abstract paintings.

DOORS

Decorate refrigerator door, change kitchen decor

And why not dress up some appliance doors? This Frigidaire model can be papered to match the walls. Trim and door handles are removed; paper is kept in place when they're returned to their proper positions.

Trim cabinet doors with wood molding

Simple molding, available in building supply stores and lumber yards, can add to the decorative motif in a kitchen. These cabinets carry out the traditional look of Armstrong's Craftlon floor tiling.

Glue on grandeur with carved trims

Any house can become a palace, or at least a mansion, with new glue-on (or nail-on) decorative carvings for doors, walls or cabinets. Made of synthetics by such companies as Filon, they look like wood. Floor is Wood-Mosaic's Gothic Oak Colonial Planking.

For fun, use swinging doors

Swinging doors lead to the "soda" room in this dream playroom for children. The rough, planked look is in the furniture, soda fountain, doors, and even Armstrong's flooring features long planks of "wood."

DOORS

Frame a doorway with folding doors

Shutter doors within an archway serve as a frame when folded back against the wall. When quiet is demanded, they shut the formal living room off from the busy entryway. Furniture is from Drexel's "Et Cetera" collection.

Paint storage doors to match wall

Folding closet doors are painted to carry out the look of the planked wood wall in this sophisticated home. Adjoining wall is natural stone. Modern upholstery and carpet is Herculon, furniture is by Kroehler.

Create windows where there are none with doors

A row of shuttered doors hide an uneven wall and help to create an indoor oasis that summons up visions of gardens abloom. The Kroehler furniture, as well as the valance and draperies, are Uniroyal's maintenance-free Naugahyde. Color scheme is a cooling blue and white.

Pierced filigree panels create custom-made doors

A delicate filigree pattern available in plywood or Masonite, is mounted in panels hinged together to create a door that closes off an unattractive view and a cumbersome air conditioning and heating unit. Bookcases flank windows. Joanna room-darkening shade was used here.

Doors open up ideas for decorating

Wood doors, like fine furniture, should be chosen with judicious attention to their detail, their quality, and what they can do to enhance the whole decorating theme throughout every room. They add elegance, distinction, and can be used to carry out any architectural effect: Colonial, traditional, contemporary, ranch or Mediterranean.

The use of the right door in the right place offers great flexibility in distinctive styling for specific areas of the home. And using the same door style throughout the house creates continuity in design—from the paneled wood entry doors to room and closet doors—to match or complement your decorating scheme.

Panel doors of ponderosa pine are particularly dramatic; they have dimension in depth, casting shadowlines that break up an otherwise flat and monotonous surface and thus provide a "sculptured" look.

Space-saving doors for closets or between rooms are folding units in panel, louver or combination panel-louver styles. These take up only a minimum of floor space and permit furniture placement close to the walls. Louver doors are particularly effective for clothes closets since they permit ventilation and help protect against mildew. Where floor space for clearance to open doors to closets is a problem, panel or louver doors can be used as sliding doors to good advantage. In combinations of two or four doors, they glide smoothly past each other or can be obtained in single or double wall pocket units to recess into the wall.

Folding doors are often a decorative answer when more storage space is needed. The panel or louver variety, hung from the ceiling can be the focus of attention in a room. Behind the wall of doors, inexpensive shelving will hold all kinds of supplies.

ideas for... ceilings

Paper a ceiling, use same pattern for accents

Buy interesting floral wallpaper and matching fabric. Cover ceiling and one wall with wallpaper. Use matching fabric on bed, for cafe curtains, perhaps as table cover. Paint ceiling border white. American Furniture's youthful bedroom set has plastic tops able to stand up to the teenage set.

Match ceiling and cafe curtains

If you can't go down, go up with wallcovering, advises the Wallcovering Industry Bureau. Start wainscoting-high, continue across ceiling. Use matching fabric for curtains.

Let wallpaper run up the wall onto the ceiling

Interestingly-patterned wallpaper covering walls and ceiling, serves as charming background for deeply sculptured colonial style cabinetry by Mutschler. A come-gather-around-the-hearth look is just right for traditional homes and family living.

Create a country lodge with a bamboo print and rough-hewn beams

This fascinating room was once a square box. Now it's a rugged delight. First, the ceiling was covered with a bamboo wallcovering. Then rough-hewn ceiling beams were nailed in place, and walls were outlined with beams, as shown. Wooden floor and doors were then added. Window really isn't a window at all, but is a wallpaper mural covered with wooden slats acting as window panes. Room designed by Bloomingdale's.

ceilings

Bring architectural splendor to any room with wooden beams

Real or imitation stick-on beams bring new interest to these rooms. In 1st photo, they enhance attic ceiling and walls. In 2nd photo, they break up a dull ceiling in unusual dining room by Colby's, Northbrook, Illinois. (3) Wooden slats cover one wall and slanting ceiling of modern attic nook. Furniture by Craft Associates. (4) Narrow beams provide interest and at same time complement furniture of traditional room. Adapt some of these ideas for rooms of your own.

ceilings

Use tile squares to cover an ugly ceiling...
or to absorb noise...or both

Ceiling tiles are now commonplace. Some are stick-on, some have to be cemented in place. Some were designed to cover an ugly ceiling, some to absorb sound, some do both. Whatever you need, you'll find these ceiling tiles at local stores. They can completely alter the appearance of any room. Shown here is "Cortega" by Armstrong.

Install a suspended ceiling... and recessed lighting as well

If those kitchen, bath, or family room remodeling plans call for recessed lighting, you needn't be an electrical engineer to install the job yourself. Thanks to the new suspended ceiling products currently on the market, any homeowner can become his own lighting "expert."

Installing your own recessed lighting begins with a suspended ceiling—2' x 2' or 2' x 4' ceiling panels supported by a metal framework or "grid" hung from the existing ceiling structure or joists by wires. To install the suspended ceiling grid, you first nail the L-shaped metal molding to the walls of the room at the desired ceiling height. This provides support for the ceiling panels around the perimeter of the room. Next, attach hanger wires to the joists at four-foot intervals and fasten the suspended ceiling main runners to the hanger wires. Then, snap in the four-foot cross tees to the main runners at 2' intervals.

With the suspended ceiling grid completed, the next step is to install a fluorescent fixture directly above the area planned for recessed lighting. Since standard, strip-light fluorescent fixtures must be fastened directly to the ceiling structure above the grid, obstructions, such as low hanging pipes or heating ducts, frequently cause installation problems. For this reason, the Armstrong Cork Company recently introduced an easy-to-install fluorescent lighting unit that attaches directly to the suspended ceiling grid and is adjustable to three fixture levels—offering homeowners unlimited flexibility in planning recessed lighting areas.

Once new ceiling was installed in this basement family room, then a kitchen bar was built. It was given recessed lighting similar to that used on ceiling. Walls were painted in two-tone combination, as shown. Old furniture was given a new coat of paint and decorative trim to match colors used on walls. Floor was treated to do-it-yourself design, using Armstrong tile.

Called "Gridmate," the new unit (shown in photos above) consists of a 4′ two-lamp fixture attached to a pair of vertical brackets mounted to the grid. Two white reflectors are fastened over both sides of the fixture and combine with the V-shaped ballast cover in providing a surface so reflective that 35% more light is distributed into the room below than with a standard strip light.

Choosing the right type of fluorescent lamps for the Gridmate fixture isn't difficult if you know what to look for. There are two basic type of fluor-escent lamps on the market today: cool white and warm white. Cool white lamps produce a light similar to natural outdoor light. Warm white fluorescent lamps resemble the incandescent lighting that is found in most homes. For this reason, warm white fluorescent lamps usually are best for most residential installations.

The final step of installing recessed lighting for your remodeling project is the easiest of all. Simply insert a trans-lucent "luminous" panel into the grid directly beneath the fluorescent fixture.

There are a number of these luminous panels on the market, ranging from the louvered or "eggcrate" style to a plain white frosted panel. Since no single type of panel is superior to the others in all respects, the homeowner will want to weigh such considerations as appearance, light transmission and cost in deciding on the proper panel for his particular installation.

*   *   *

Be daring, mix several exciting patterns

Only a courageous and knowing designer would wallcover almost every surface, including the floor, in three different designs. For a Wallcovering Industry Bureau setting, James Hyde Daggett, AID, unabashedly chose an impressionistic floral background for living room walls with a contrasting Navaho design for foyer. Floor throughout is covered with a Portuguese design. Note: if floor is covered with wallcovering, it must receive at least two coats of a polyurethane varnish which will protect the handsome design and make such an unusual choice and effort well worth it.

WALLS

Be conservative, use one pattern overall

Here, one gay floral print was used to cover the walls, make bedspread, draperies, cafe curtains, and window seat covers. All woodwork was painted white, as was ceiling. Result is a charming room any young miss would feel right at home in. Designed by Celanese.

WALLS

Light up a dark wall with an artificial fireplace

Here's a simple, yet grand, way to bring life to any dark wall. Just install an artificial fireplace and let the light from the "flames" brighten the wall and the whole room. Fireplace here, along with all furniture, is by Craft Associates. Love seats are flexible polyurethane in chrome-plated framework.

For summertime living, a sea-like wallcovering turns a humdrum screened porch into a garden-like dining room

In most parts of the country a screened porch is a dandy idea . . . if you don't mind it's being out of use on rainy days. Why not capitalize on its true potential and create a garden-like dining room that has much to offer, decoratively speaking? If you add fold-out shutters, the room becomes practical no matter what the weather. Here both they and the wall have been treated to David & Dash's "Aspen" fabric of Eastman Verel, a ripply blue and green stripe that suggests both garden and sea. A large part of the room's appeal lies in the fabric-lined shutters. When open, they look like awnings, but come wind or foul weather, they fold down flat into the window frames to become part of the walls. The carpet is easy-care stuff. It is of Kodel in a garden-grass-deep shag by Trend called "Touche".

Outline a room with painted wooden strips... use them to accent the bed wall, too

Walls are just walls unless you do something to give them distinction. Here the trick involved a quick trip to the lumberyard and the paint store. Inexpensive wooden strips, first lacquered in a finish to accent the silvery glow of American of Martinsville's "Affinity" furniture, then nailed to the walls, give this contemporary bedroom its unique look. Note how the vertical lines of the panels of the headboard are repeated in the wooden strips which embellish the bed wall. As a final flourish in creative wall work, a spray of dogwood blossoms was slipped into a vase, then stapled to the wall above the dresser, so that spray stands erect.

Repeat wallcovering on cabinets or appliances

Cover walls, then glue same wallcovering to cabinet or appliance doors. Some appliances come with removable fronts which can be changed whenever you desire. Dishwasher shown here is Maytag's trim kit model, the front of which can easily be made to match wallcoverings or curtains whenever you desire. Just cover two panels of ¼-inch plywood that fit the chrome strips for this model.

WALLS

**Go nostalgic
with a patchwork print**

Make circular plaques from
wallcovering . . . cover a table, too

Non-stop fashion comes to this den via "Clan," a new pre-pasted
wallcovering design by Thibaut. The rousing plaid also covers a trio
of wall plaques and a parson's table, interesting touches in this
family room with its swing chair hung from ceiling.

Each circular plaque is cut from a 30x40-inch sheet of double
thick illustration board. To make a large circle, tie a piece of string
to a pencil. Tie other end of string to another pencil and place it in
the center of the cardboard. Make a circle, keeping the string taut
at all times. Cut out the circle with a mat knife or x-acto knife. Do
not try to cut through the cardboard on the first cut. Make three
or four gradual cuts until the circle is cut out. Cover circles with
"Clan" wallcovering which is pre-pasted and strips off easily in case
you make any mistakes.

Play up a corner with a marvelous mural

The eyes of one entering this room are drawn instantly to the twin "tapestry panels" hung gallery-style in the corner. Displayed against a neutral vinyl-covered wall and silk-screened in soft blues and greens, the mural is entitled "A Gentle Pleasure, Roaming in Indiana." A Jack Denst Design, it was inspired by a vista of sand, sky and lake.

Schumacher's "Swatches" pattern was used for wallcovering, draperies and bedspread in this pert bedroom for a young girl. Carrying out the nostalgic feeling is Early American furniture by Ethan Allen. Note that even clutter becomes attractive when placed in bookcases, vanity, etc., which neatly rounds the wall.

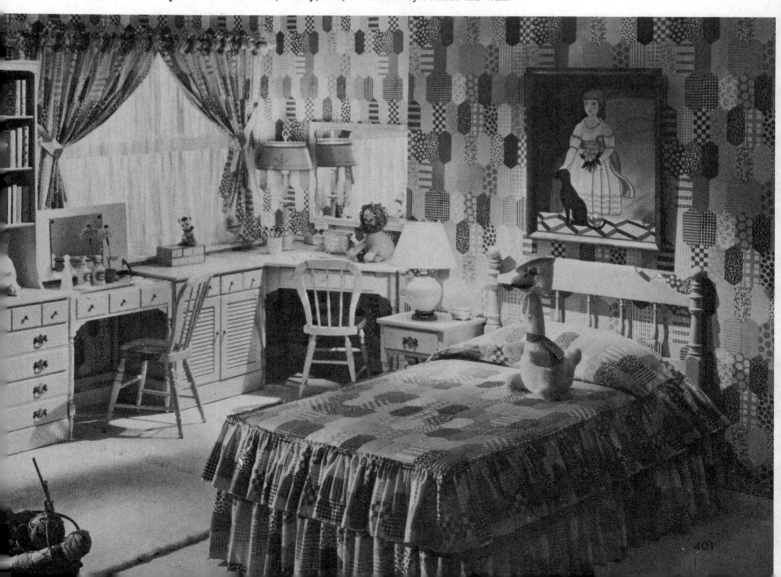

WALLS

Use your derring-do . . . paint a rainbow on your wall

Although you won't find a pot of gold at the end of this rainbow, you can be rewarded with a spectacular effect without the major investment of an expensive wallcovering. For your own personal rainbow, begin by lightly penciling the arcs on the wall. Then, get out pots of your favorite rainbow hues and fill in your outline. You might want to reflect one of the prismatic colors that Thomasville has introduced in the glossy lacquered finishes of its new "Critique" furniture collection. Styled with updated Chippendale detailing, it comes in four primary colors as well as white.

Add character with molding, interestingly arranged

A plain box-like room takes on individuality when walls are trimmed with wood molding from local lumberyard. Arrange molding in interesting panels, breaking up the space into areas. Use ornamental wooden trim over fireplace. Furniture here is from Drexel's "Marchesa" collection.

Wallcovering and flooring unite a spacious kitchen-family room

Anyone who has struggled through meal preparation in a capsule-size kitchen will appreciate the lack of clutter in this roomy kitchen-family room. Here you can make all kinds of goodies, chat with family and guests, and keep an eye on the small fry too. The counter space is more than ample, appliances up-to-date and the number of storage cabinets by Mutschler generous enough to stow away everyday cooking gear and gadgets for occasional gourmet splurges. Wallcovering in a neat stylized motif and color-flecked hard surface flooring sweep the room into a handsome entity.

Make a stunning screen by hinging together pine boards covered with wallpaper

Cut four, five or six pine boards for desired height. Cover each board with a fashionable wallpaper of some kind, cementing in place and overlapping edges neatly and carefully so they don't come undone later on. When wallpaper has dried, hinge the boards together to form screen.

Use shingles and paneling for an outdoor effect

The spirit of the rugged outdoors can be brought into a room by covering one wall with shingles and the others with pine paneling, as shown here. Combined with "Leather 'n' Brass" furniture by Kemp, the area is masculinely accented with a tiger skin rug. Simple window treatment and a few, large-scaled accessories retain the room's understated atmosphere.

Completely alter the appearance of a room with wood paneling

It's almost hard to believe both these pictures were taken of the same room. But, they were. The hefty ceiling beams take on new excitement; the niche becomes a useful closet; the arched entranceway takes on a contemporary look; the fireplace loses its mantel . . . all through the installation of U.S. Plywood Weldwood paneling. Wall-to-wall carpeting adds to the overall effect and the modern metal sculpture commands a focal point.

WALLS

White-on-white room features a do-it-yourself wall trim ...a three-dimensional collage

Designed by Colby's of Northbrook, Illinois, this bed-sitting room contains furniture in various shades of white (the white shag carpeted pouffs were once ice cream cans) and a very interesting wall decoration. To make it, paint a large sheet of plywood, masonite, hardboard, etc., silver. Then paint pieces of wood of various sizes white. Plan your design, then nail pieces to hardboard, and nail this to the wall.

Use one zingy pattern everywhere!

A good decorator trick is to pick a pattern and then use it everywhere for a socko effect. Here, pink and orange flowers on a white background cover the walls, dress the studio couch, and even are used for tie-back draperies which frame the sleeping alcove. Simple cubes, painted pink and orange, provide table-top space.

WALLS

Today's wallcoverings know no bounds ... here they're disguised as woven damask and wood moldings

This bedroom has all the elements expected in an aristocratic villa along the Mediterranean. But all are the result of All-American efficiency, and available to every man. The back-drop, for example, is not hand-woven damask accentuated by moldings. Actually its two wallcoverings by Imperial, one with a damask effect, the other cut to simulate moldings and both strip off easily when you're ready to move. So do treat yourself to this kind of Mediterranean mood.

Let this "before-and-after" serve as inspiration

Time, effort and lots of elbow grease transformed this kitchen into a perfect gem. The ugly duckling version was enough to make any homemaker hate cooking. With renovation, the free-standing stove was eliminated, and built-in range top and cooking surface were moved into an area where counter space could be added. Double ovens are built into wall cabinet. Counter island juts into kitchen. Backsplash fashioned of multi-colored ceramic tiles by American Olean.

WALLS

Add glamor and gleam with corrugated aluminum panels

Corrugated aluminum panels are used to cover the wall in a narrow foyer, giving sparkling reflections to this dining area. Mini-sized, the dining alcove wins color excitement from the bold palette of the round Egetaepper rug. Steel and glass table by Brueton and modern chairs by Stendig are in perfect scale for the area. Aluminum panels used here are from Barney-Brounum Shanker Steel Co., 24 Wyckoff Ave., Brooklyn, N. Y. They should be available locally, too.

Paint on a supergraphic

You may have trouble following the New Math, but it's really a snap to conquer the circles and rectangles of the New Geometry. Let's take a crash course under the talented direction of famed furniture designer Milo Baughman who created this "ultimate room." First, a powerful curve of white, a great sofa upholstered in textured wool and set on a rosewood plinth, captures our eye. Then, repeating its roundness, there comes a marble table on a sleek pedestal base. For his setting, the designer turned to contrasting supergraphics. In opposition to the curves of the furniture units in the foreground, the background is squared off. Slashes of orange, purple, yellow, pink and green stripe the walls. Room photographed at Colbys, Northbrook, Illinois. Furniture by Thayer Coggin.

WALLS

Establish a reflective mood with shiny silver foil wallpaper

Glittering, reflective wallcoverings are much the news these days, and here's a room that shows why. Silver foil wallpaper is a perfect setting, too, for ultra-modern furniture designed by Milo Baughman for Thayer Coggin. Upholstered pieces are foam covered in creamy fleece and can be arranged in many ways, as can the lacquered semi-circular table in the foreground.

Cover a wall with mirrors to make room twice its size

Stunning effects can be achieved when one wall of living room is covered with mirrors. Room looks bigger and is more interesting to look at. Room here also features swirling supergraphic on other walls, modern furniture by Thayer Coggin, and "Vitality" carpeting by Lees.

Contrast brick panels with floral print

Today you can buy a brick wall just by buying fake brick panels and sticking them onto the wall. Here, we've paired such a wall with an exciting floral print on another wall. Then we've introduced another pattern, the hounds-tooth carpeting on the floor. It's "Cricket" by Viking, comes in a variety of colors. As you can see, the three different patterns mix nicely and are ideal background for modern furniture used here.

Get special effects with special VINYLS

Mediterranean splendor is captured in first photo left by use of Congoleum's "Camerarillo" vinyl floorcovering, which sets the pace for the whole room. Other photo features Congoleum's "Villager" design, a handsome reproduction of a parquet floor of natural slate and wood.

Build PLATFORM, carpet it and floor in same material

Overnight guests would delight in this room, where the bed is placed atop a raised, carpeted platform, then covered with a fur throw and decorative pillows. "Seventh Heaven" carpeting by Lees flows from wall to wall, as well, giving a restful, cozy effect. Interesting placement of furnishings lets room function fully, twenty-four hours a day. The platform also works as an end table, fitted with lamp and ashtrays. Desk in corner serves as game table, too. Wall unit holds books and trophies, and acts as a focal point above the bed.

Build CONVERSATION PIT into a vacation home

Focal point of this spacious living room is the conversation pit, surrounded with multi-colored seating cushions, facing the massive black fireplace. The pure simplicity of the furnishings is underscored by the use of Murray Quarry tile flooring by American Olean.

DIVIDE a room into areas with a raised platform

Large rooms often are more successful when they are divided into areas. Here, a raised platform, with a step approach, divides a large country living room. The use of paneling along the window wall and on the base of the platform accentuates the country flavor. Interesting medley of furnishings from many periods gives room an eclectic effect. Designed by Bloomingdale's.

FLOORS

CUTOUTS Trim draperies and floor

The next time you have your sofa upholstered (or buy new slip covers), get some additional fabric. Cut out designs (flowers, here), and applique some to draperies and glue others to the floor. Shellac those on floor so they'll stand the wear and tear. Waverly's "Gaite Parisenne" fabric used here by McCanless Custom Fabrics.

Divide A ROOM with AREA RUGS

This simple trick always works. Use a large rectangular area rug to hold living room area together, and a smaller, circular area rug to underscore round dining room table, thereby creating a dining room. Both rugs here are by Egetaepper.

Instead of one large rug, use several SMALL ONES

In this era of mix and match, a series of bright rugs, such as these by Egetaepper, can add a vervy touch to a bedroom. A pair of useful etageres by Brueton on either side of the bed gleam against the deep chocolate wall. White and chocolate brown in the wood-grain bedspread and drapery design spark the contemporary atmosphere.

TILE a floor, trim shelves with same material

You don't have to be in Holland to create a Dutch mood. In this charming kitchen, Amtico's 12x12 inch "Nieu Amsterdam" vinyl tiles have been quartered and set into a sunny yellow vinyl laid in brick fashion. Contrasting orange vinyl bands extend wall to wall across the interior, helping to create the illusion of lengthy extra dimensions. The same "Nieu Amsterdam" vinyl tiles, cut in half, are used to cover the face of a beam used as a display shelf.

Make use of new UN-REAL FUR rugs

(Left) Here's a convincing double for those distinctive made--in-Greece shag textures. It's called "Flockati" and it brings real zip to this family room. Sturdy knit-backing has non-skid latex coating.

(Below) Now anybody can out-fox winter's chill with a toe-toasting chairside rug that mimics the silky texture and distinctive markings of cross fox pelts.

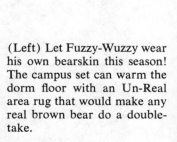

(Left) Let Fuzzy-Wuzzy wear his own bearskin this season! The campus set can warm the dorm floor with an Un-Real area rug that would make any real brown bear do a double-take.

414

All the Un-Real Fur rugs shown on these two pages were born in a test tube, not in a forest. All have an amazing likeness to the real thing. All can be washed or dry cleaned. All were knitted by Norwood Mills, Janesville, Wisc., for the Rug Corp of America, Dallas, Texas. You'll find the rugs at major department stores.

(Above) Imagine waking up on a cold morning and sinking your tootsies into the velvety warmth of sheared Canadian beaver! You can with this imitation.

(Left) When the fireside chat turns to heated debates, the question may well be: "Is it or isn't it genuine red fox fur on the floor?" So set conservationist minds at ease by revealing that the amazing likeness to fox pelts are manmade.

(Right) Why settle for a little luxury when a lot can do so much more for a modern apartment interior? A fun-fling at winter white ermine fits well within most decorating budgets.

FLOORS

Carpets and Rugs

They can do all kinds of things these days

A tailored, masculine theme is maintained by subtle Cabin Crafts area rug whose softly-etched geometric design is simply contained within a fringed border. To complete mood, add scaled wood furniture, tweed and leather upholstery.

These area rugs establish style, define conversational areas

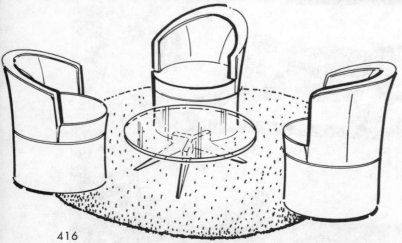

A play on shapes can bring any corner of a room to life. Everything comes across round in this snappy vignette which places three barrel-like leather chairs on a rug circle, around a round glass-topped coffee table. Same thing can be done with all rectangular furnishings.

Start with a dramatic area rug, then add a sleep sofa, a fireside bench, a polished hexagon coffee table, a handmade leather chair from Mexico. The finished look, which is exciting and personal, is the popular eclectic style with a strong Spanish flavor.

Spanish accent is underscored by the choice of "Oporto" area rug by Cabin Crafts, a loop pile texture featuring a raised border, and delineated in a combination of three colors.

Psychedelic colors are worked out in a simple weave stitch in an over-and-under interlacing for striking area rug (left) designed by Nell Znamierowski for Regal Rugs, Inc. "Plain Weave" pattern will add a "now-pow" look to any contemporary room setting. Here it enlivens an interior furnished with streamlined, upholstered and wood furniture.

Area rug is tufted in all Caprolan nylon and comes in such exuberant color combinations as vivid blue and green on red.

Carpets and Rugs

Carpet pillows
for down-to-earth seating

Instant down-to-earth seating is provided by carpet-covered floor pillow, an idea borrowed from the Persian Pashas by Regal Rugs, Inc. The white pillow gets a bold pattern of black and brown geometric symbols and the added touch of four fluffy black tassels. Black vinyl covers the underside of the cushion which is also available in other patterns and colorations.

For L-shaped room and staircase,
cut rug to fit, then fringe

The clever use of carpeting can go a long way toward underscoring the salient architectural features of an interior. Here it has been used to frame and ornament the charming staircase of a room designed by Abraham & Straus. L-shaped carpet and stair runner have been treated to a trim of fringe which home owner sewed on himself. Staircase is ornamented by gay floral wallpaper which dances upstairs.

Use a bold accent rug as a modern painting

Why not use a spectacular modern accent rug as you would use a painting? It's a marvelous idea, especially for small-apartment dwellers who find that their dining arrangement must be placed against a windowless wall. The brilliant exclamation of the vivid accent rug brings the area to life and provides an interesting focal point.

Carpets and Rugs

Carpeting covers the floor...and then some

Colorful, printed carpet runs over the floor and up the wall of delightful music-sitting room (above). Designed by Paul Krauss, A.I.D., for Barwick Mills, setting mixes an assortment of lighthearted, spray-painted wicker furniture with metal and fabric covered tables. Built-in wall unit houses speakers and supports shelf containing high-fidelity equipment, records. Carpet backdrop is simply glued or nailed to wall.

Carpet-covered ottomans (left) is an amusing do-it-yourself idea. Make cube by building plywood box with 2x4 framing inside for strength. Glue pieces of foam rubber to top for cushioning. Cover box in several ways: (1) Cut "red cross" from rug remnant, lay on top of box and nail and glue in place. This method obviates seams at the top where most wear will occur; (2) Cover top with one piece of carpeting, then wrap long piece of rug around sides; (3) Cover each side individually with rug remnants, matching pieces as closely as possible.

A single bed set on a carpeted platform and ensconced in a strikingly colorful plaided corner, is the focal point of handsome teenager's bedroom (above). Wallpaper-covered plywood panels frame the window thus providing pattern continuity. White walls, white metal and plastic furniture counterpoint the bold colors of the plaid and the vivid tone of the heavily-textured shag carpeting by Barwick Mills. A scrap of the same shag is used to cover the side of wooden frame supporting foam rubber mattress, effecting a continuous flow. Room designed by Paul Krauss, A.I.D.

Another do-it-yourself idea, which is actually a variation on the teenaged sleeping platform, is carpeted bunk-bed for a ski lodge (right). Base of bunk is built of plywood, then cushioned with foam rubber, then covered with a large piece of carpeting. A separate remnant finishes the exposed end.

Carpets and Rugs

Use carpeting for bath, laundry room, and pool

The obvious advantages of wall-to-wall carpeting are probably most fully enjoyed in the bathroom. Carpet of all Herculon olefin fiber flatters a room fitted with stainless steel tile, modern plumbing and lighting fixtures.

Leisure living in the laundry room becomes a practical idea with colorful tweed carpeting, also made from Herculon fiber. Rug is moisture-resistant, has rubber backing to make hours at ironing board easy on feet, muffles sounds of appliances.

Luxury and unique practicality merge in densely-looped indoor-outdoor carpeting of Monsanto's acrilan, a good poolside idea.

Give your bed a carpeted platform and backdrop

An impressive bedwall offers an alternative to the canopy bed as an effective way of dramatizing your bedroom.

Sketch seen here was suggested by a room designed by Edmund Motyka A.I.D. for Herculon.

Bed is set up on raised wooden platform covered by rug in contrasting color to rug used on floor. Backdrop is large sheet of plywood or Masonite covered with same carpet used for platform. Architectural unit frames panel and windows.

Carpets and Rugs

Current kitchen look: patterned carpets

The charm of delph tile and the comfort of carpeting merge in handsome printed floor covering directly above, designed, engineered and colored especially for all-purpose use by Barwick Mills. All nylon carpeting, which is available in an assortment of colorations, requires no more than vacuuming for day-to-day maintenance. If stains do occur, they can be taken out with an application of soap and water. Vinyl-coated grasscloth paper and bold floral Roman shade combine with patterned floor to create a rich, warm look.

A carpet cut-out can give your kitchen a personal signature. The floral motif of carpeted kitchen floor (top left) blooms on a field of sky blue Hearthstone carpeting by Viking, whose unique woven construction makes this kind of inset possible. A design this size should be cut by the mechanic who installs the carpet, but smaller simpler patterns can be done by the average handyman. Pattern used here restates the floral watercolor. Why not repeat the motif in your window curtains or invent something striking, even way out?

Bold pattern gives this streamlined, highly-efficient looking kitchen (left) its measures of warmth and excitement. Printed, loop pile, all-purpose nylon carpeting by Monarch, is installed wall-to-wall for easy maintenance, rugged wear and a comfortable base for stand-up kitchen work. Pattern emulates the look of ceramic tile, comes in an assortment of lively, brilliant color ways.

breakfast bar, carpet the base and the floor

Easy on the eyes, and on the feet is captivating "mini" kitchen (right) that counterpoints sleek walnut cabinetry and white Formica counter tops with richly colored tweed carpeting by Beattie Mfg. Co.

Central to the setting is ingenious breakfast bar with carpeted base, a great do-it-yourself idea (instruction and diagram given below). Oversized lighting fixture, and metal stools complete the arrangement.

To make breakfast bar: Make a simple, open-bottomed box from plywood or scrap lumber for base unit. Make it whatever size you wish.

Cover sides of box with carpet material used on floor. Use glue and nails. Position carpet on box so that ends of carpet meet at center of box on side facing nearest wall; this way the joint will be the least noticeable.

Then make table top section, which is merely a very narrow box with a top piece and a bottom piece screwed and glued together with narrow pieces, to form shelves. See diagram.

Screw and glue entire top section to carpeted base piece.

Weight of table will keep it in place, but for built-in rigidity, nail a length of 2x4 (same size as interior of box) to the floor with a few finishing nails. Set the table down over the 2x4 and drive a few nails into it through the bottom sides of the box to hold table in place. Nail set will hide nail heads.

Carpets and Rugs

Set the stage for terrace design with a patterned outdoor carpet, as shown (right). Carpeting, which is part of a new group by the Ozite Corp., is quite easily self-installed, as photograph illustrates.

Note that identical carpeting has also been used in adjacent living room.

The current generation of weatherproof carpets can go anywhere—inside the home or for outdoor living. Flame red Topside outdoor carpeting (below) by Lees makes a handsome base for redwood deck designed by Abby Chapple, N.S.I.D. Carpet's tufted, tip-sheared texture looks elegant enough to be used in the living room, comes in vivid colors.

Relate indoor
and outdoor
with
indoor-outdoor
carpeting

A stretch of carpeting that goes beyond the interior confines of a home really seems to make the outdoors a part of the total scene. It's a particularly effective technique when both areas are done in a similar style, such as the Spanish theme used here.

You can make the lattice window trim shown here by nailing strips of wood across each other and forming a panel which slips into window area. This can be removed whenever desired.

Fashion a family room with wooden beams

Wood paneled walls and wooden beams set the pace for this charming playroom. The floor has been made new with Amtico's "Beacon Hill" brick tiles. Tufted hanging sofas of Naugahyde vinyl from Uniroyal are aided by decorative chains. Swivel-y chairs are also covered in Naugahyde. A hanging-chain lamp above one sofa provides light for chess game or mystery book. A series of globular lamps bubble above the ping-pong table.

Add that much-needed extra bedroom

Here, walls were covered with treillage-patterned vinyl wallcovering, while matching bedspreads, draperies, table topper and pillows were made of wash-and-wear Kodel polyester and cotton fabric. Carpeting is also easy-care Kodel polyester, styled by Wunda Weve.

Letter a snazzy supergraphic on one wall

Letters were cut from plywood, painted strong colors, nailed to white wall. Area around letters was masked off with tape and wall was painted, as shown. Under supergraphic is "The Swinger," something new from Kroehler for Debut '72. Available as a single chair, loveseat or three-section sofa, "The Swinger" becomes a sleeper without any mechanism. The back and seat cushions, which are connected, pull forward and stretch out on the floor to form a sleeping pad over 6' in length, more than 8" in thickness, Upholstered in teddy bear pile, "The Swinger" is as good to touch as it is to sleep on.

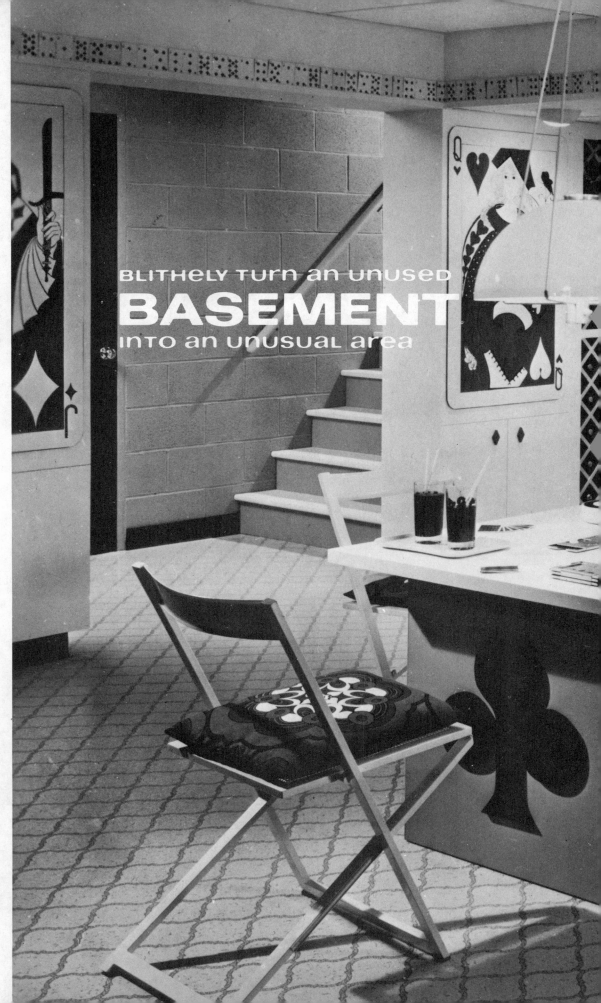

Bid for attention with an exciting game room

Here's how to create this stunning game room. Cover walls with white paneling. Install hanging ceiling of acoustical tile by Armstrong. Cover floor with Armstrong's new "Place 'n Press" excelon tile with adhesive backs (just set tile in place and press). Note how design "flows" from one tile to the next, creating seamless look.

Build kitchen-bar unit, paint same color as walls. Decorate it and ceiling border with row of playing cards, glued in place.

Cut card motifs from felt or colored cardboard, glue on kitchen-bar and on sides of table made by nailing five pieces of plywood together.

Decorate wall in sitting area with mod wallpaper murals. Add mod furniture, and you're all set for the card players to descend.

BLITHELY TURN AN UNUSED **BASEMENT** INTO AN UNUSUAL AREA

BASEMENTS

Plan family room that doubles as utility room

Family room shown below doubles in brass, as photos indicate. Serving counter hides clothes presser on rolling table, which wheels out from under, while counter against wall has folding doors which open up to reveal clothes hamper, drier and washer. When utilities are not in use, room is in perfect shape for parties of all kinds. Walls of room were paneled in pine, floor was covered with Armstrong tile.

Hit a new high with a ski lodge built down under

You can't say this isn't different! Here, walls of basement were covered with light pine wood paneling, while ceiling was painted white. One wall was covered with a giant photostat to give illusion of view seen from wide picture window atop mountain. Another wall takes a modern storage unit, while rest of room is outfitted with exciting plastic furniture, the seats being hung from beams in the ceiling. All furniture here is from Hudson's, Detroit, Michigan.

Make it your TV room

Ceiling of this TV room was covered with acoustical tile (Armstrong) and wooden beams, as shown. Storage unit to hold TV, books, record player, etc., was built to cover one wall. Area looking out into patio was bricked in, as shown, with windows looking out and allowing a little sunshine to come in. Floor was covered with stick-on vinyl floor tiles (Armstrong). Main piece of furniture in room is great big coffee table, built by the man of the house ... which could be built by anyone with a little handyman aptitude. The top is two big sheets of plywood nailed and glued together. Edges were trimmed on an angle with power saw. Legs are store-bought, merely screwed in place.

433

Make it a summer living room . . . for year 'round use

This porch was enclosed with small-paned windows, then treillage panels were nailed inside around tops of windows to form frames for Roman shades. Floors were carpeted with a thick shag rug ("Fat 'n' Sassy," one of carpets selected by Lees for Debut '72). Then room was furnished simply, mainly with wicker furniture. That's a faence stove in the corner of the porch, at rear . . . a keepsake of France. Accent rug is "The Hot Tin Zinnia" by Lees.

Make it a sitting room for one . . . maybe two

Create a special place for yourself . . . somewhere you can retreat to and re-group the forces. Here, a porch was enclosed with small-paned windows, then floor was covered with charming vinyl pattern ("Martinque" by Congoleum), and plants were placed here and there. With all this as a soothing background, a basket-like swing was hung from the rafters, and a little table, just big enough to hold coffee for one or two, was added.

Transform a PORCH
into an
extra room

Divide areas: Large porches have plenty of room for everyone when designated into areas. Two rugs divide this one into an entertainment section and a game area, with movable serving cart to keep all the family happy! Game table is a pleasant place for Sunday evening meals, Saturday football lunch. Room-darkening shades and draperies aid TV watching.

Make it a family room for one and all

Panel porch: If you're tired of rattan or wicker, and don't fancy a porch that resembles a playroom, why not the sleek built-in look? This do-it-yourself Weldwood oak paneling has been used for walls, planters and built-in seating. Underneath the cushions there is plenty of room for storage of games, dining accessories and records.

Preserve view: Large panels of insulating glass replace the many-paned windows of this porch, making it a comfortable place for the family to gather all the year round. Simple cafe curtains were chosen as an accompaniment for the Early American furnishings, and the even earlier American mountain in the world beyond.

decoratinc ideas for Patios and Pools

Build an elevated sun deck for outdoor living

Although most people think of a deck patio as being suited to a hillside, this photo shows that it also gives character and depth to a flat-land yard. Elevated one foot above grade, the deck allows cooling air to circulate underneath and between the boards. Weathered Douglas fir 2x4s on edge do not retain heat or cause sun glare. The framing should be pressure treated, and the deck board should have a liberal application of clear water repellent-preservative. Built by Western Wood Products Association.

Create a patio out of cement blocks set in your lawn

Here is the very simplest kind of patio you can build, yet see what a terrific effect it provides. It's made just by putting oblong cement blocks into the ground and bordering them with grass for added beauty. This kind of installation has the added advantage of simple expansion—just add a few more blocks as you see the need. Furniture can be as simple or as elaborate as you wish.

Build your patio around a beautiful swimming pool

This elegant patio features a pool. Area round pool was filled with sand, then cast cement patio blocks were laid in place with the brushed sand filling in the cracks. These blocks come in several colors. Fence around pool is made from ornamental cement blocks. Non-folding patio furniture is by Telescope Folding Furniture Co, Granville, N.Y.

Patios and Pools

Create outdoor living rooms with exciting, functional patio furniture

Transform your patio into a decorative asset with handsome and durable furniture. The attractive strap pieces can be combined with your own choice of accent tables. All glass tops are tempered, therefore unbreakable. Straps and frames come in a choice of colors. By Salterini Co., 305, E. 63rd St., N.Y.C.

Crisp contemporary outdoor furniture is executed in aluminum and vinyl. The round dining table has a rigidized aluminum top; comfortable chairs have two-tone vinyl strapping. Group is available in eight weather-wise colors. Meadowcraft, P.O. #1911, Birmingham., Ala.

Variety, comfort and tailored good looks are offered in versatile redwood furniture. Seating group is shown in foreground while dining furniture is seen beyond it. John Hancock Furniture.

Delicate looking tracery furniture is also sturdy and durable.—built for years of low-maintenance service and beauty. The 48-inch round dining table has a sparkling top of translucent tempered safety glass. Seat cushion covers are zippered across their full width to facilitate easy removal. By Meadowcraft.

Juggling paper plates on your lap is now a thing of the past. New outdoor Snak-Rak is a marvelous boon to outdoor entertaining. This unique, sturdy, stick-in-the-ground product holds a plate and a glass (or bottle) firmly anywhere you put it. Colorful plastic tray anchors to the ground on metal stem. By The Marketplace, Box 8627, St. Paul, Minn.

Elegant but practical four-shelf etagere is ideal for both outdoor and indoor use. Beautiful vine-like textured metal forms the supporting frame, while the shelves are made of expanded metal mesh. Shelves can be used to display accessories or to assist in serving. By Meadowcraft.

Handsome, contemporary outdoor furniture features a unique blending of the A-form and sleigh-runner legs. Frames are made of ⅞-inch round and oval tubular aluminum, ruggedly welded. Seating is provided by 2-inch-wide vinyl straps, individually attached for easy "at home" changes. Brown-Jordan, Box 1269, El Monte, Cal.

Styled for all seasons is sculptured metal framed furniture covered with unique fluidized "leisure-cote," making it impervious to the elements. Frames come in white only, while cushions are offered in a choice of patterns. By The Bunting Co., 18th and Allegheny Ave., Phila., Pa.

New trends in the development of outdoor wrought iron furniture is seen in these designs distinguised by gracefully sculptured frames with vinyl straps. Weather resistant vinyl straps come in a choice of high fashion colors. Metal finishes are guaranteed against rust for ten years. Lee L. Woodard Sons, Inc. Owosso, Mich.

Patios and Pools

Build an easily-constructed gardener's workshop

Fencing does double duty when combined with gardener's workshop. Protected potting bench has space under slat roof for shade-loving blooms. Upper front panels go up or down to control light inside or display plants. Behind are storage fence and mulch bins. Douglas fir used.

Erect high walls for outdoor sitting room

High walls create a roofless sitting room, delightfully open to sun and sky. The walls are western red cedar siding panels applied horizontally to match the style of the house siding. Resawn cedar has weathered to a lovely silvery grey. Simple patio furniture outfits the room.

Build a storage shed for patio-garden tools

This shed was built from rough-sawn, silvered western red cedar, framed with Douglas fir 2x4s. Doors swing open to allow easy passage of lawn mower, wheelbarrow, other garden tools. For northern climates, line interior with building paper to keep the frost out.

Include a fireplace as part of your fence

Interesting idea: build a fireplace as part of your outdoor fence. Secret of this corner fireplace is the raised circular hearth, made by an inverse pyramiding of poured concrete circles. Square and tapered cement patio blocks are used for all facings.

Add a fountain

Outdoor fountains continue in favor, and much of this favor is due to the creation of fountains that form water into sculptured shapes. Fountain shown here, for example, is "Shower of Diamonds" by Rain Jet Corp., 301 S. Flower St., Burbank, Calif. Rotating nozzles break the water stream into individual droplets, each droplet acts like a prism of light.

Add a partition

Direct vision the way you want with a partition. This handsome vertical louvel screen, only five feet long, gives a feeling of privacy and enclosure to the patio, and with planting beds on both sides joins the patio gracefully to the lawn beyond. Louvers are western red cedar 1x6s set at a 45 degree angle in a frame of 2x4s, with 4x4s as posts.

Photos courtesy Western Woods Products Association

Patios and Pools

Build fences or screens for privacy

Seven-foot split cedar fencing brings privacy to this Japanese-American garden. Tea House enclosure was built from cedar posts, bamboo panels and slats for roof. Pea-sized pebbles are ground cover with larger, flat-sized rocks serving as pathways. Rattan-woven furniture with aluminum frames is by Telescope Folding Furniture Co., Granville, N.Y.

Concrete blocks piled atop each other and then painted white create a fence for this terrace-patio in mid-town Manhattan. Bricks form the flooring. Wrought-iron furniture by Bunting is available in white or antique green finish with upholstered cushions in co-ordinating floral prints. Add plants, grow vines on wall.

Sculptured decorative panels from local lumberyard or hardware store can also be fashioned into fences and screens for your patio. Just build a simple wood frame and fit panels into the frame, as shown here.

Taking advantage of a slight slope in the lawn, this concrete deck affords fun for both family and guests. The garden house, an integral part of the plan, provides for both garden and patio materials storage. Note fence made of concrete blocks.

Elegant looking, but actually simple, this curved screen of ready-made concrete forms gives both privacy and good ventilation. If you have artistic tendencies or just want to have fun, try your hand at a piece of concrete sculpture, too, such as the turtle in the foreground.

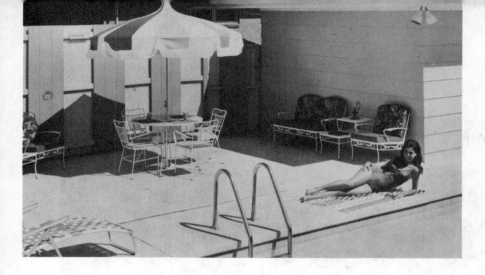

An attractive fence around the home swimming pool keeps out intruders and maintains privacy. This one, built in two weekends by the home owner and a friend, was made by alternating panels of sturdy, moisture-resistant Masonite Ruf-X-90 Grooved Siding on two sides of the framework. The textured surfaces, facing the poolside, were painted alternately bittersweet orange and off-white. Sides of paneling facing the yard were finished in bittersweet. A feature is the three-inch overlap which permits circulation of air. One of the 2x7-foot panels is hinged to serve as a door.

Even if your lot is so small that the patio has to be in the front yard, you can still find privacy. Here, a secluded nook was created in front yard by the addition of a delightfully designed screen. It gives privacy to first floor windows, but permits unrestricted view out. Built of Douglas fir lumber, it is painted black as an accent to the design of the house.

A screening wall can add interest and variety to your patio, protect it from visual intrusion to that too-close' house next door. Here a series of concrete forms gives a curving look, plantings add grace and color. Study the fences and walls shown on these pages and adapt the ideas to fit your patio, pool, or porch. A great deal of improvisation is possible.

A circular wall defines this patio, built wide enough for extra seating for bigger parties. Just add cushions for comfort, and you are in business. Center of interest is the handsome tree, set into its own well of dirt. Neat, nice, and very effective.

Here is another way to achieve a dramatic effect using simple, easily available materials. This screen wall was fashioned from a variety of colorful brick in a pattern whose beauty expresses varying moods in changing light and shadow, provides welcome ventilation, too.

Patios and Pools

Give your pool an interesting shape

Fan-shaped pool, two views of which are seen right and below, has three 3-tread ladders, ultra-modern diving standard. This 20x40-foot pool was built by Starlite Pools, Southfield, Michigan.

Spring-fed lake pool, shown above and at left is enhanced by magnificent gardens, charming brick wall and pool house. The 20x40-foot design was installed by Midwest Pool & Court Co., St. Louis, Mo.

Patios and Pools

Style pool to suit land and house

Turn your outdoor swimming pool into a year-round family fun center with an Aquadome cover, made of clear, sun-proof, non-cracking vinyl, that can fold back, accordion-style, to permit full exposure in warm weather. By Cascade Industries, Edison, New Jersey.

Shape of pool, above left, matches the overhang of ranch house roof. Angular, oblong, pneumatically-applied concrete pool is 22x45 feet. Paddock Pool Co., Phoenix, Ariz.

The mountain-lake-shaped beauty of pool directly above is enhanced by the landscaping that surrounds it. Pool has a surface area of 700 square feet. Viking-Aquatech, King of Prussia, Pa.

Modified kidney-shaped pool, 16x32-feet, has large built-in steps. Pool was built directly off the back of the house. By Starlite Pools, Inc., Southfield, Michigan.

Perched high on a Brooklyn apartment house, commanding a spectacular view of New York harbor, this extraordinarily-shaped penthouse was designed to provide a family of four with a totally new and modern environment. That this feat was accomplished with almost no structural alterations (even the old-fashioned moldings were left intact) is almost entirely due to the success of a beautifully cohesive, subtle but strong, decorating plan.

The project was a collaborative venture between the architectural firm of Savoia and Bararo, A.I.D., and interior designer Eve Frankl, A.I.D. It involved two major architectural changes: a new kitchen and the addition of a dressing room to the master bedroom.

The serene, light-hearted modern style of this rambling 8-room apartment derives almost completely from purely decorative elements — the skillful and often inventive use of color, furniture and home furnishings that are purely modern in shape and pattern, and a purposefully spare choice of window decoration in deference to the view. Also effective throughout the home is the strategic use of built-in cabinetry to store, conceal and display.

Walls were painted soft white as a counterpoint for colorful woven wall hangings, bold colors of interior cabinetry, primary tones of rugs and upholstery fabrics. Other brilliant color accents include the red and orange checkerboard tile floor in the kitchen, the vibrant blue ceiling of the tower room, the enchanting top level room, windowed on all four sides.

In addition to the pointed use of exuberant colors, oversized furniture was chosen to complement the generously proportioned, high-ceilinged rooms. Teak is the favored wood both for furni-

ture and specially designed cabinetry, while fabrics are understated and informal — linen, Mexicotton, monochromatic textures and leather.

Cabinetry was designed to conceal old fashioned radiators and to provide built-in storage facilities for various rooms, while a ceiling-high entertainment cabinet housing high-fidelity equipment, record storage and bar provisions, was fitted into an existing niche in the dining room.

The fresh, contemporary environment achieved by Mrs. Frankl contrasts rather strikingly in look and approach with the popular collected style in which the interior is deliberately made to appear as if it were put together in a random, amusingly haphazard kind of way. The strong, disciplined personality of Mrs. Frankl's interiors emerges from a precise floor plan, a careful selection of elements skillfully related to one another.

contemporary living in an old penthouse

THIS MODERN EIGHT-ROOM APARTMENT SITS ATOP A FORTY-YEAR-OLD BUILDING IN BROOKLYN

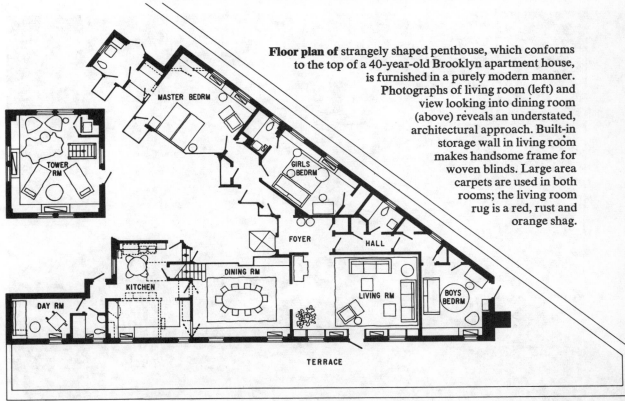

Floor plan of strangely shaped penthouse, which conforms to the top of a 40-year-old Brooklyn apartment house, is furnished in a purely modern manner. Photographs of living room (left) and view looking into dining room (above) reveals an understated, architectural approach. Built-in storage wall in living room makes handsome frame for woven blinds. Large area carpets are used in both rooms; the living room rug is a red, rust and orange shag.

TOWER RM

MASTER BEDRM

GIRLS BEDRM

FOYER

HALL

KITCHEN

DAY RM

DINING RM

LIVING RM

BOYS BEDRM

TERRACE

449

penthouse

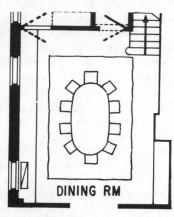

DINING RM

Photos below show two views of dining room, each from different end of room. Photo at right shows built-in entertainment cabinet, opened. Cabinet provides space for glasses, liquor storage, trays, high fidelity equipment and records.

To enclose the old-fashioned radiators and offer ample storage and serving facilities, a long, teak cabinet with serviceable black slate top was placed beneath the windows. Oval dining table and chairs are also teak.

Inside of the entertainment cabinet is vivid red-orange lacquer—a bold accent for the teakwood tones.

View of dining room (left) shows stairway leading up to the tower room above it. While original moldings were left intact, dining room (and all other areas) was furnished with understated, beautifully designed modern pieces which rely for their decorative appeal upon the honest and inventive use of materials.

Tower room, a marvelous place to meditate, is on a level of its own. Windows open on all four sides to the magnificent view. Black and white furnishings are defined by a brilliant blue ceiling, floor cushions in green, lime and aqua.

Two walls of the room are fittted with shelving units that offer the necessary storage space for games, books, and for charming planted areas.

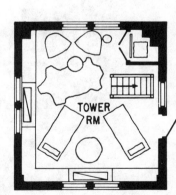

TOWER RM

451

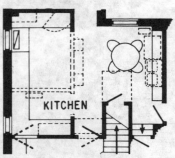

KITCHEN

U-shaped kitchen, one view of which is shown above, has rich, deep-walnut stained cabinet, backsplash and work surface of white thermoset plastic.

Dinette adjoining kitchen (below) is enlivened by bold red-striped Mexicotton fabric of seat covers and shade. Floor throughout is red and orange vinyl tile.

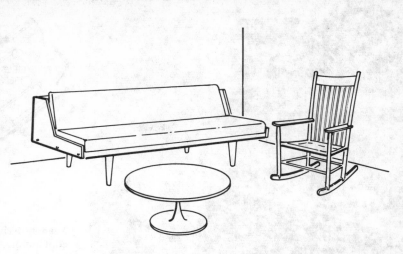

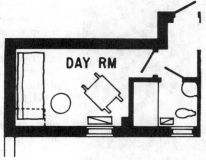

DAY RM

Furnishings for day room, sketched here, were kept to a minimum. Room is used as a retreat, study area or guest room. It is located at the far end of the penthouse, beyond the kitchen.

For foyer (above) a pristine, modern environment is achieved against a backdrop of wall moldings by pedestal stools, black and white floor, tapestry. From foyer one sees master bedroom at far end.

Master bedroom (above) was planned in a serene scheme of oatmeal, olive and mustard gold.

Plain linen used for window wall and window shade matches the background of linen bedspread print.

Closet was removed (see plan) to permit the installation of wall-length walnut cabinets.

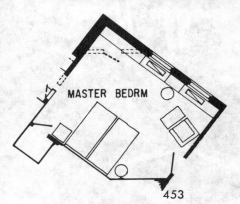

MASTER BEDRM

453

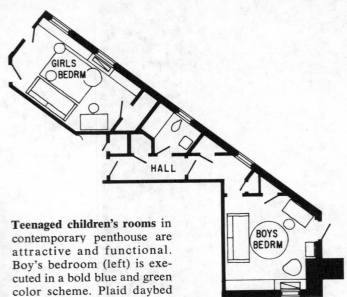

Teenaged children's rooms in contemporary penthouse are attractive and functional. Boy's bedroom (left) is executed in a bold blue and green color scheme. Plaid daybed cover is wool, chair is covered in royal blue Naugahýde. Walnut commodes have white plastic tops.

Girl's room (below) features, as a bedspread, a Spanish rug similar to the one used on the floor.

Dark cork wall displays this teenager's artwork. Room is Delft blue and white.

penthouse

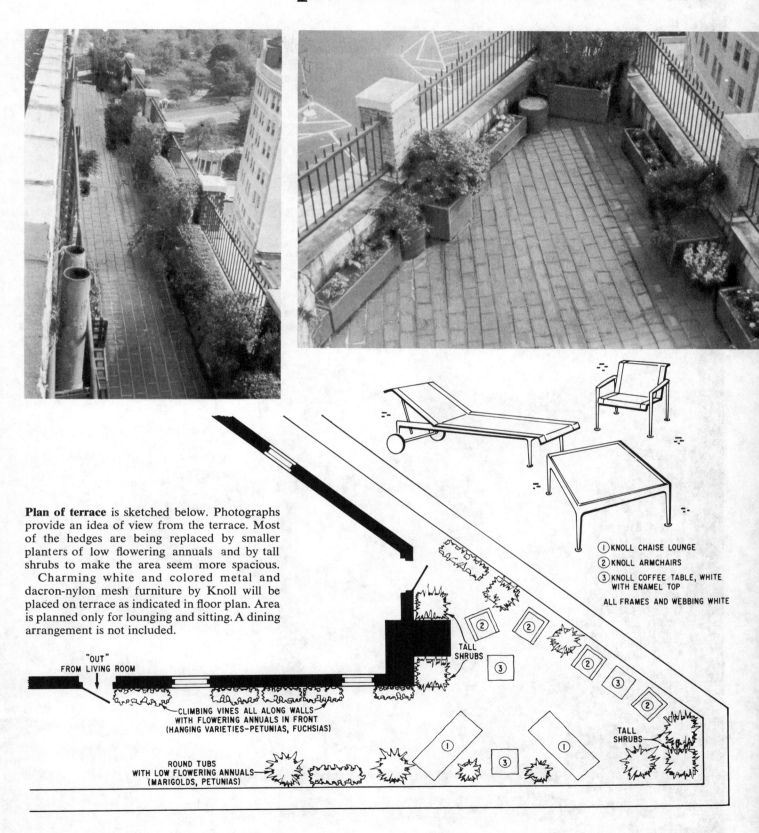

Plan of terrace is sketched below. Photographs provide an idea of view from the terrace. Most of the hedges are being replaced by smaller planters of low flowering annuals and by tall shrubs to make the area seem more spacious.

Charming white and colored metal and dacron-nylon mesh furniture by Knoll will be placed on terrace as indicated in floor plan. Area is planned only for lounging and sitting. A dining arrangement is not included.

① KNOLL CHAISE LOUNGE
② KNOLL ARMCHAIRS
③ KNOLL COFFEE TABLE, WHITE WITH ENAMEL TOP

ALL FRAMES AND WEBBING WHITE

"OUT" FROM LIVING ROOM

CLIMBING VINES ALL ALONG WALLS WITH FLOWERING ANNUALS IN FRONT (HANGING VARIETIES—PETUNIAS, FUCHSIAS)

ROUND TUBS WITH LOW FLOWERING ANNUALS (MARIGOLDS, PETUNIAS)

TALL SHRUBS

TALL SHRUBS

DESIGNERS' TRICKS FOR ROOM TREATS

Cover a wooden pedestal with wallcovering

Make something to match the exciting wallcovering you've used on the walls . . . a pedestal, for example. It'll give the room a custom look. Directions for making a pedestal are on opposite page. Wallcovering used here is "Aquarius" from Thibaut's new "Beautiful" collection, which is pre-pasted, strippable and completely washable.

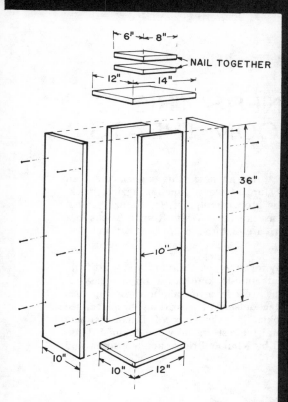

How to make pedestal: The measurements given in the diagram are for a unit 38½ inches in height. If you wish to make a taller or wider unit, adjust the measurements. The unit can be built to any size and still retain its basic design.

Materials: Two pieces of 1x10x6-feet pine wood; two pieces of 1x8x6-inches; one piece of 1x12x14-inches; one piece of 1x10x12-inches; 1½-inch finishing nails; hammer; sandpaper; wood saw; pencil; ruler; nail set; wood filler; self adhesive plastic or wallcovering and glue.

Directions: Cut the two pieces of 1x10x6-foot wood in half. This will make four pieces 36-inches long. Assemble as shown in diagram and nail together at sides.

To make top, nail together two pieces of 1x8x6 wood. Sandpaper edges smooth and paint desired color. Let dry, sandpaper again and paint once more. Repeat sanding and painting steps for 1x12x14-inch piece of wood.

When dry, nail all pieces together. Then nail in position to top of platform. Use nail set and tap nails slightly below surface of wood. Fill holes with wood filler and sandpaper smooth. Touch up sanded areas with paint. Nail piece to bottom.

Cover unit with same wallcovering used on wall—in this case, "Aquarius" by Thibaut. It's pre-pasted so can be positioned easily.

Cubes are really "in" . . . here's how to make some of your own

From sheet of ¾-inch plywood, smooth on one side, cut two pieces 18x 18-inches for sides of cube. Cut two pieces 18x19½-inches for top and bottom. Sandpaper edges. Assemble the four pieces, as in diagram shown below. Before nailing pieces, place white glue between joints. Nail together, using 2-inch finishing nails. Cut two pieces 19½x19½-inches each. Sandpaper, glue and nail to front and back of cube. When all sides are attached, fill in holes with wood filler, sandpaper smooth. Cover cube with plastic adhesive. If desired make a table top by placing a 24x24-inch piece of plywood on top of cube, nailing it in place.

CUBE

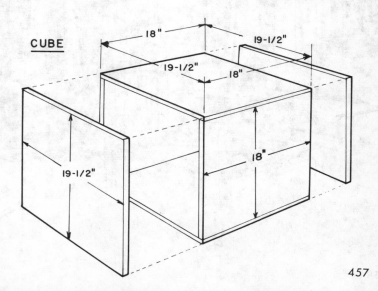

DESIGNERS' TRICKS FOR ROOM TREATS

An interplay of textures keynotes this sophisticated entrance hall. The texture of wood paneling against brick. Of brick against the bronze sculpture. Of bronze against glass. Of glass against greenery. White Roman Bricks in a "stack bond" pattern are pictured in this application.

Although it's strictly for show, who's to know that artificial bricks make an authentic-looking cover on the easy-to-build alcove of this walk-in artificial, non-working fireplace. (To cover the outside of a working fireplace, see the instrucion booklet in every box of Dacor Miracle Bricks.) The textural interest on the wood-beamed flanking walls is created by Klinker Bricks, applied hither and yon.

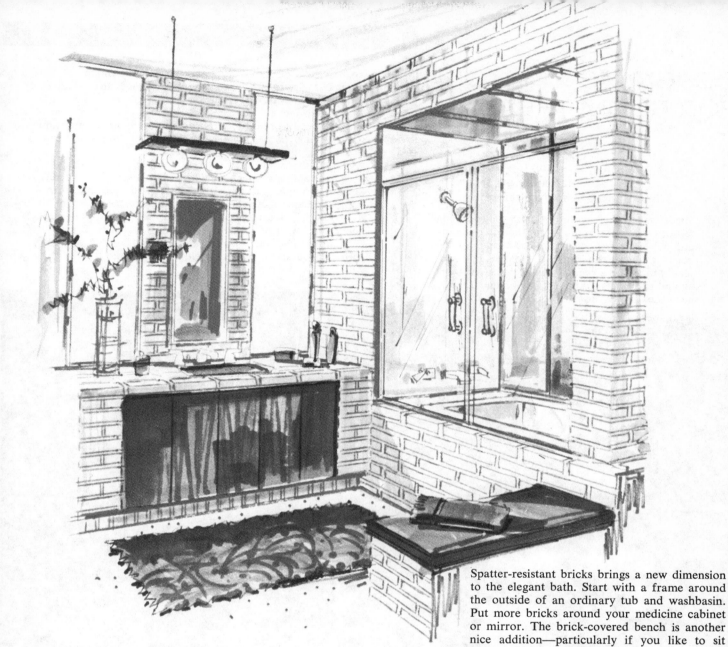

Spatter-resistant bricks brings a new dimension to the elegant bath. Start with a frame around the outside of an ordinary tub and washbasin. Put more bricks around your medicine cabinet or mirror. The brick-covered bench is another nice addition—particularly if you like to sit and admire your own handiwork.

Become a modern bricklayer ...use lightweight imitation brick for these effects

Yes, you can become an honest-to-goodness bricklayer . . . except you won't be mixing mortar or be carrying a back-breaking hod. Instead, you'll be using the new Dacor Miracle Bricks which are made of lightweight, high-density polyester. Only ¼-inch thick, they're easy to apply to any indoor wall or floor or to any plywood skeleton with their own ready-m i x e d, authentic-looking Adhesive Mortar. Dacor Bricks are available at hardware stores, lumberyards, etc. Instructions for working with the bricks are on the package, but the basic steps are shown in illustrations at the right.

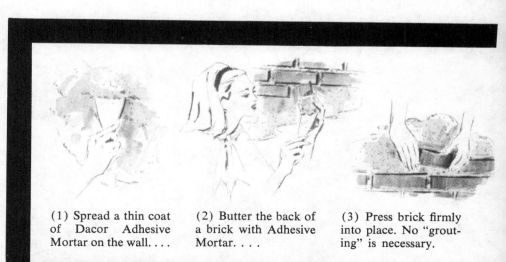

(1) Spread a thin coat of Dacor Adhesive Mortar on the wall. . . .

(2) Butter the back of a brick with Adhesive Mortar. . . .

(3) Press brick firmly into place. No "grouting" is necessary.

DESIGNERS' TRICKS FOR ROOM TREATS

Take a tiger ... and lots of other wild animals and put them to use in a boy's safari bedroom

Paper wall with jungle print. Cut "paws" from felt or Con-Tact plastic, glue to floor. Use leopard print for bed cover. Make "cage" headboard as described at right. Scatter toy animals around the room. Adorn the walls with animal placemats. Furniture is all from Kemp's new "Leather 'n Brass" collection.

To make "cage" headboard, first determine amount of felt needed. Measure height of ceiling over bed and width of bed. Then cut two rectangular strips and one triangular shape of colored felt to sizes needed. Then collect long cardboard tube; colored gift wrap paper; yarn; staple gun and staples; paper party animal head, bought at dime store; scissors; white glue; ribbon; foam block.

Directions: Staple the triangular felt shape to the wall over bed. Staple one end of both rectangular pieces of felt, to ceiling. Staple one side of each piece of felt to wall, forming tent shape shown in diagram. Glue piece of foam to felt on wall. Glue animal in position on foam. Cover cardboard tube with colored paper. Make hole in each side of tent, insert tube and trim ends with ribbon. Glue strips of yarn to tube and hang from felt, forming cage.

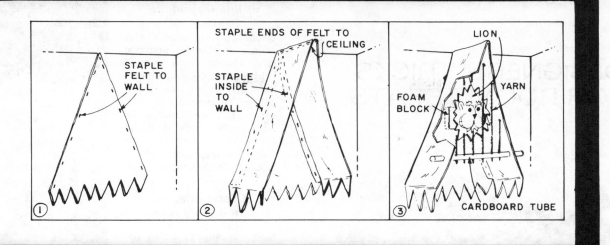

① STAPLE FELT TO WALL

② STAPLE ENDS OF FELT TO CEILING — STAPLE INSIDE TO WALL

③ LION — FOAM BLOCK — YARN — CARDBOARD TUBE

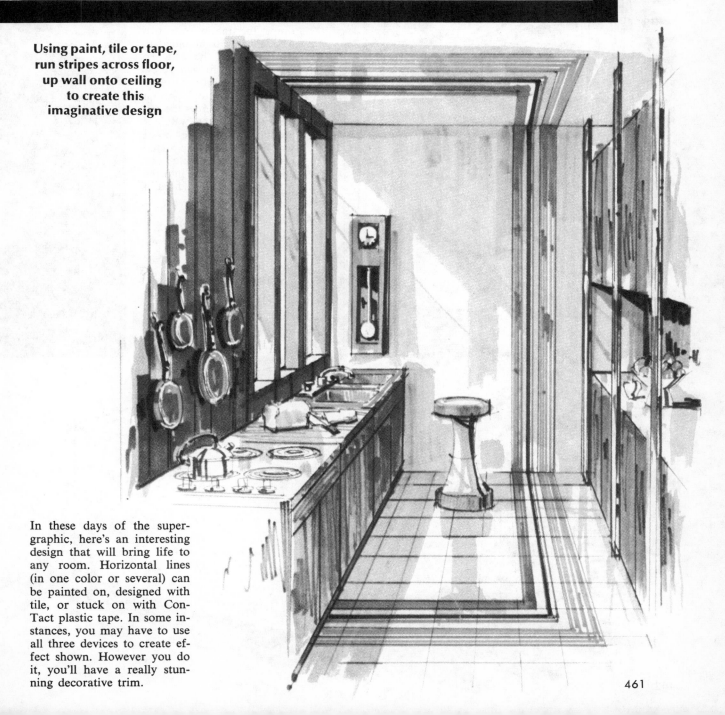

Using paint, tile or tape, run stripes across floor, up wall onto ceiling to create this imaginative design

In these days of the super-graphic, here's an interesting design that will bring life to any room. Horizontal lines (in one color or several) can be painted on, designed with tile, or stuck on with Con-Tact plastic tape. In some instances, you may have to use all three devices to create effect shown. However you do it, you'll have a really stunning decorative trim.

DESIGNERS' TRICKS FOR ROOM TREATS

Work wonders with wallpaper and tile

Exciting paisley print covers ceiling, scalloped plywood trim around windows and cabinet doors. Complementing the print are solid-colored ceramic tile counter tops. Contoured and raised border tiles prevent liquid spills or rolling utensils from reaching floor. By Tile Council of America.

Create interest with draped fabric

Make a canopy out of the same material you've used to make bedspread. Simply drape the fabric over two wooden dowels mounted to the wall over the bed. To mount dowels to wall, screw two angle irons into each dowel, one on top, one on bottom. Then screw the angle irons into the wall. Or use hanger bolts, one end of which will screw into a stud in the wall, and the other end of which will screw into the wooden dowel and hold it straight.

Put an old antique to new use

This old-style coal stove was bought at an antique shop, painted white and topped by a circle of plywood bolted to the stove. Table top can be covered with plastic adhesive (such as Con-Tact) or you can buy rounded piece of Formica at your local lumber yard. If you can't find an old stove to convert, see what other treasures you come up with at a local antique shop.

DESIGNERS' TRICKS FOR ROOM TREATS

Make headboard from floral pattern used in rest of room

Custom-made by Norman's of Salisbury is this delightful room—sassy enough for the young "in" generation, yet not too far out to use for a guest room. Room takes its cue from the quilted bedspread. Matching material was laminated to the shades. Flowers cut from the material adorn one wall. Other flowers were cut out for headboard. To make this headboard, cut piece of 2x4 to the width of the bed. Sandpaper smooth and paint desired color. Cut flowers including stems from fabric. Glue to heavy cardboard with aerosol spray adhesive or white glue. Cut out shapes with x-acto knife or single-edge razor blade. Place 2x4-inch piece of wood horizontally, and drill small holes in wood. Insert stems of flowers. Find studs behind wall, and nail 2x4-inch piece of wood horizontally, to studs, as shown in diagram.

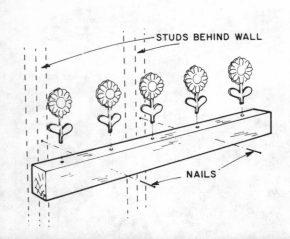

STUDS BEHIND WALL

NAILS

Build a hidden bedroom in your living room . . . or in your dining room

Here's an excellent way to hide a guest room in a wall . . . either in the living room or in the dining room. In both instances, one entire wall was covered with rich Weldwood panels which conceal bed and storage units.

In living room, bookcase was built on one side of bed closet, other side was simply paneled wall. In dining room, bed was built into corner, middle section displays art and other part has door which opens into kitchen; when door is closed, wall gives effect of one solid panel.

Both rooms were designed by Albert Herbert for U.S. Plywood to show how to increase living space in any room in any house. Since sturdy, hinged hardware anchors bed to floor in recessed area, other wall areas can be framed out to accommodate paneling and doors resulting in a beautiful accent wall with no indication of the hidden bedroom. Diagram shows basic construction which should be altered to individual needs.

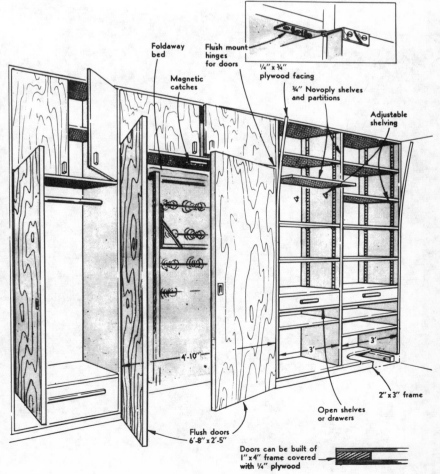

Foldaway bed

Flush mount hinges for doors

Magnetic catches

¼" x ¾" plywood facing

¾" Novoply shelves and partitions

Adjustable shelving

4'-10"

3'

3'

2" x 3" frame

Open shelves or drawers

Flush doors 6'-8" x 2'-5"

Doors can be built of 1" x 4" frame covered with ¼" plywood

DESIGNERS' TRICKS FOR ROOM TREATS

Glue mirror tiles to wall for modernistic look

Put a really different mirror on a wall by gluing on new mirror tiles. Made by Beylerian, the tiles come in three versions, each silk-screened in white and grey on mirror surface. Each is designed so it matches the next one, tile by tile by tile . . . but the end result is highly individualistic. A Giant snow flake, definitely lacy. But no two designs exactly alike. The tiles are 15¾" x 15¾", 10½" x 10½" and 5¼" x 5¼".

Partition a basement into fun areas

Basement space can perform in a multitude of ways, by separation. Here, a basement has been portioned off via the use of wooden beams, making three separate areas from the large whole. The foreground spotlights the game and snack area, with furry backrest pillows. To the left is the party area, complete with bar set-up. Conversation and television viewing take place in the area with the large fireplace. Note the interesting use of shingles and the practical, easy-to-care-for flooring by Armstrong.

Combine small mirrors or small aluminum trims into one great big dramatic wall decoration

Today's market is filled with all kinds of interesting decorating items: three-dimensional mirrors, aluminum graphics, crazy little do-dads of all kinds that can be glued together to create some of the wildest effects ever seen. This room, photographed at J. L. Hudson's, Detroit, features a really spectacular piece of wall sculpture. With a little imagination and daring, you can come up with something like this, too. All furniture for this "French Room" was made in France.

Make an inexpensive desk from plywood, paint or cover it with plastic adhesive

Make it from ¾-inch plywood smooth on one side. If you use a power saw to cut plywood cut with the good side down. If you use a hand saw, cut with the good side face up. Keep saw low when cutting. Cut two pieces for the sides 20x28 inches. Cut one piece for the back 27x28 inches. Sandpaper smooth and assemble the pieces as shown in the diagram. Pour white glue on the joints and then nail them together. Use 2-inch finishing nails. Cut bottom support piece 8x25½ inches long. Glue and nail as before. Screw one 1½-inch corner brace to each side of the desk, as shown in diagram. Cut piece 25x40 inches wide. Place top on desk in position, glue and nail to desk. For extra support screw top to corner braces underneath. Paint the bottom part of desk or cover with a self-adhesive plastic. The top was covered with a Con-Tact woodgrain self-adhesive plastic, but could be painted, too.

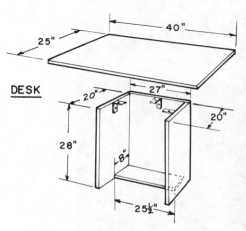

DESK

40"
25"
27"
20"
20"
28"
8"
25½"

467

DESIGNERS' TRICKS FOR ROOM TREATS

Build four-poster canopy from 4x4's

Four 4x4-inch posts serve as posters for this bed canopy. They were attached to a box-frame for top of bed. Before frame was assembled, however, all pieces were covered with fabric, glued in place. After unit was assembled, bands of fringe were glued to top for trim, as shown. Plaid spread was made by McCanless of Salisbury.

Turn a large closet into a "baby care" center

This built-in requires the installation of sink, shelves and cabinet in a long, narrow closet. Sink acts as tub when baby is very little, and for quick wash-ups in later years. Long counter serves for powdering and dressing, while storage space holds diapers, towels, cotton and other necessities. Bottom cabinet space holds rubber toys, extra blankets, etc. Colorful floral fabric used in door insets color-blends with the striped paper used on one area of ceiling and wall. Plastic mattress on floor serves as soft, safe underpadding for baby's first crawling ventures. Woodwork is painted one color, rest of room another color. Designed by Sherwin Williams paint people.

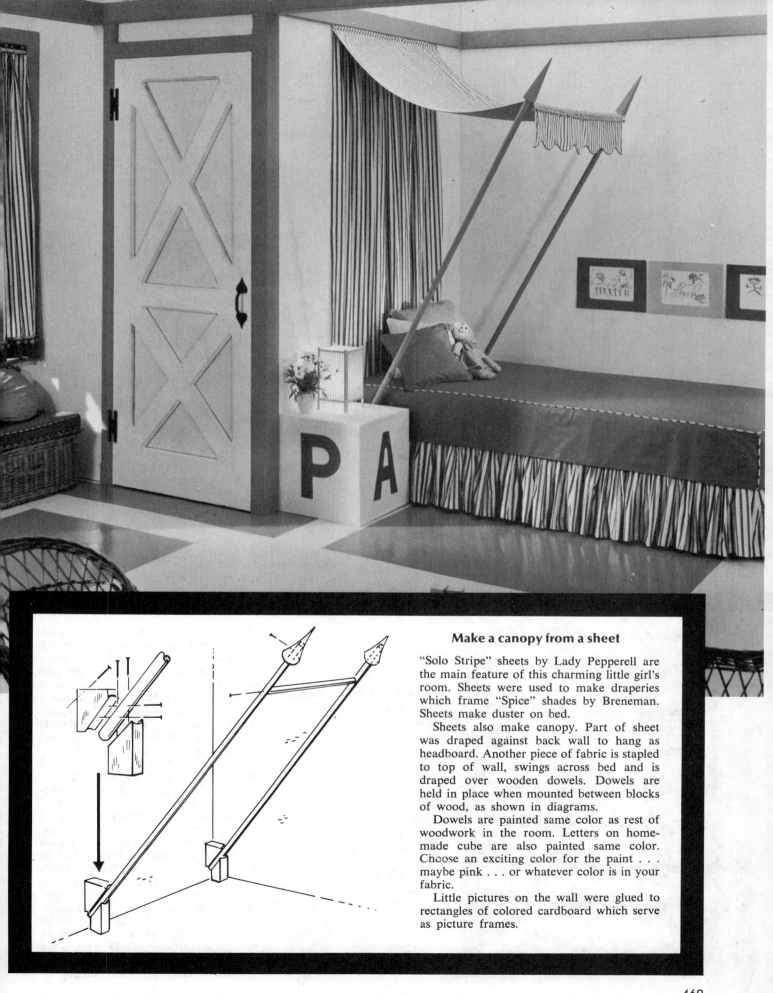

Make a canopy from a sheet

"Solo Stripe" sheets by Lady Pepperell are the main feature of this charming little girl's room. Sheets were used to make draperies which frame "Spice" shades by Breneman. Sheets make duster on bed.

Sheets also make canopy. Part of sheet was draped against back wall to hang as headboard. Another piece of fabric is stapled to top of wall, swings across bed and is draped over wooden dowels. Dowels are held in place when mounted between blocks of wood, as shown in diagrams.

Dowels are painted same color as rest of woodwork in the room. Letters on home-made cube are also painted same color. Choose an exciting color for the paint . . . maybe pink . . . or whatever color is in your fabric.

Little pictures on the wall were glued to rectangles of colored cardboard which serve as picture frames.

DESIGNERS' TRICKS FOR ROOM TREATS

Build a combination stage, storage and sleep unit for the children

This project is for the home handyman who's good at building things. Actually, it's just a series of plywood platforms which form a stage and have doors for storage space underneath. Similar horizontal units fit against walls. Bed is plywood box with latex foam rubber mattress and storage slots.

Buy unpainted furniture, trim with wood molding, then paint a gay color

Buy an unpainted chest at store, make it grand by trimming it with wood molding from local lumberyard.

Wood molding used on drawers, plus a combination of two moldings around the perimeter of the base (see diagram) will give depth and a finished appearance to the chest. Wood moldings are available in a wide variety of sizes and patterns at most lumber yards.

To trim a chest you'll need: wood molding; miter box; saw; finishing nails; hammer; white glue; nail set; fine sandpaper; wood filler.

Directions: cut molding to desired length. Using miter box and back saw, make two 45 degree cuts, one at each end of the molding (see Fig. 1). Cut all pieces this way. Sandpaper edges smooth. When placed together on the chest, the pieces will form a right angle, and can be glued and nailed in place. For a tight miter joint, glue and nail at joint. Use nail set to drive nails slightly below the surface. Fill in with wood filler, sandpaper smooth.

Chest is now ready for painting or staining.

Go wildy modern with an attic

Just look at the photo above and you'll see what can be done with that old attic of yours! It can take on a completely new appearance with some imagination and effort.

"Light boxes" on either side of window are made from plywood with panes of translucent glass fitted into them and lighting fixtures mounted inside so that they become huge lamps when turned on.

These boxes (which could hide all kinds of unsightly beams and pipes) and window create modernistic look, which is carried out in the sculptured foam and plastic furniture used in the room.

Room created by J.L. Hudson's of Detroit.

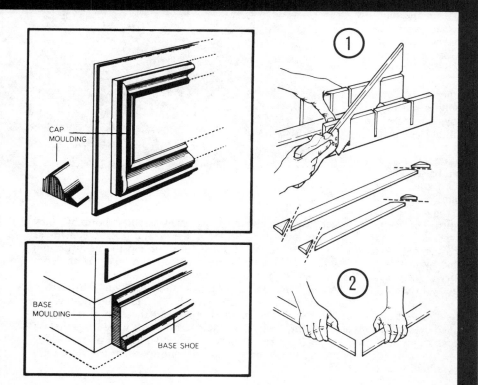

CAP MOULDING

BASE MOULDING

BASE SHOE

DESIGNERS' TRICKS FOR ROOM TREATS

Re-do your basement, turn it into an fun-filled ski lodge

Any unfinished basement (small photo above) can acquire a delightfully rustic ski lodge atmosphere with a little ingenuity and modern building materials. Here's how one family of skiers did it—by laying out three fluid but distinct areas: a lounge area, a bar and eating area, and a game area with a pool table.

An acoustical ceiling was suspended first from the bare rafters to absorb the noise of the family's teen-agers at play so that adults in other parts of the house wouldn't be disturbed. The clean, white surface of the ceiling panels also reflects the last ray of illumination from the room's cozy lighting arrangement.

A bonded fiber indoor-outdoor carpet in cherry red contrasts brightly with snow (which may exist only in memory during much of the time that the family enjoys the room). Besides, the carpet made by Armstrong is durable enough to withstand a succession of Saturday night parties.

Cinder block walls were covered with a textured wall paneling that resembles old, weather-beaten barn siding. For easy installation, it was glued to the wood studs.

The room serves several purposes and satisfies many family needs. It is the repository of souvenirs from ski trips. Posters and ski trail charts decorate the walls. The walls also double as storage space for ski gear. One poster has been lacquered and studded with pegs for stacking skis horizontally. Further storage space is provided by cabinets under the bar. Refrigerator and heating units (a furnace, oil tank, and hot water tank) were tucked away in closets where they are instantly accessible.

The Lally columns, those cylindrical steel poles that are the headache of many a remodeler, were handled creatively. Painted red and adorned with ski resort decals, they add to the room decor.

A curtain trick makes small casement windows seem larger. By hanging curtains from window bottoms, they give windows an illusion of depth and preserve them as a valuable source of daylight in a mostly belowground room. Potted plants or other objects can be set in the concavity outside the sunken windows.

A red contemporary fireplace and red light fixture over the pool table carry the accent color to different sections of the room. The rustic flavor is enhanced by the exposed dark beams, really just rough-cut boards nailed together.

A perfect time to tackle a remodeling job of this scope is during the summer and fall months when the slopes are bare.

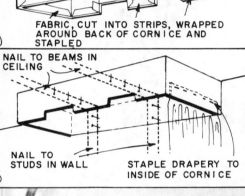

①

FABRIC STAPLED AT TOP

②

FABRIC, CUT INTO STRIPS, WRAPPED
AROUND BACK OF CORNICE AND
STAPLED

③

NAIL TO BEAMS IN
CEILING

NAIL TO
STUDS IN WALL   STAPLE DRAPERY TO
                     INSIDE OF CORNICE

④

Turn an everyday daybed into a thing of splendor

Do it by making a cornice and draperies from same material used to cover daybed. Then hang an interesting collection of pictures or prints on the wall, as shown. The cornice is made from 1x12 inch pieces of pine wood. To determine the amount and length needed, measure the length of daybed. Using that measurement as a guide, determine the size you wish the cornice to be. You'll need five pieces of wood. A piece for the top, front and back and two sides pieces. Cut them to the size and shape desired. Nail together with 2-inch finishing nails. Wrap fabric around front and sides of cornice. Fold fabric at top and staple in place. Cut bottom of fabric into strips. Wrap around back of cornice and staple in place as shown in diagram. To attach cornice to ceiling, find the ceiling beams and studs behind the wall. Place the cornice in position on the ceiling, and nail or screw it to the ceiling beams. Nail the back of the cornice to the studs behind the wall. Staple draperies to the inside of each end of cornice, as in diagram.

DESIGNERS' TRICKS FOR ROOM TREATS

Create a canopy from a piece of plywood and fabric

Stunning canopy shown here is nothing more than a square or oval of plywood, covered with fabric and mounted to the ceiling. Then four long pieces of fabric are nailed or stapled to the plywood piece and draped downward to the top of the four bed posts. Use same material on bed too for unified effect. Use on shades, too, if desired.

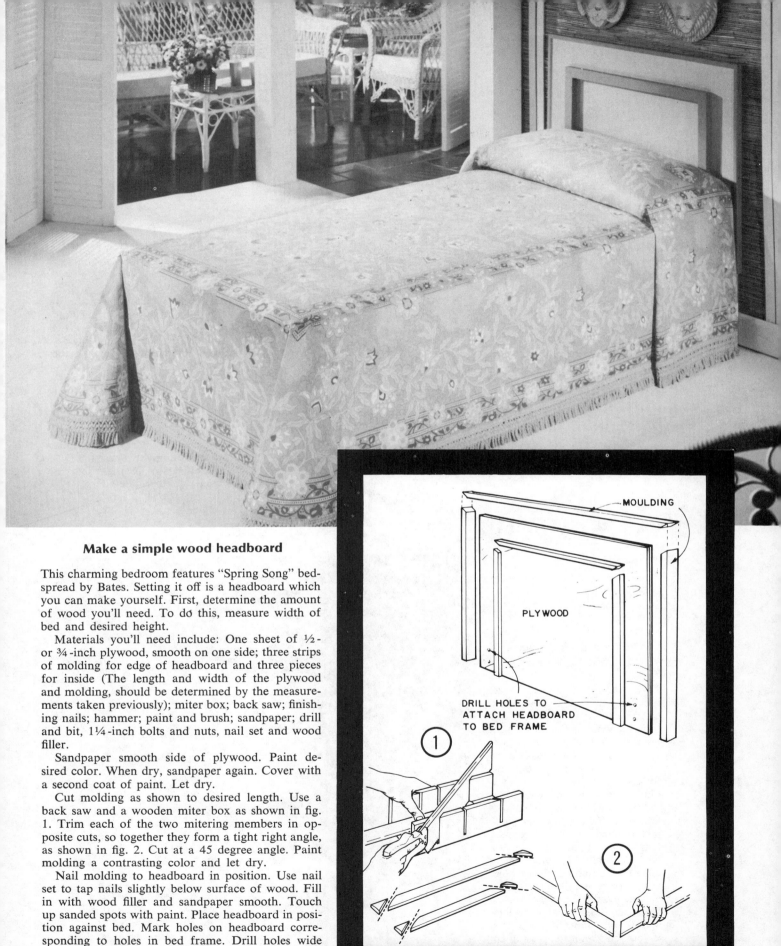

Make a simple wood headboard

This charming bedroom features "Spring Song" bedspread by Bates. Setting it off is a headboard which you can make yourself. First, determine the amount of wood you'll need. To do this, measure width of bed and desired height.

Materials you'll need include: One sheet of ½- or ¾-inch plywood, smooth on one side; three strips of molding for edge of headboard and three pieces for inside (The length and width of the plywood and molding, should be determined by the measurements taken previously); miter box; back saw; finishing nails; hammer; paint and brush; sandpaper; drill and bit, 1¼-inch bolts and nuts, nail set and wood filler.

Sandpaper smooth side of plywood. Paint desired color. When dry, sandpaper again. Cover with a second coat of paint. Let dry.

Cut molding as shown to desired length. Use a back saw and a wooden miter box as shown in fig. 1. Trim each of the two mitering members in opposite cuts, so together they form a tight right angle, as shown in fig. 2. Cut at a 45 degree angle. Paint molding a contrasting color and let dry.

Nail molding to headboard in position. Use nail set to tap nails slightly below surface of wood. Fill in with wood filler and sandpaper smooth. Touch up sanded spots with paint. Place headboard in position against bed. Mark holes on headboard corresponding to holes in bed frame. Drill holes wide enough for 1¼-inch bolts. Insert bolts, add nuts, and tighten.

MOULDING

PLYWOOD

DRILL HOLES TO
ATTACH HEADBOARD
TO BED FRAME

1

2

DESIGNERS' TRICKS FOR ROOM TREATS

Glue a fabric headboard onto the wall

Make cover for your daybed. Use same material for headboard you can glue right onto the wall. Simply scallop the material in some interesting design, and then glue it onto the wall. For a little more dimension, you can cut headboard first from heavy cardboard or ½-inch plywood, then cover this and nail it to the wall. However you do it, the final result will have a smart, custom look to it. You might repeat the fabric elsewhere in the room to create an ensemble effect.

Create a dining nook in your bedroom

Not everyone likes to have breakfast in bed. (Those toast crumbs, you know. Not to mention a spilled cup of coffee.) A good bet for those who do appreciate seclusion and relaxation at the breakfast hour, or for a snack, is the creation of a dining nook in the bedroom. All that is needed is a table and adequate light. Here the former is skirted in Bates' "Crazy Dazy" tablecloth, a gay daisies and diamonds pattern which comes in red and green or blue and orange. It's illuminated by a graceful chandelier in Art Nouveau design that is widely available in copies in the stores if you don't want to invest in an original. A small area rug sets off the dining nook.

476

Let yourself go! Create a conversation cave!

The Tile Council of America shows what can be done with a little imagination and good deal of work. Their conversation cave (really just an extra room in a house) lets the outdoors in with a wealth of natural materials including rectangular quarry tiled floor, brick fireplace and natural wood ceiling and beams. Once available only in earthen-red, 6-inch squares, today quarry tile comes in a range of decorative shapes and colors, including hexagonal and Mediterranean contours.

work
wonders
with
ceilings

Ceilings are having a high old time with marvelous new decorating ideas to give cohesion and balance to other background elements. Wrap-up an entire kitchen (1) with scrubbable vinyl floral-patterned wallcovering from James Seeman for eternal springtime. Both ends of a living kitchen (2,4) have wallpapered ceiling and wall border coordinated with American Olean's "Arabesque" tile floor. Stripes on Azrock floor (3) flow into three-dimensional striped wallcovering which also makes "false" ceiling over sofa. For an entirely new dimension and dramatic effect, raise a ceiling with mirrors by Conwed which fit into a grid system (6). A new tile ceiling by Armstrong (5) can be cemented to existing ceiling, has no bevel edges to interrupt flow of textured design. Lightweight polyurenthane beams have texture and color of aged wood (7) and blend well with old brick and fabric-covered wall.

work
wonders
with
folding
screens

Screens go back to the Middle Ages. In the eighteenth century they became important decorative accessories as they are today. A pretty screen serves many useful purposes—to keep off draughts, set off a handsome sofa, mask an ugly corner, highlight a window. Sometimes they do nothing more than stand around and look beautiful. A clutch of highly imaginative uses to which screens may be put are shown on these pages. Incidentally, screens can easily be built by covering pine boards with fabric, wallpaper, etc., and hinging them together.

To double the size of living room (1) use a tall mirrored-screen as shown. Furniture is by Simmons. If you are lucky enough to own a treasure such as the Oriental beauty (2) give it star billing in an uncluttered area. Or hide a bedroom radiator with a little half-screen covered in fabric to match the bed cover (3). This one is by Cannon. Repeat a strong pattern (4) by upholstering window screens in the same fabric as used on sofa. In this case, washable Herculon. Cover flake board panels (5) in a smashing paisley in brilliant colors to offset dark Tontine shades. For sheer elegance (6) back a sofa with ceiling screen covered in silver-gilt Chinese tea paper. Furniture by Simmons.

work
wonders
with
fireplaces

A fireplace is the heart of a house, the inevitable focal point of a room. Design emphasis should reflect the spirit and theme of the room. For example, (1) hand-made tiles and a provincial mantel work well in a room with a Spanish accent. For a weekend country house, a double fireplace (2) provides log storage. A beguiling black iron stove (3) has a raised hearth backed by matching white brick wall, gives a contemporary sitting room nostalgic charm. Trim as a sea dog's cabin (4), a masculine retreat has a shipshape fireplace in keeping with the nautical theme. Lounge chairs are washable, suede-like Frontera.

A massive jagged opening (5) in blonde driftwood rock makes stunning if unusual fireplace in a family room. Cafe au lait color scheme has black accents including Italian onyx tile hearth. The cozy, open-hearth stove (6), beloved by generations of Northwest hunters, is not expensive, installs easily and comes in great colors. Weldwood paneling of pre-finished Nakora is warm setting for old brick (7). Extended hearth, log storage and eye-level grill are nice extras.

work wonders with room dividers

Room dividers can be as handsome and durable as a piece of "real" furniture, or as simple as a fabric-covered plywood panel. Room dividers are a nifty way to create space, mask awkward spots or achieve an interesting effect in a boxy room. Here, dividers solve a clutch of situations with wit and imagination. (1), A tall piece by Hooker does double-duty as a storage unit while separating the dining area from the seating area. A see-through, plastic storage system (2), despite its size, seems to stretch the small room whilst dividing it. Widely-spaced bamboo poles (3) "fence" a kitchen from the breakfast room without obstructing the view. Bamboo lattice on dado and kitchen cabinet mouldings give a planned, total look. Armstrong flooring looks like sun-drenched stone. Pullout Shoji screens (5) are handsome, functional separator in oriental-minded home by Armstrong.

A screen of shiny beads and a ceiling-hung curtain by Beadangles (5) frame a bed for privacy. Ornate wrought iron panels by Alhambra (6, 7) could be a full length screen or on easy-to-move tension poles. Plywood panel covered to match bed cover (8) makes decorating point in studio room by Sears.

work
wonders
with
shelves

Whether you live in a big house or a small apartment, space limitations are always a problem. The more kept "off the floor" the better. Wall-hung shelves solve many perplexing situations of too much furniture and too many "legs" in a room. Shelves can be as decorative as a fine piece of furniture. They should bear some relation to the character of the room.

Replace the traditional buffet in a dining room or dining area (1, 7) with a long serving shelf. A TV-stereo installation from hardboard paneling in a foyer (2) has the controls imbedded in shelf hung between beams. It also works as a buffet-cocktail server. Bedroom shelves have endless possibilities—as a dressing table (6), bedside tables (3, 5). Capitalize on space under windows by building a long, low shelf for books, plants (4). The wall-hung "box" (8) houses reading materials handy to Dad's favorite easy chair.

work
wonders
with
windows

Shades now come in a variety of weights, textures, cloths, colors and stripes. With a jot of imagination, the home decorator can turn a standard shade into a window treatment worthy of a professional designer.

For example, gussy up store-bought shades with trimmings including braid, felt, ribbon, fringes, tassels or other interesting pulls (1, 3, 4, 6, 8), or add a band of matching fabric (5) to a plain shade to unify a window wall treatment. The ultimate is the custom-made shade (2) with your own fabric—a really chic idea. With Stauffer's iron-on laminating kit it is possible to get professional results (9). Directions are clear and explicit. Another glamorous trick with shades is to applique motifs cut from fabric (7). This requires little more than a good eye, sharp scissors and paste.

Window Shade Manufacturers' Association

work
wonders
with
paintings

Pictures should be hung to achieve a creative mix of aesthetically pleasing subjects and styles. Bold abstracts, for example, are as effective in a contemporary room (2) as they are in an Empire-inspired sitting room (3). Do not hesitate to hang paintings low enough to be part of the surroundings (8). A contemporary room with an oriental flavor enjoys soft touch of antique Chinese scroll (10).

Art inspires exciting color schemes, too. The giant abstract in primary colors (9) is the basis for the total room color. Collections of small prints look better when hung en masse. A group of costume prints (1) balance a too-narrow mirror. Mounted trophy loses "hat rack" look to become important part of well-hung group of lithographs (7). Stunning prints by Aubrey Beardsley (5) team well with strong geometric design to make pungent point. Kitchen-dining areas are great spots for off-beat art, e.g. still life (4) over a stove, country primitive (6) over bench.

work wonders with area rugs

Area rugs come in many sizes and shapes. A colorful rug is a catalyst to focus attention on a conversation group (1), highlight a fireplace (2), cushion a kitchen floor (3) (not impractical if rug is machine washable), to underscore a beamed ceiling (4) with matching lines and rectangles.

A tiny foyer seems to grow larger with a "stepping stone" rug (5) to extend the outside flag terrace indoors. A lightly marbeled design is a creamy touch in a dark area (6). The soft touch of an oval shag rug emphasizes a dark polished Spanish tile by Armstrong. Odd spots become distinctive living areas (8, 9, 10) courtesy of strongly patterned, shaggy rugs. For sheer panache hang a beautiful abstract rug (11) on the wall.

V'Soske

2

Bigelow

3

Regal

4

Regal

5

Aldon   *Regal*

6

7

Ozite

9

Regal

8

Regal

10

11

Bigelow

Egetaepper

493

work
wonders
with
designer
carvings

1

2

3

"Designer Carvings" are made by Filon, sell at local lumberyards, hardware stores, etc. They're made from special polyester resins, but look like wood, handle like wood. They come in circles, quarter-circles, strips, squares, etc. Just nail or glue them in place, then paint or stain the whole unit. On these pages we show the carvings trimming a bathroom cabinet (1), a dressing table (2), a hallway cabinet (3), a folding screen (4), a front door (5) and a headboard for a bed (6). As you can see, the possibilities are limitless for use on furniture of all kinds. Carvings can also be used to form interesting wall designs.

INDEX